Great Outdoor Getaways
to the
Southwest

by Bill McMillon

ISBN 0-935701-42-7

Foghorn
Press
BOOKS BUILDING COMMUNITY™

Foghorn Press
555 DeHaro Street #220
San Francisco, CA 94107
415-241-9550

Foghorn Press titles are distributed to the book trade by
Publishers Group West, Emeryville, California. To contact
your local sales representative, call 1-800-788-3123.

To order individual books, please call Foghorn Press at
1-800-FOGHORN (364-4676).

Library of Congress Cataloging-in-Publication data:

March 1995
Great outdoor getaways to the Southwest.
ISSN 1079-6924

Printed in the United States of America.

Great Outdoor Getaways
to the
Southwest

by Bill McMillon

Foghorn Press
BOOKS BUILDING COMMUNITY™

Credits

Managing Editor/Book Design—*Ann-Marie Brown*
Editors—*Howard Rabinowitz, Emily Miller*
Maps/Layout—*Michele Thomas*
Cover Illustration—*Ray Marshall*

Dear Readers,

While our information is as current as possible, changes to roads, fees or facilities are sometimes made after we go to press. Please be certain to call every getaway location for updated information before traveling there.

We are committed to making *Great Outdoor Getaways to the Southwest* the most accurate, detailed and enjoyable Southwest outdoor book ever published. We welcome your comments and suggestions. Please mail in the enclosed postcard or write to us at: Foghorn Press, 555 DeHaro Street #220, San Francisco, CA 94107.

Please enjoy and protect the outdoors—

Ann-Marie Brown
Managing Editor

How To Use This Book

The layout of this guide is simple. Each of the states covered—Arizona, New Mexico, Utah, Nevada and Southern California—has its own section. Most of the states are further divided into northern, central and southern areas. Outdoor getaways within each state are noted on grid maps at the beginning of each section, and included in the text under the designated numbers.

You can search for your ideal Southwest getaway in two ways:

1) If you know the name of the area you'd like to visit, use the index beginning on page 433 to locate it, and turn to the corresponding page.

2) If you'd like to travel to a particular state or part of a state, and want to find out what getaways are possible there, use the table of contents on page 6 to find your area and turn to the corresponding pages.

•Note that sometimes a number will appear more than once on a map, as some of the getaways cover more than one location or a large range of territory.

About the Author

Bill McMillon is the author of over a dozen travel and nature books, including the bestselling *Volunteer Vacations* and *Best Hikes with Children* guides. He has also published over 400 articles in regional and national publications in the past decade. A former teacher and environmental educator, Bill spends his non-working hours traveling the West in search of great outdoor getaways.

Contents

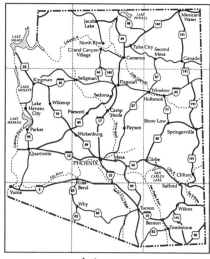

Arizona

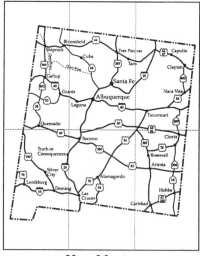

New Mexico

Nevada

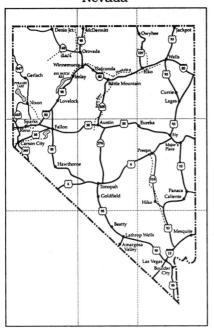

Utah

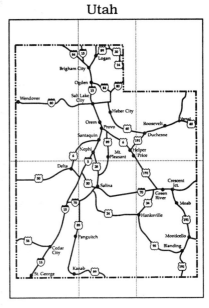

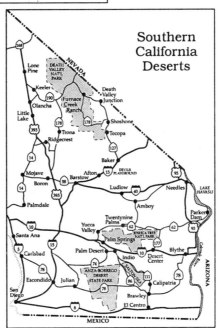

Southern California Deserts

Introduction

Great Outdoor Getaways to the Southwest is about desert country. That means country where summer temperatures at ground level may reach 200 degrees, where what water you find is at best undrinkable and at worst poisonous, where torrential summer rainstorms bring roaring flash floods that sweep away everything in their paths—including cars, trucks and 20-ton boulders—and where freezing nights frequently catch the unprepared by surprise.

Add to these horrors plants and animals that are armed and dangerous—cacti, mesquite, scorpions, rattlesnakes, peccaries and scarab beetles. They all stick, prick, bite, sting, hook or tear anything and everything that comes too close.

Most people avoid these hellholes called deserts, and well they should. How can you feel safe in a place where even plants jump out and attack the unwary?

But not everyone is repelled by the prickly world of sand and sun that stretches across Arizona, New Mexico, Nevada, Utah and Southern California. Such varied personalities as Edward Abbey, my idol and the prince of curmudgeons, and Joseph Woods Krutch, the urbane professor from the Northeast, both wrote kindly of their attractions to the desert. They approached the desert in very different ways, however, both in their lives and writings.

The region's diversity is one of the things that most attracts me to the Southwest. As I travel here, I often spends days and weeks without talking with anyone—but when I do encounter people, I find an amazingly varied bunch. From desert rats hiding from civilization to elderly couples escaping from the frigid Midwestern winters to thrill-seekers in search of adventure, desert travelers tend to be different from most other travelers I run across. They are more individualistic and generally more reclusive.

Of course, the hundreds of thousands of snowbirds who flock to RV parks across the Southwest are a different breed altogether. Year after year, they come for the warm winters, not to explore one of the most forbidding and mysterious wild places in our nation.

The treasures travelers seek here are many. Gems and minerals lay hidden beneath the surface of the rugged mountains of the Southwest, and rock hounds and prospectors spend weeks on end digging for rich deposits. Others search for hidden treasures spoken of in tales passed down through the generations. These include treasures from Spanish times, such as the one supposedly buried by Spanish soldiers in the Chiricahua Mountains of southeastern Arizona, or from more recent times, such as the Lost Dutchman Mine in the Superstition Mountains outside Phoenix.

By far, though, the treasure most sought-after by visitors to the desert is solitude. With solitude, travelers find they can best explore and enjoy a primitive, even primeval, region where animals and plants that are found nowhere else in the country survive, and where the views and pastel colors are unsurpassed in stark beauty.

Most people visit the Southwest during the winter when the temperatures in the lower desert lands are mild. The foolhardy among us venture out in summer into even the hottest regions when the fancy strikes us. We know that most desert travelers have migrated to the higher elevations of the Colorado Plateau and the Basin and Range Province where the temperatures are at least livable, leaving the inhospitable low desert to the plants and animals that have adapted to its high temperatures and lack of water.

Whenever and wherever we go, we know that we will find large tracts of desolate land where we can camp far from the city lights and look across the low-lying desert to distant mountain ranges with no signs of civilization in between. Unfortunately, these vast stretches of desert are broken occasionally by metropolitan areas—Phoenix, Tucson, Albuquerque, Salt Lake City, Las Vegas and Los Angeles—that have grown around oases and prospered using water diverted from the Colorado and other rivers of the Southwest. All of these cities depend upon water from once-wild rivers for their very survival.

These metropolitan areas have spread over the desert as an uncontrolled mass that drives the wildness from the land. Edward Abbey so disliked them that he once called Phoenix "the blob that ate Arizona." Instead of accepting the prickly and uncomfortable desert, transplants from the East and North have tried to make the desert bloom. They try to make it more like what they were used to "back home," except that they want the warmth of the winters that make year-round living easier on the bones.

Today, large dams rise above rivers canyons as they impound lakes. Turbines turn deep in the dams to provide electricity for air conditioning, which residents insist upon, and water from the artificial lakes flows hundreds of miles across the sandy desert to nurture green lawns and golf courses that grow where cactus and mesquite once grew.

Fortunately for those of us who search for outdoor getaways where we can look out over sharp-edged mountains rising from the flat desert floor in the silence of the evening, the "blobs that ate the Southwest" have been only partially successful. The human fear of being bitten, stung, heat-struck and torn keeps most of the desert untarnished. City residents usually don't venture too far into the wild areas of the desert, and they discourage visitors from doing so. Instead, they point them in the direction of green golf courses and air-conditioned malls where life is "civilized."

I want to point you in another direction, away from the greenery and frigid air of the urban gardens, toward the rugged land where you always carry several days' water with you wherever you go—and where you shake out your boots before you put them on in the morning to avoid scorpion bites.

Why would you want to go there? How about chancing upon a roadrunner sitting on her nest deep within the folds of a prickly-pear cactus in the Sonoran Desert? Or watching a cactus wren flit in and out of his nest among the spines of a cholla cactus? Or watching a sidewinder slither up the side of a sand dune? These are all unforgettable moments that desert wanderers witness regularly. And there are others—looking out over the snow-covered spires at Bryce Canyon during a winter trip...watching wisps of sand blow off the ridges of the Algodones Dunes as nature constantly shifts her vast sandbox in the Mojave Desert...walking among bristlecone pine, the oldest living things, on the slopes of Wheeler Peak in Great Basin National Park.

The Southwest boasts three major desert areas: the Sonoran of Arizona and New Mexico, the Mojave of Southern California and the Great Basin of Arizona, Utah and Nevada. Each has its own identity and attractions, yet they share certain characteristics. Little rain falls on any of them—so little that some spots go for as much as a quarter of a century without measurable rainfall. High temperatures permeate all—so high that the nation's daily highest temperature is generally found in the region. Cold temperatures reach even the lowest desert during frigid nights—so cold that more people die of hypothermia in the desert each year than do of thirst or hyperthermia.

All of these facts lead many to assume that the desert regions are barren and lifeless places. That isn't true. You just have to take a different perspective on how you look for life in the desert. To do that, you have to head out into unpopulated and uncivilized regions. There, you can touch the prickly things without fear, because you know in advance that they are sharp and spiny. You can cross large arid regions, because, knowing there is no water, you have brought extra with you. You can withstand the torrid heat of midday without wilting, because you are ready to shade yourself from the enervating sun.

It is easy to make long lists of do's and don't's for exploring the desert country covered in this guidebook. Most authors include a comprehensive one as a warning to those who are going where perhaps they shouldn't be going and who might fall victim to their own negligence, or, shall we say, stupidity.

Traveling in the desert isn't like going to the nearest

county park. It is more dangerous, and there are many small traps that can lead to disaster, but a word or two to the wise should be sufficient. The desert truly is an inhospitable place for the unprepared. It is a place where you can quickly come face-to-face with your lack of resources. The trick to survival is to know what your resources are, how to use them, and how not to overextend yourself.

The earliest European explorers to the region did not understand how different the desert was from their homelands, and many perished as they attempted to cross the inhospitable lands. We know about the problems of living and adventuring in the desert and can prepare ourselves.

We can cover our faces and heads with hats. With sunscreen, we can protect our skin from the scorching rays of the desert sun that so characterize the Southwest. And with extra equipment and tools, we can prevent a flat tire or a water leak from leading to a major catastrophe.

The last item is far from least, because cars make it easy to get into trouble in the desert. We can head off on any side road that appears to be maintained, and is—until our car gets stuck in a dry wash.

Don't drive on desert roads as though they were freeways where help is just a call away. When driving in the desert, do it slow and easy. That keeps you out of trouble, and allows you to go just about anywhere you want, at least anywhere you should go with limited resources.

Edward Abbey often railed against four-wheel-drive vehicles. He thought a good pickup could take you as far away from civilization as necessary. If you wanted to go any farther, he thought, you should walk. That would keep you from overextending your resources and getting into trouble.

Here's a good rule to follow: Anytime you absolutely have to engage your four-wheel-drive in the desert, you are flirting with disaster. A five-gallon can of water and all the repair equipment in the world can't keep the unexpected from happening.

Prepare your vehicle as if expecting to get stuck somewhere. Always carry a can of water in your car, maybe several cans. And don't forget a large tarp that can act as a sunshade during the day and a windbreak at night. Have extra food in case you do get stuck. But don't let these provisions make you overconfident.

The one item I always carry with me when I venture into the desert, on-road or off-road, is Stop Leak™. In all my travels across the deserts of the Southwest I have been stranded only once. On my way south from Death Valley to Interstate 40, my radiator sprang a leak. I had water. I had tape. I even had an extra radiator hose. But I didn't have anything that would plug up the hole in the radiator.

I lucked out. Within an hour, a couple from Los Angeles stopped, and took me 50 miles to the nearest gas station where I bought some Stop Leak™. A California Highway Patrolman took me back to my vehicle. It was a simple process to pour in my Stop Leak™, add water, and start up my engine.

As I drove by the gas station on my way home I purchased another can of Stop Leak™, and have never left home without it again.

Here are a few guidelines that everyone should follow when exploring in the desert:

•Always carry at least one gallon of water per person per day.

•Always have extra warm clothes or bedding in case you get stranded during the night when the temperatures drop.

•Always have a large tarp that can be set up to provide shade during the day if you are stranded.

•Always have enough food to last you for several days more than you plan to be out traveling.

•Always wear sufficient sunscreen and a good, wide-brimmed hat to protect you from the sun, even in the winter.

•Always be aware of flash floods and don't stop for extended periods of time in washes and narrow canyons during rainstorms.

•Always set up camp on high ground.

•Always let someone know where you will be headed and when you will be back. Leave a map of the area with them.

•Always check with someone (a ranger, a local outdoors expert, etc.) who knows the area before heading into unknown territory.

•Always act as though the desert is an inhospitable place. Use common sense at all times.

If you follow these basic guidelines, you should not get into trouble—and if you do, you have provided yourself with a few safety nets. If you are planning to do much exploring in desert country, I recommend that you buy and read one or more of the many guides that are devoted specifically to desert survival. It is impossible in these few pages to provide you with all you need to know about surviving in the desert, but there are excellent books available specifically for that purpose.

Arizona

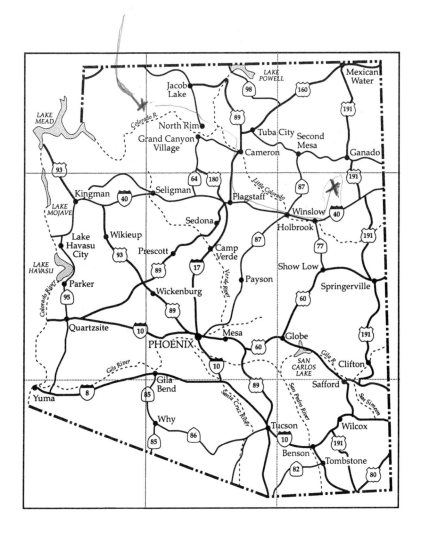

Introduction to Arizona

The landscapes of Arizona are more varied than the state's predominant image—a lone cactus in a desert—would lead you to believe. However, the resilient desert plants and animals, and the unique environments in which they thrive, are still the major outdoor attraction here. In Arizona's 140,000 square miles, you will find canyons where rivers can roar thunderously, but generally remain quiet trickles of water, streams with rich riparian habitats, mountains that rise above 12,000 feet and are capped with snow for much of the year, red-rock country where the surfaces of cliffs and boulders have been worn slick and smooth by wind and water, and expansive grasslands where pronghorn still roam.

In the lowlands of the southwestern part of the state lie the northern reaches of the Sonoran Desert. Here, it is not unusual for daytime temperatures to reach over 115 degrees during the summer. This land is covered with desert shrub. Venturing into the Sonoran region, you'll find a wide variety of plant life, including Palo verde, mesquite and ironwood. These trees survive in the hot, arid climate of the region thanks to their hard wood, rough bark and tough leaves, which keep water inside, and their deep-digging roots, which reach beneath the sand to find underground water supplies.

The desert bushes catclaw, bursage, ocotillo, brittle

bush, jojoba and creosote are smaller than the desert trees (except for ocotillo, which has large limbs). They have adapted to the dehydrating environment of the desert by developing small leaves that drop off when there is no water present, thus protecting their limited water supply. Their spines and thorns catch and hold anything moving through their territory. While this grabbing and holding doesn't accomplish much, the plants' spines and thorns discourage browsing animals from devouring them.

Barrel, fishhook, hedgehog, cholla, organ pipe, prickly pear and saguaro are cacti that fill the spaces between the bushes and trees. Young cacti frequently make use of the taller trees and bushes to provide shade until they are able to withstand the strong rays of the sun. Cacti have no leaves; their chlorophyll is in their outer skin. Leaves would only lead to loss of the plant's critical water, which is stored in its pulpy interior. You can tell by their names that these are plants that grab and tear. The cholla is even thought to jump out and catch passing animals. This is only an illusion, but one that you can readily believe as you feel the sharp, barbed spine of the cholla enter your hand or leg at the most casual contact.

Among these plants, peccaries (small wild pigs also known as javelinas), road runners, pygmy owls, gila woodpeckers, deer, coyotes, ravens and cactus wrens feed, breed and live. Closer to the ground, you'll find the reptiles—slithering snakes, lizards and toads that are frequently a symbol of desert life. The gila monster, the only poisonous lizard in North America, is seldom seen, feeding only once or twice a year, and spending the rest of the time secluded in a cool subterranean hideaway. The horny toad (it isn't really a toad, but it does have horns) is a favorite of children since it easy to catch and doesn't sting, bite, grab or tear.

In the higher country of central and southern Arizona are the desert grasslands. Here, between 3,000 and 5,000 feet in elevation, expanses of grasslands extend to the horizon. Few large plants rise above the grass, but in some areas mesquite forms dense, impenetrable thickets where mountain lions, coyotes and smaller mammals live and hide. Golden eagles and ravens rule the skies above, while scaled, Gambel and Montezuma quail scurry about below.

Even higher are the ponderosa pine forests where the state's residents flock during summer to escape the heat below. There they find cool mountain streams, trout-filled lakes and easy hiking trails that lead through open forests.

Most of these forested sites are found north of the Mogollon Rim that divides the state almost in half from east to west, but others are found in the Sky Islands of southeastern Arizona. The Chiricahua, Santa Rita, Santa Rosa and Huachuca mountains are small, isolated ranges which rise rapidly above the surrounding deserts to catch the rain from summer storms. This moisture feeds forests of pine and oak, and make the region one of the top five birding locations in the U.S.

Even farther north is Arizona's red-rock country. Here the Hopi and Navajo natives have lived for hundreds of years in a barren and stark land where wind and sun combine to shape all that live here, animal or plant. Sage brush, greasewood, rabbit brush and deer bush—all are low-growing scrub that cover most of this open land. Along the slopes of slightly higher country, you'll find large stands of pinyon pine and juniper.

As you drive through Navajo country, you are also assailed by the smell of pine as the smoke from hogan fires drifts across the flat country.

Each region has its own special attractions, whether it's world-class birdwatching in the southeast portion of the state, rafting on the Colorado River, or seeing in person the cinematically familiar wonders of the Grand Canyon and Monument Valley. Whether you wish to hike through a river canyon or camp in the desert, Arizona provides a plentiful supply of outdoor getaways.

Chapter 1

Northern Arizona

Maps 1, 2, 3

Map 1

Map 2

Map 3

Map 1

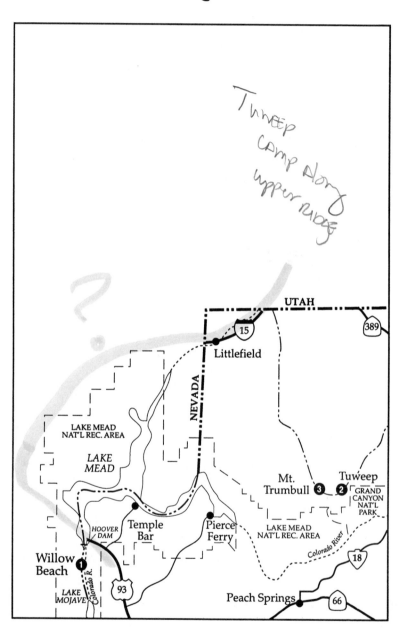

Map 2

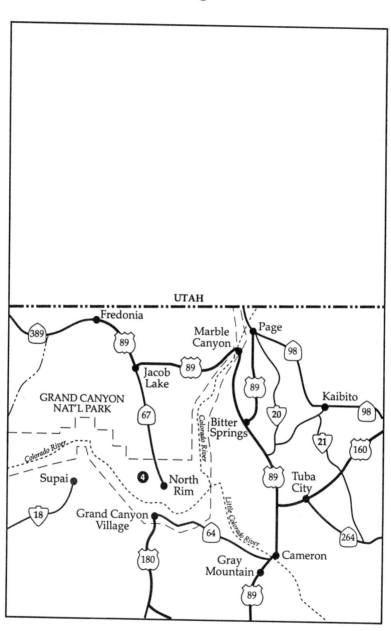

Map 3

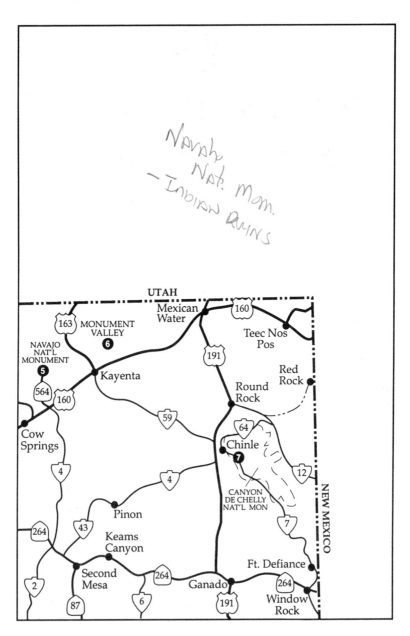

Willow Beach & Ringbolt Hot Springs

On the Colorado River, in Lake Mead National Recreation Area

My first impressions of the Lake Mead area were garnered as I pitched a tent late at night in a crowded, RV-oriented campground on the Nevada side of Hoover Dam. The next day, I saw the vast marinas and heard the sound of hundreds of motor boats as they towed waterskiers around the open waters near the dam. I had a sudden urge to leave and never come back.

It was only later that I discovered the less-crowded parts of the recreation area that lie along the Arizona side of the lake, both above and below the dam.

On a second trip, we were headed for Willow Beach, a popular boating, swimming and fishing spot along the Colorado River below Hoover Dam. You wouldn't have known that it was popular for swimming by the landscape. The dirt road heading to the west from US 93, about 13 miles south of the dam, traversed what seemed to be an interminable table. The river was nowhere in sight, nor were the canyon walls rising hundreds of feet above it. Scanning as far as the low sun in the west, you

---

could see nothing but endless, open grasslands.

Then signs that the river was ahead began to appear. A side canyon to the south began to grow wider and deeper as we skirted its edge. Soon after, we could see the steep canyon walls on the west side of the river.

As we began our slow descent down to the river, we rounded a blind curve and spotted a herd of desert bighorn sheep grazing on the steep slope above the road. For anyone who has never seen these sheep up close, a sighting of even a small herd is a wonderful experience. These wild beasts were once on the edge of extinction, but have made a good comeback on some of the protected lands in the Southwest.

The facilities at Willow Beach weren't impressive. It was just another marina, but it had one thing we needed to reach our destination—boat rentals. A motor boat was essential for the trip upriver to Ringbolt Hot Springs.

Ringbolt is one of the real natural wonders of the Lower Colorado River Canyon. It is one of three side canyons between Willow Beach and Hoover Dam where hot springs seep and flow from the canyon walls at temperatures of up to 125 degrees. The other two hot-spring destinations are farther upstream—Boy Scout and Gold Strike.

While all three are popular spots, Ringbolt Hot Springs is the only one that you can access easily by motor boat. Boy Scout and Gold Strike are both set in whitewater territory, above Ringbolt Rapids. Travelers with rafts or kayaks can launch just below Hoover Dam and float to them, but they must get special permits from the Lake Mead National Recreation Area to do so. Be prepared for turbulent water on the rapids, which may be impassable during high water. (While some intrepid souls make the trip upstream to Boy Scout and Gold Strike by motor boat, we weren't up to the adventure on this trip.)

As we motored upstream to Ringbolt, we kept an eye out for the two small warning buoys on a submerged rock just downstream from mile marker 60. We were rushing now, for we had not reached Willow Beach until late in the afternoon. We didn't want to be on the river as dusk approached, and we wanted to set up camp while there was still some light.

Soon we spotted the buoys and the wide, sandy beach on the east side of the river. We pulled our boat high up onto the sand, because water levels below the dam are known to fluctuate widely and rapidly and water discharged from Lake Mead can wash away lightly tethered boats.

A canyon mouth opened up beyond the beach, and that was where we headed. As night fell, we set up camp in the lower canyon and slept well, anticipating the next day's soak.

The next morning, we trekked upstream through beautiful rock formations and over jumbles of rocks. (Don't attempt the walk barefoot, as there are plenty of sharp rocks along the streambed.) In less than a mile, we reached a 25-foot-high waterfall. Since it is fed by Ringbolt Hot Springs, the waterfall sends a curtain of warm water over the rocks and into a small pool below. We doused our heads and climbed a small ladder leading up the falls.

At the top of the ladder, we got our first view of the series of five or six soaking pools. Constructed by hot-springs-loving volunteers, the pools are dammed in with sandbags and rocks. Hot mineral water flows from the rocky sidewalls of the canyon at approximately 106 degrees into the highest of these pools, then grows progressively cooler as it moves down from pool to pool. By the last pool, the water is a tepid 95 degrees.

It's hard to beat the experience of soaking your tired bones in the hot springs, surrounded by high cliffs and gazing down over the falls and the river. In addition to enjoying the soaking pools, keep an eye out for the desert bighorn sheep that come to the river for water in the early morning and late evening.

Directions: Take US 93 south 13 miles from Hoover Dam and turn west on a well-maintained dirt road. Follow this dirt road for about three miles to the developed area at Willow Beach.

Fee or Free: This a free area. Concessionaires offer food services and boat rentals for a fee.

Camping: The closest campgrounds are along the north shore of Lake Mead. Primitive camping is allowed on BLM land off the road and along the river.

Lodging: The closest lodging may be found in Boulder City to the north and Kingman to the south.

Contact: Lake Mead National Recreation Area, 601 Nevada Highway, Boulder City, NV 89005; (702) 293-4041.

❷

Tuweep

Along the North Rim of the Grand Canyon

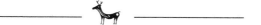

Millions of tourists clog the roads to both the North and South Rims of the Grand Canyon, where hotels and curio shops abound, but there are still primitive regions in Grand Canyon National Park where you will see few people during a week's exploration and find campgrounds with plenty of empty spaces. And they aren't in Havasupai Canyon.

Although Havasupai was the place to go to enjoy the Grand Canyon 25 years ago, today it is overused and overcrowded. Even long dirt roads don't keep large numbers of tourists from descending upon the waterfalls and creeks of Havasupai and the lower canyon.

For unobstructed vistas of the canyon, where you can find a parking place without having to wait in line and take photos without pushing the crowds aside, head for the Tuweep Point Overlook on the North Rim. Here you can look upstream along the Colorado River over spires, towers, talus slopes and cliffs, which together create one of the most breathtaking views in the park.

Miles and miles of thick lava have formed steep, dark flows over ridges and canyons. As you look downstream, you can see these strange, frozen, black lava falls hanging over cliffs.

The walls of the canyon make a sheer drop of 3,000 feet to the river below, which has cut a meandering route through blocks of glittering columnar basalt. Across the chasm of the Grand Canyon, the waters of Prospect Wash, a feeder stream for the Colorado River, have sliced a canyon right through the center of a cinder cone.

What you won't find are crowds or controls. What you will find are almost unlimited camping options. There is a small number of designated primitive campsites with tables, but your choices are not limited to those. Surrounding the overlook is plenty of space where you can camp among pinyon and juniper, protected from wind by natural rock outcroppings.

The wind does blow hard near the overlook, sometimes so hard that it drives campers away. For greater protection, head back along the road about a mile to the site of some rustic restrooms. Turn off the road here and head behind the restrooms for less than a hundred yards to a campground in the lee of a sandstone overhang. The wind is much less of a problem in this site, and you will still be camping in relative solitude.

Even though this getaway is within Grand Canyon National Park, don't expect the usual amenities. There are a few ranches along the 70 miles from Route 389 to Tuweep Point, but don't count on finding gasoline or emergency help along the way. Fill up with gas, check your water supply, and ask about road conditions before you make this trek to the far corners of the park.

Directions: From Fredonia, drive eight miles west on Route 389 to County Road 109. Take County Road 109 (which is a graded road) 65 miles from the turnoff to the Tuweep Ranger Station, and another five miles on unimproved road to the overlook. The road has signs that lead to the ranger station.

Fee or Free: There is no fee for camping or entry.

Camping: This is primitive camping at its best.

Lodging: If you don't want to camp at Tuweep, your choices are limited.

The region is far from population centers having lodging and food. Only head out to this destination if you plan to camp.

Contact: Grand Canyon National Park, P.O. Box 129, Grand Canyon, AZ 86023; (602) 638-7805.

❸

Mount Trumbull

In the Mount Trumbull Wilderness

Just to the west of the Tuweep Point Overlook, outside Grand Canyon National Park, lie vast expanses of open, desolate country, administered by the Bureau of Land Management. From the generally flat plateau rises 8,029-foot Mount Trumbull, the highest point for miles.

I didn't know what to expect as I headed to the peak for the first time. The surrounding countryside was covered with low-lying desert scrub, and nothing indicated what we would find on the higher slopes.

Just as evening fell, we reached the Nixon Springs area. Here, at Nixon Flat, the BLM maintains a primitive campground with water. The pinyon pine and juniper on the lower slopes of the peak were just a dark cover in the shadows cast by the dying sun. Higher up still, the fading light hit old-growth stands of ponderosa pine and aspen. We could glimpse our next day's hiking destination, the old-growth forest on the higher slopes of the mountain.

The trail to the top of the mountain from the primitive campground is 2.5 miles one-way. For just over the first mile, the trail was easy to follow, but it petered out about a mile from the top of the peak. From here, we had to use our map- and compass-reading skills to reach the top as we skirted the north edge of a basalt flow extruding from the side of the upper slopes.

When we made it to the top, we looked south over

the top of the Grand Canyon. In every direction, we could see for miles across wide-open country—not another soul was anywhere within miles of us. No civilization intruded upon the grey-green sagebrush. Even our view over the Grand Canyon was blissfully free of hotels and RVs.

After resting at the peak, we began our trek downslope to the campground. Along the way, we encountered a flock of wild turkeys as they scurried into the trees above. As we cooked dinner that night, a herd of wild deer came to the springs near our campsite to drink and browse in the surrounding meadow. It was a fitting end to a great day in the wilderness.

Directions: From Fredonia, drive eight miles west on Route 389 to County Road 109. Follow County Road 109 for 46 miles to County Road 5 and a major fork in the route. Keep to the right and follow the signs toward Mount Trumbull. You will reach Nixon Flat after about six miles.

Fee or Free: There are no fees.

Camping: The Bureau of Land Management maintains a primitive campground at Nixon Springs. Water is available.

Lodging: The nearest lodging is in Fredonia, and it is limited. I recommend that you visit Mount Trumbull only if you plan to camp.

Contact: BLM Vermillion Resource Area, 345 East Riverside Drive, St. George, UT 84770; (801) 628-4491, ext. 232.

Forest Service Roads to the North Rim

In Kaibab National Forest, North Rim of the Grand Canyon

The Kaibab National Forest covers two-thirds of the Kaibab Plateau to the north of the Grand Canyon, while Grand Canyon National Park covers only one-third. And the national forest has more roads that lead to canyon views than you'll find in the park.

As traffic jams form during the summer months along Route 67 from Jacobs Lake to Grand Canyon Village along the North Rim, I head along the well-maintained forest service roads to the west. These lead to Crazy Jug Point and Timp Point where the vistas of the canyon are as spectacular as any in the park, yet few visitors ever leave the main road and head across the unpopulated national forest lands to see them.

This is fortunate for those of us who like to drive through ponderosa pine forests with an open understory—where it is not unusual to see deer browsing in meadows surrounded by quaking aspen—rather than along paved roads with stop-and-go traffic to paved parking lots and overlooks where you have to elbow your way up to get a view.

It isn't difficult to reach these lightly used overlooks. Crazy Jug Point is along Forest Service Road 292, which heads west about 20 miles from Jacob Lake to Big Springs. Timp Point is west of the Kaibab Lodge and Route 67, outside the park. A forest service road heads west about 15 miles from the lodge through Quaking Aspen Canyon to Timp Point. This is an especially scenic drive with plenty of aspen groves and meadows where wildflowers carpet the ground during early summer. The last section of road is only occasionally maintained, but it is not difficult to drive.

One attractive feature of the Kaibab National Forest is that you can camp anywhere within the forest. You just have to make sure that you are outside the national park boundaries. This means that you can avoid the summer crush at the improved campgrounds in the area, and still can enjoy the ponderosa pine forests and views of the canyon.

Directions: Take US 89 and 89A north about 170 miles from Flagstaff to Jacobs Lake. At Jacobs Lake, head south on Route 67 about 35 miles to Kaibab Lodge and the road to Timp Point, or southwest on Forest Service Road 292 about 45 miles to Crazy Jug Point.

Fee or Free: There are no fees in this area.

Lodging: There is lodging at Jacob Lake, Kaibab Lodge and Grand Canyon Lodge, but reservations are required. You can reserve rooms at the Grand Canyon Lodge by calling TW Recreational Services at (801) 586-7686.

Contact: For information about camping and road conditions in Kaibab National Forest, and for a map of the forest lands, contact the North Kaibab Ranger Station District, P.O. Box 248, Fredonia, AZ 86022; (602) 643-7395.

5

Navajo National Monument

Northwest corner of the Navajo Indian Reservation

State Road 564 heads north off US 160 between the reservation towns of Tuba City and Kayenta in the northwestern part of the vast Navajo Reservation. It leads across wind-carved lands where sandstone monuments rise above wide washes. Here, the pastel pinks and reds of the sandstone cliffs fade to muted colors during midday sun only to become deep, bright hues at sunset. Forests of pinyon and juniper cover the hillsides as you near the end of the road.

At the end of State Road 564 lies Navajo National Monument, with two of the best-preserved prehistoric cliff dwellings in Arizona. Although Mesa Verde in southern Colorado is much better known, and consequently more visited, the Betatakin and Keet Seel ruins both provide visitors a chance to explore ruins that seem to have been deserted only yesterday.

There is a small campground near the monument headquarters for those who wish to stay overnight, which you must do if you want to inspect the ruins in depth. There is also a Navajo crafts store and an exhibit of a hogan, a log and mud dwelling, where you can view how traditional Navajo live.

Betatakin is visible from an overlook about a half mile from the headquarters, but to explore among the ruins close-up you must take a guided tour to this multi-story, multi-unit dwelling that rests inside a huge cave in the canyon wall. These tours are ranger-led hikes; they take about three hours, and the climb back out of the canyon is strenuous.

But the fascinating tour is worth it. As you walk along the paved path that leads through the ruins, you can look into the rock apartment houses, which were built four centuries before the Europeans ever set foot in North America. Although the structures have not been restored, there has been little deterioration over the centuries, thanks to the dry climate and protected setting of the buildings. It is easy to imagine that the former residents have only gone on vacation and will be back any time to resume residence in the well-preserved apartments.

Keet Seel is even farther from park headquarters than Betatakin. This 160-room village, the largest surviving cliff dwelling in Arizona, is located eight miles north of Betatakin along a well-maintained trail. Those who were impressed by Betatakin will be awestruck by Keet Seel. This village, which once housed hundreds of people, maintains a majesty that is hard to imagine. Only a limited number of hikers and riders are allowed on the trail each day and you should make reservations up to two months ahead of your trip. At the time you make reservations, you can also arrange to hire horses from Navajos for the 16-mile round trip.

Hikers must obtain a free permit to spend the night near the ruins. For those attuned to the spirits, this is a "don't miss" trip. Try to make your trip during a full moon, and plan to stay up late to see the moonlight gently illuminate the ruins as it washes over the canyons. If coyotes are out and about, the experience is incredible.

Directions: Take US 160 (Navajo Route 1) 50 miles northwest of Tuba City to State Road 564. Follow State Road 564 nine miles north to the monument headquarters.

Fee or Free: There are no fees at the monument.

Camping: There is an improved campground at the headquarters, and backcountry camping is allowed with a permit.

Lodging: The nearest lodging is in Kayenta and Tuba City, both of which have limited numbers of modern motels.

Contact: Navajo National Monument, HC 71, Box 3, Tonalea, AZ 86044; (602) 672-2366.

❻

Monument Valley

Along the Arizona/Utah border

Anyone who has seen television commercials, magazine ads or Western movies has likely encountered pictures of this strange land with red-rock spires, towers, stacks, buttes and mesas that rise above a red sand desert. The exotic shapes have become as familiar to Americans as they are to the Navajo who have lived in the region for hundreds of years.

Monument Valley sits 5,000 feet above sea level, and many of the rock formations rise several thousand feet above the valley floor. First-time visitors are overwhelmed by the size of the towers and spires in the monument, much as they are with the breadth and depth of the Grand Canyon, for photos cannot convey the immensity of these natural phenomena.

For centuries, the Navajo have considered the rock monuments in the valley to be sacred, and it is easy to see why. Visit the valley during a night with a full moon, during a summer thunderstorm, or after winter snows have left white caps atop the rock formations, and you will understand the awe that the natives feel for this area.

The valley is a Navajo tribal park and access to many regions is limited. However, you can still reach many of the most famous sandstone formations. The maintained but often rough Valley Drive leads from the visitor center to the Mittens, disembodied hands reaching for the sky;

the 470-foot-high Totem Pole; the Three Sisters and other renowned landmarks on a 17-mile loop drive. This is the only developed road that leads into the monument.

Several guided horseback and four-wheel-drive tours are permitted to go beyond the marked roads to lead groups into the outback where the Navajo people continue to follow traditional ways of life. These are moderately priced excursions, costing about $30 for a half-day and $60 for a full-day trip, and can be arranged through Goulding's Lodge and the Navajo tribal park headquarters.

Guided tours generally include a visit to a hogan, the traditional Navajo residence built of mud and logs. Many Navajo continue to live in these eight-sided, cabin-like structures during winter. In summer, they live in shelters where limbs are braided across a timber frame to give shade from the midday sun.

As you come upon one of these settlements, you will see young Navajo herding sheep across red-sand slopes, and find women weaving their traditional blankets on handmade looms beneath the shade of the summer home. If you are lucky, the guides will have arranged for you to enjoy a lunch of fry bread and mutton stew, a Navajo specialty.

Directions: Drive north on US 163 from Kayenta. The formations are visible within several miles, but the entrance to the monument is actually about a half mile across the Utah stateline. Turn right to the visitor center.

Fee or Free: Auto tours cost approximately $30 for a half-day, $60 for a full day. Park admission is $2.50 per person.

Camping: There is a small campground, Mitten View, within the monument. A private campground is operated by Goulding's Lodge nearby.

Lodging: Goulding's Lodge is the traditional place to stay near the monument, but modern motels are found in Kayenta and Mexican Hat. Reservations are advised.

Contact: Monument Valley Navajo Tribal Park Headquarters, Box 93, Monument Valley, UT 84536; (801) 727-3287.

❼

Canyon de Chelly National Monument

Red rock canyons of the Navajo Reservation

———————— 𝄞 ————————

For more than 300 years, the sheer rock walls and narrow entrance of Canyon de Chelly (pronounced "de-shay") provided sanctuary to the Anasazi and Navajo tribes as they sought shelter from various enemies who wished to subdue or destroy them. Kit Carson was one of those enemies, and today's Navajo claim that not even he managed to round up hundreds of Navajo who hid in the far reaches of the canyon during the period when the U.S. Army herded the Navajo on their "trail of tears" to Bosque Rondo in New Mexico.

Today the Canyon de Chelly and adjoining Canyon del Muerto offer sanctuary to Navajo who wish to follow the ways of their ancestors in peace and tranquility.

Unlike the Grand Canyon farther west, Canyon de Chelly does not overwhelm the senses. The canyon and its surrounding red-rock cliffs are at human scale. The sheer walls rise from 30 to 1,000 feet above the canyon floor, and the 100 miles of canyon contain over 100 prehistoric sites, most dating from the 11th and 13th centuries.

———————————————————————

You must be accompanied by an authorized guide to enter any part of the canyon except for the 2.5-mile hike from the canyon rim to the much-photographed White House Ruins, the most accessible cliff-dwelling ruins, which sit in a south-facing cliff near the mouth of the canyon. This hike takes you down the canyon wall, by a Navajo home, across a creek and sand bottom, and to the cliffs below the ruins. Here you can see the handholds that the Anasazi chipped into the sandstone cliffs so they could reach the village above. The sheer, red sandstone walls above the ruins are streaked with dark desert varnish that contrasts with the slick rock.

I like to take this hike in the late afternoon so I can get pictures of the ruins and the cliffs that rise above as the rays of the setting sun highlight the shadows of cracks and ledges in the face of the cliff.

During summer, rangers lead hikes into the canyon from the monument headquarters, and concessionaires lead full- and half-day horseback and four-wheel-drive tours deep into the canyons. (Stay close to the guides; quicksand is said to pose a risk to those who stray from the beaten path.) The tours take you along the canyon floor where the red cliffs rise high above as they appear to reach for the sky itself. During spring, cactus and wild-flower blooms add a spot of color to the red soil, and the bright green of the new leaves of the willow and cotton-wood along the streams stand out brightly against the red background.

There are also scenic drives along the rims of both canyons, with many pullouts. These overlook the spires and towers of the canyons below and the sheer walls on the far side of the canyons. Again, late afternoon is the best time to take these drives. The midday sun tends to wash out the cliffs' many colors, but the low afternoon sun highlights their subtle differences. These drives begin near the monument headquarters outside Chinle.

Directions: State Road 264 bisects the Navajo Reservation between Tuba City to the west and Window Rock to the east. US 191 runs north and south through the eastern portion of the reservation. Chinle sits along US 191, 35 miles north of State Road 264. The monument headquarters is three miles east of Chinle on Navajo Route 7.

Fee or Free: There is no fee to visit the monument, and camping at Cottonwood Campground is free. Guided tours of the canyon, either hiking or by four-wheel-drive, are $10 per hour for groups up to 15 people (with a three-hour minimum).

Camping: Cottonwood Campground, operated by the National Park Service, has 92 units, is located near the visitor center and is open year-round.

Lodging: Thunderbird Lodge is located near the mouth of Canyon de Chelly. There are several modern motels in Chinle.

Contact: Canyon de Chelly National Monument, P.O. Box 588, Chinle, AZ 86503; (602) 674-5500.

Chapter 2

———— ✍ ————

Central Arizona Maps 4, 5, 6

Map 4

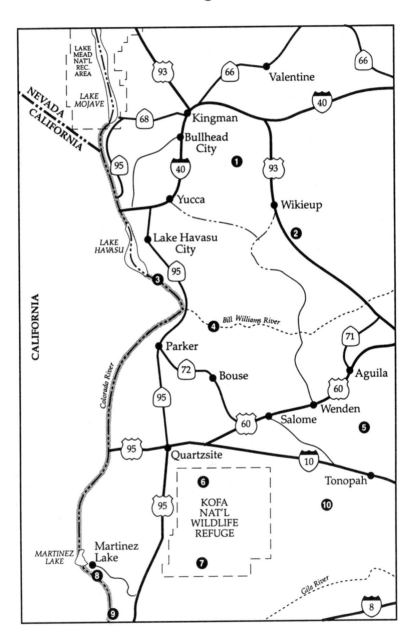

Map 5

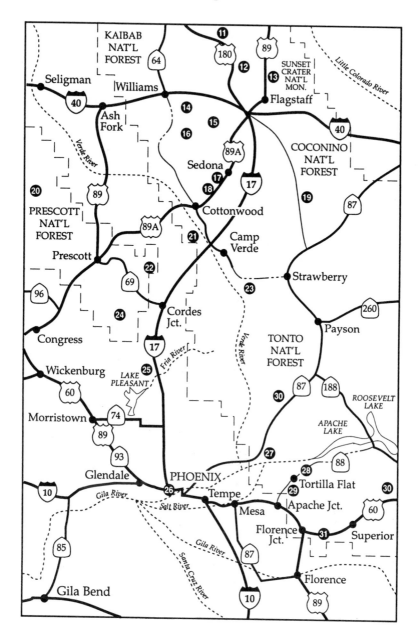

Map 6

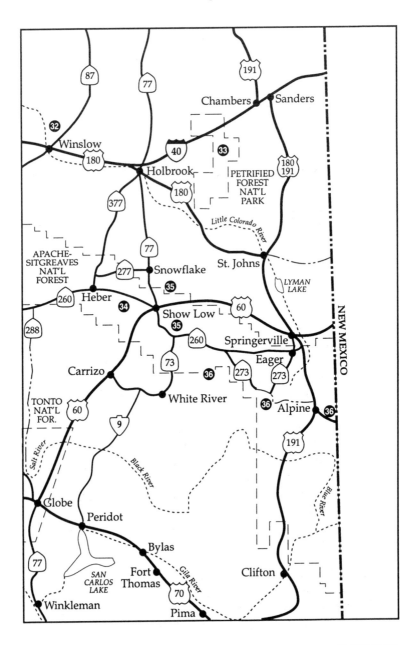

Hualapai Mountain Park & Wabayuma Peak

In the Wabayuma Wilderness Area

County parks generally can't be described as wilderness getaways, but this is one that very much fits the description. Although only 30 minutes by paved mountain road from downtown Kingman, the cool forests of the park offer visitors a respite from the 100-plus-degree weather that wilts Kingman during the summer.

Kingman is just over 3,000 feet in elevation, and the entrance to the park lies at almost 5,000 feet, where temperatures are 20 to 30 degrees less than those at Kingman. Temperatures are even lower as you climb the slopes of the higher peaks in the park, which reach 8,417 feet in elevation.

I avoid the traditional parts of the park—playgrounds, recreation areas with sports fields, and large picnic areas—and head for parts where nearly undisturbed wilderness is home to the flummalated owl, coyote and even cougar. The flummalated, a rare owl that resides in only selected sites in the Southwest, attracts hundreds of birders to the park each year. It is only one of over 100 bird species that you can see here. Once you get beyond the developed section of the park, you'll find over 10 miles of hiking trails that lead through the wilderness forests, where you can find solitude in the hills.

For spring wildflowers, Wabayuma Peak, on Bureau of Land Management land some five miles southwest of Hualapai Mountain Park, is unbeatable in west-central Arizona. The 7,601-foot peak rises 5,000 feet from the surrounding desert in less than five miles, and its slopes rise through five life zones from the Sonoran desert scrub through chaparral and pinyon pine-juniper country to ponderosa pine and Gambel oak. The slopes of the mountain are the northernmost site of saguaro cactus in the state of Arizona.

The area was once heavily grazed and the remains of mining activity still dot the slopes, but it is slowly recovering from these depredations. Many of the old roads are still usable for some moderately strenuous hiking, although most have vegetation encroaching upon them as the wilderness reclaims its territory.

My favorite hike in the region is the three-mile Wabayuma Peak Trail, which follows a gentle route up through the ponderosa pine forest to the peak. At times, the trail almost disappears, but the trail blazes on the large ponderosas keep you on track.

Although midsummer temperatures at the lower elevations reach searing proportions, those on the higher slopes frequently drop into the 30s, so pack warmly if you plan on early morning hiking or overnight camping.

Directions: One-and-a-half miles east of the junction of US 93 and State Road 66, turn right on Hualapai Mountain Road. Follow the signs to the park. The paved road winds up the mountainside for 14 miles to the park entrance.

For the Wabayuma Wilderness Area, continue past the county park and turn right on the dirt road marked with signs for Flag Mine Road and Wild Cow Springs. This road takes you to the trailhead for Wabayuma Peak, 13.5 miles past the campground at Wild Cow Springs.

Fee or Free: There are no park fees, but camping costs $6 a night per vehicle.

Camping: There are both group and individual campgrounds in the park. For those who want a little more wilderness in their camping, the BLM's Wild Cow Campground is located five miles past the park on a winding dirt road.

Lodging: There is plenty of lodging in Kingman, a major rest and overnight stop along Interstate 40, as well as cabins in the park and Hualapai Lodge about a mile past the park.

Contact: Hualapai Mountain Park, Pine Lake Star Route, Kingman, AZ 86401; (602) 757-3859. BLM Kingman Resource Area, 2475 Beverly Avenue, Kingman, AZ 86401; (602) 757-3161. For cabin reservations, call Mojave County Parks, (602) 753-9141.

2

Burro Creek

Along the Joshua Tree Parkway

Burro Creek Canyon drops from Goodwin Mesa, a large, rolling, grassy area to the northeast of US 93, over several vertical rock faces. These descend over 1,500 feet in a half mile to the floor of the canyon where several tributary canyons join with the larger Burro Creek Canyon as it winds around small buttes and hills.

In Lower Burro Creek Canyon, on the southwest side of the highway, a large volcanic butte stands above an intricate series of seven small canyons that have carved overhangs, spires and ridges out of the surrounding cliffs into an area known as Hell's Half Acre. Burro Creek meanders through an open but steep-walled canyon for about eight miles here.

The Bureau of Land Management administers about 50,000 acres of this fascinating area along the Burro Creek watershed of the Hualapai Mountains. Plenty of water, at least by Arizona standards, nourishes a wide variety of plant and animal life here, and the scenery is some of the most dramatic in the region.

The management area is divided into two parts: Lower Burro Creek, on the west side of US 93, has a good, developed campground; the Upper Burro Creek area, a large, roadless area to the east of US 93, offers good hiking opportunities.

There are two reasons to avoid hiking here in summer. One is the high heat that settles in the canyon during the long summer, and the other is the danger of roaring flash floods in both the main and tributary canyons after summer thunderstorms.

The region ranges in elevation from 2,000 to 5,000 feet, with the average about 2,500 feet. This keeps the winters mild and makes backpacking enjoyable throughout much of the year. Spring and fall are the best times to come to the canyon, though; there are plenty of wildflowers blooming during both seasons, and the temperatures couldn't be better.

Both management units have numerous microhabitats with prime birdwatching (over 150 species have been seen in the area), both large and small mammals in good numbers, and a wide variety of plants.

Burro Creek Campground features a desert garden but has no formal trails, although it is easy to explore around the campground without them. The views of the buttes, mesas and rugged canyons make this one of the most scenic campgrounds in Arizona.

Directions: Burro Creek Campground is 58 miles north of Wickenburg and 15 miles south of Wikieup along US 93. Primary access to the Upper Burro Creek area is off Pipeline Road, which you take east off US 93 about halfway between Wikieup and the Burro Creek Campground.

Fee or Free: Day use is free; camping costs $6 per site.

Camping: Burro Creek Campground has over 30 sites, available on a first-come, first-served basis.

Lodging: There is lodging in Wickenburg to the south and Kingman to the north.

Contact: BLM Kingman Resource Area, 2475 Beverly Avenue, Kingman, AZ 86401; (602) 757-3161.

3

Lake Havasu State Park

On the Colorado River

I personally don't like the loud and busy activities that take place around the artificial lakes that are strung out like pearls along the lower Colorado River. Motor boats, huge RVs and drunken revelry are what spring to my mind when these lakes are mentioned, as opposed to solitude and quiet enjoyment of the natural world.

That said, I do occasionally choose Lake Havasu State Park, the largest and busiest state park in Arizona, as an outdoor getaway. The lake itself covers over 25,000 acres, and the park includes another 13,000 acres of the surrounding desert. With a hotel, several restaurants, a golf course, tennis courts, a waterslide and a huge, 1,250-site campground, the park certainly cannot be described as an outdoor getaway in the truest sense. Even with the congestion and noise associated with such a large, developed park, though, the park has places where you can find wilderness.

Large chunks of the 25-mile shoreline are roadless and can only be reached by boat or foot, and that is where you will find wildlife, solitude and undisturbed desert. Along the rugged road south of Lake Havasu City, with its famous, transplanted London Bridge, is the Aubrey Hills Natural Area. Easy hikes into hills lead to great views of the lake and geological outcroppings worth exploring.

I like to boat into one of the more isolated 250 boat-in campsites along the lakeshore. Keep an eye out for a herd of 50 to 60 desert bighorn sheep that live in the hills near the lake. They frequently come down to the water's edge to drink during early morning and late evening in the dry summer months.

There is no off-period for this busy state park. During the warm winter months, the campgrounds are filled with snowbirds who head for the Southwest to escape the harsh Midwest winters. During the hot summer months, water lovers of all types head for the large lake where they can enjoy its wide expanses as they waterski and participate in other aquatic pursuits.

Directions: Take State Road 95 south 23 miles from the Arizona Inspection Station on Interstate 40 to Lake Havasu City. The park is another 15 miles beyond the town.

Fee or Free: The day-use fee is $5 per vehicle. Campsite fees vary.

Camping: The area has huge campgrounds dedicated to large RVs, and an outlying campground with 40 sites where tent campers may feel more comfortable. The best sites are the 250 boat-in campsites along the shore of the lake.

Lodging: There is plenty of lodging in Lake Havasu City and at a hotel at the park.

Contact: Lake Havasu State Park, 1801 Highway 95, Lake Havasu City, AZ 86403; (602) 855-7851.

Bill Williams River

From Alamo Lake to the Havasu National Wildlife Refuge

Humongous parks sit at both ends of this section of the Bill Williams River, but the stretch of river between the two offers outstanding outdoor adventures.

Of all Arizona state parks, Alamo Lake State Park is surpassed only by Lake Havasu State Park in the number of available campsites. Both cater to the RV crowd and feature motor boating, waterskiing and group activities, which do much to hide the natural wonders of the riparian habitats along this desert river.

The invasion of civilization pretty much ends at the dam that holds back Alamo Lake, however, and I like to hike along the river as it winds its way downstream through an 800-foot gorge and camp on the higher banks. The eight-mile-long Bill Williams Gorge makes an excellent overnight hike. It's generally easy hiking, but be forewarned: During the occasional high water, you may have to scramble over some rock outcroppings to avoid walking in the river itself.

For longer hikes, I continue along the 35 miles of river through the Bill Williams Gorge and Banded Canyon downstream to Lake Havasu. Want to find out if Banded Canyon, which stretches for 15 miles along the river, lives up to its name? Just watch the setting sun cast longer and longer shadows against the horizontally layered cliffs. The reds, pinks and whites in the cliffs change from light to dark as the sun sets.

Perennial streams, some with waterfalls, enter the river along the way from side canyons, and the groves of willow and cottonwood that rise from the banks of the river offer excellent habitat for both large and small animals. It's pleasant to just sit and watch the numerous birds that use the habitat. At dusk, generally you can spot a deer or raccoon sneaking down to the water's edge for a long drink of water.

Since the flow of the river is regulated by releases from the dam upstream, you should check with the BLM to see what the water flow of the river is going to be for the period you wish to hike. Avoid getting trapped unexpectedly.

At the end of the 35-mile stretch of river below the dam is the Bill Williams Unit of the Havasu National Wildlife Refuge. This refuge is located along the delta of the Bill Williams River near Parker Dam, and it's one of the prime bird- and wildlife-watching areas in the state.

I explore this 4,356-acre parcel of the larger refuge on foot, since it has a variety of habitats that range from marsh to rocky hillsides covered with cactus. The largest stand of Fremont cottonwood along the Lower Colorado River rises from the bottomlands here and little vegetation grows on the refuge's higher slopes. The wide variety of habitat makes this great birding country. Between February and May, you can view active heron and double-crested cormorant rookeries in the tall cottonwoods.

Directions: Head north from US 60 in Wenden for 38 miles on a scenic drive through the Harculvar Mountains to Lake Alamo. Large stands of saguaro, chollo and ocotillo grow on the hillsides along the way.

Access to the river at the dam at Lake Alamo takes some scrambling, since the road to the dam is gated and locked. Park employees appear to know little about the surrounding BLM lands, so they are of no use with directions and rules and regulations.

From Parker, take State Road 95 14 miles north to Planet Ranch Road. Head east about one mile to Havasu National Wildlife Refuge and the mouth of the Bill Williams River.

Fee or Free: These are free areas.

Camping: Camping is permitted along the river or in Lake Havasu and Alamo Lake state parks.

Lodging: There is lodging in Lake Havasu City and Parker.

Contact: Havasu National Wildlife Refuge, P.O. Box 3009, Needles, CA 92363; (619) 326-3853. Bill Williams River National Wildlife Refuge, 60911 Highway 95, Parker, AZ 85344; (602) 667-4144.

5

Harquahala Mountains

West of Wickenburg

To the north of Interstate 10 and the Eagletail Mountains rises another, higher mountain range. This is the Harquahala, my favorite range in the region. The name supposedly means "running water up high" in the native Papago language, and the range is one of the few in southwestern Arizona where you can actually see running water year-round.

Harquahala Peak rises to 5,681 feet, and is the highest spot in southwestern Arizona. From the top, you can see landmarks that are as far as 100 miles away.

Steep peaks and deep canyons are trademarks of the region, and I am never disappointed by the new canyons I discover each time I explore in the area. The green campsites you'll find here, with water from springs, seeps and creeks, are luxuries one seldom encounters in desert camping. Occasionally, I have even found a seasonal waterfall to camp beside.

Nothing beats going to sleep on a desert night with the sounds of a waterfall in the background. Beware of some of the wet areas, though, for bugs and mosquitoes flourish in the warm desert where they have a constant water supply.

For first-time visitors, I recommend the 5.5-mile Harquahala Mountain Pack Trail, which was built originally for hauling supplies to the top of the peak where the Smithsonian Institution had a solar observatory in the 1920s.

The trail is not well marked or maintained. At times, you cross rocky terrain where the trail is almost invisible, but there are a number of rock cairns along the way that indicate which direction to go. Although the hike is only moderate in length, it is difficult in spots as you must scramble over boulders and talus material. At the peak, you can explore the remains of the old observatory. Views of the surrounding desert extend for miles in every direction. You may also look down into the deep canyons that cut into the slopes of the mountain below.

I have seen a wide variety of wildlife in this range, including rare desert tortoise in Brown's Canyon. Raptors are abundant, and you fall asleep to coyotes yipping almost every night. The BLM says there are more mule deer per acre in the mountains here than anywhere else in western Arizona. A large herd of desert bighorn sheep roams the steep higher slopes of the canyons.

November to April is the best time to wander here, and the wildflower blooms in the late spring are as profuse as anywhere in the state.

Directions: The best access to the wilderness area is from US 60 west of Wickenburg. Continue west past Aquila for 14 miles to a rest area on the south side of the highway. Head south on the dirt road at the rest stop and follow it to the wilderness area. Park in the designated area, and head into the wilderness along the old jeep trail that leads from the parking area.

Fee or Free: This is a free area.

Camping: You can camp throughout the area, but there are no improved campgrounds nearby.

Lodging: The best chance for lodging is in Wickenburg.

Contact: BLM Phoenix District, 2015 West Deer Valley Road, Phoenix, AZ 85027; (602) 780-8090.

Crystal Hills

In the Kofa National Wildlife Refuge

The Kofa National Wildlife Refuge, which was established to protect one of the few remaining habitats of the desert bighorn sheep, is a wild and barren place—a true desert with little to attract visitors. The mountains of the refuge rise from the flat desert to the east of US 95 as it heads south from Interstate 10 and the town of Quartzsite, on a long, lonely stretch to Yuma far to the south.

Few roads lead into the wildlife refuge, but I found myself driving on one about 10 miles south of Quartzsite, which led far up into the refuge toward the mountains to the east. We were in search of rocks—large quartz crystals—and the mountain we were heading toward in the Crystal Hills was the only site in the refuge where you could actually dig for them. In other areas, you can collect rocks from the surface, but you may not dig. In the Crystal Hills, you can dig for and find quartz crystals on the slopes of an ancient volcanic fumarole.

Nothing is ever really easy in the desert, but the drive to the Crystal Hills is across some of the most desolate land I have ever traveled. It crosses desert flatland with few plants, fewer animals and even fewer birds. I have been in some remote areas, but the desolate feelings evoked on this drive were the strongest I had ever felt. And they didn't subside as we pulled up to the abandoned campground near the base of the fumarole. The ruins were a sign of human intrusion that had failed, as any such effort was doomed to do.

Once we began our explorations around the fumarole, though, these feelings disappeared, replaced by the excitement of a search for things of beauty buried beneath the hard surface of this hard place. As the day wore on and the sun sank in the west, I even began to enjoy myself. We were nowhere, with no one, and on the way to nowhere. We were doing something we enjoyed in a place where we had no other distractions.

Since the campground near Crystal Hills has been closed, there is primitive camping only in the wide-open spaces of the wildlife refuge. It's allowed as long as you are more than a quarter mile away from a water hole and your vehicle remains less than 100 feet from the roadway.

The night sky darkened and the winter stars filled the dome overhead to overflowing. We sat around camp, talking about how we felt about this barren plot of land where, of all large mammals, only desert bighorn sheep choose to live. By the time we went to sleep, we were already looking forward to another day of digging, and hesitant to return to less barren places and their many distractions.

Directions: Take US 95 south from Interstate 10 at Quartzsite for just under 10 miles. Turn left at the sign to Crystal Hills. The road may be rough, but high-clearance vehicles should have no problem.

Fee or Free: This is a free area.

Camping: Primitive camping is allowed in the refuge.

Lodging: Some lodging is available in Quartzsite, but the best bet is Yuma, 75 miles to the south.

Contact: Kofa National Wildlife Refuge, P.O. Box 6290, Yuma, AZ 85366-6290; (602) 783-7861.

A word of advice: No matter how caught up you get in your crystal-gathering, don't forget to constantly rehydrate yourself. Summer temperatures are extreme here. There is no water in the refuge, so be sure to bring a good supply.

7

Palm Canyon

In Kofa National Wildlife Refuge

As you drive down the first 30 miles of the lonely stretch of US 95 between Quartzsite and Yuma, the Kofa Mountains are a constant companion to the east. This rugged range rises abruptly from the desert plains to almost 4,000 feet, but unlike most desert mountains, their elevation does not bring vegetation. The peaks of this range are as barren as the surrounding desert, and seem to have no more water.

The desert bighorn sheep that roam the mountains in search of the barest supply of food and water do manage to survive in this harsh environment, however. You can see them occasionally as they jump from ledge to ledge high up the steep cliffs of the Kofas. One site where you may be able to spot this elusive animal is near Palm Canyon, a steep and narrow canyon in the middle of the refuge.

There are several water holes, or tanks, that provide water year-round to the sheep and other wildlife around Palm Canyon. Vegetation, even if it is not what you would call lush, does grow a little better here.

One rare plant that you'll find here is the California Fan Palm, which is the only native palm tree found in Arizona. It is also the tree for which the canyon is named. You can reach a small grove of these by climbing a rough

---

mile up the side of the steep canyon wall near the mouth of the canyon, to the base of the high cliffs that reach to the sky overhead.

The day I made the hike I wondered about my sanity. The air temperature had to be in the high 90s, and the solid rock cliffs that rose upward for 2,000 feet on both sides of the narrow canyon reflected the heat of the sun. I could feel the sweat surface on my skin, and then just as quickly evaporate in the dry, hot air. A full quart of water was gone by the time I reached the palms, and I was glad this was only a short side trip from my vehicle and water supply.

The road to Palm Canyon is maintained, but it's still rough. That means your drive in must be slow, allowing you to keep an eye on the side of the road for various types of desert wildlife, including roadrunners that skit here and there on the desert floor. From the parking lot at the head of the canyon, you can take a marked trail a half mile up the canyon, but you must then bushwhack your way through the prickly vegetation that grows on the side of the canyon to reach the palms. (This sticky stuff includes palo verde, ironwood, various cacti and a few bushes of Kofa Mountain barberry, a rare plant found only in the southwest corner of Arizona.)

With its defined parking lot and plaque describing the canyon, Palm Canyon is the most developed area of the Kofa National Wildlife Refuge. And with roughly a couple of dozen visitors a week, it is also the refuge's most visited area—you are likely to encounter other folks here. If you want to head into even more desolate wild country, where you are not likely to find anything other than desert bighorn sheep, check with the refuge headquarters for maps and current information on the roads that lead away from Palm Canyon and into the wilderness.

Directions: Take US 95 about 18 miles south of Quartzsite (and 68 miles north of Yuma). A signed road leads east from US 95 into the refuge. Follow it for nine miles to the parking area. Just past the halfway mark, there is a fork in the road. Take a right and continue to Palm Canyon.

Fee or Free: This is a free area.

Camping: Camping is allowed within the refuge, but your vehicle must be in the parking area or no more than 100 feet off the road.

Lodging: The best bet for motels is in Yuma, which is about 70 miles to the south.

Contact: Kofa National Wildlife Refuge, P.O. Box 6290, Yuma, AZ 85364; (602) 783-7861.

Imperial National Wildlife Refuge

Along the Colorado River north of Yuma

Mention Arizona birding and most serious birders only think of the Sky Island region in the southeastern part of the state. During winter, however, one of the great birdwatching sites in Arizona is along the Colorado River in the Imperial National Wildlife Refuge. The refuge's more than 25,000 acres of water and marsh are surrounded by some of the driest and harshest desert in the country.

The sharp contrast between the desert and marsh also marks a contrast in the type of wildlife you'll see here. In the desert nearby, birdlife is scarce, but waterfowl and wading birds congregate in large numbers among the riparian growth along the waterways. During winter, ducks and geese that nest in the Far North come here to feed and fatten up for their spring migration back to the Arctic.

The refuge is comprised of a number of lakes that were formed after Imperial Dam was built almost 30 miles downstream, early in this century. Only Martinez, the largest of these, is named. The others are simply backwater lakes that formed in the river bottomland as Imperial

---

Dam flooded the main river.

The refuge's headquarters, just past Martinez Lake, has a viewing platform that overlooks the river, marsh and surrounding agricultural land where the waterfowl cackle and quack as they feed. Along Red Cloud Mine Road to the north of headquarters, there are four more lookouts from which you can scan the river for birdlife.

In addition to the large collection of waterfowl and shorebirds, you can also spot several species of dove, roadrunner, screech and great horned owl, lesser night-hawk and dozens of LBBs (little bitty birds), which feed on the insects that breed in the refuge's shallow waters.

The Painted Desert Trail, off Red Cloud Mine Road about three miles north of the headquarters, is a one-mile self-guided hike that leads through interesting eroded red, white and blue sandstone formations. Beware: This is one spot where you are almost assured of seeing rattle-snakes.

I used to explore the river and its surrounding riparian areas in a canoe, but no more. In recent years, there has been such a dramatic increase in motor boat traffic that I now feel I am placing my life in danger by venturing out on the lakes along the river above Imperial and Laguna dams. If you stay near the shore and in the shallow waters near the marshes, I suppose you can still enjoy canoeing here, but be careful.

Directions: From Yuma, take US 95 north for 23 miles to Martinez Lake Road. Turn west and follow the signs for 13 miles to the refuge headquarters.

Fee or Free: This is a free area.

Camping: There is a private campground at Fishers Landing (on Martinez Lake), and a large public campground, the Imperial Oasis Campground, just north of Imperial Dam.

Lodging: There is plenty of lodging in Yuma.

Contact: Imperial National Wildlife Refuge, P.O. Box 72217, Yuma, AZ 85364; (602) 783-3371.

9

Mittry Lake Wildlife Area

Along the Colorado River north of Yuma

Just south of Imperial Dam, an oxbow-shaped lake lies to the east of the Colorado River. Mittry Lake has a rich and well-developed wetland that has been improved to provide habitat for waterfowl and wading birds, which are found here in abundance. Even the reclusive and endangered Yuma clapper rail, although seldom seen, is common here.

If you visit during the hot season, tall cottonwood trees rise along dry portions of the waterways and provide shade against the hot desert sun. The best time to head for the lake is between November and February when thousands of wintering waterfowl can be observed feeding along the edges of the lake.

Unlike in the waters of the Imperial National Wildlife Refuge, canoeing is still an excellent way to observe the wildlife here. If you think you see a beaver as you quietly paddle near shore in the early morning or late evening, you are probably right. While they do inhabit the area, they are tough to spot. They build their lodges in large holes in the soft banks of the wildlife area, instead of in the more traditional log-and-twig dams. You are more likely to see muskrats as they scurry about on the shore or swim in the shallow waters.

Fishing for largemouth and smallmouth bass is excellent in the lake, and the surrounding lands of the wildlife area are home to several thousand dove and quail. During open seasons, hunters come from the Yuma area to stalk these game birds, as well as geese and ducks.

If you are not canoeing, the best views of the wildlife area are from atop the access road to the Gila Gravity Canal. Since this road is elevated above the surrounding wetlands, the view from it is excellent.

The wildlife area includes the 400-acre, three-mile-long lake, several smaller lakes and about 3,500 acres of surrounding land. The BLM administers adjoining land where you can hike and look for the numerous songbirds that are attracted to the marshlands.

Directions: Go seven miles east on US 95 from Yuma and turn north on Avenue 7E (Laguna Dam Road). Continue 10 miles, past Laguna Dam and Betty's Kitchen, to the Mittry Lake Wildlife Area.

Fee or Free: This is a free area.

Camping: Primitive camping is allowed, but there are no improved facilities.

Lodging: There is plenty of lodging in Yuma.

Contact: BLM Yuma Resource Area, 3150 Winsor Avenue, Yuma, AZ 85365; (602) 726-6300.

Eagletail Mountains

South of Interstate 10, west of Phoenix

Near the small crossroads community of Tonopah, between Phoenix and the Colorado River, are several mountain ranges that are part of the same large *despladado* (desolate uninhabited area) as the Kofa and Castle Dome mountains farther to the west. All were bypassed by early explorers, who saw them simply as large barriers that delayed trips across the vast wasteland of what is now southeastern Arizona.

Today, although a few intrepid souls venture into these desert ranges, no one could ever call them crowded. Most of the adventurers who head for the Eagletail Mountains Wilderness Area to the south of Interstate 10 are rock climbers bound for the southeastern end of the range, in particular for three freestanding feathers of rock which rise more than 2,000 feet above the surrounding desert.

Even non-climbers who just like to hike in desert mountains can enjoy the three-mile trek along the crest of the range to the three peaks, and there is a good camping site at the base of Eagletail Peak. From here, it is a simple hike to the top where you have outstanding vistas in all directions. To the east are the rich agricultural lands of the Harquahala Valley where the deep green, irrigated fields present a stark contrast to the dry desert lands reaching to the horizon in all other directions.

On your hikes, keep an eye out for desert bighorn sheep. You are most likely to spot them near V-notch passes in the range where *tinajas*, or rock tanks, collect water during the wet season. Try to avoid lingering near any water hole, however, for the sheep depend upon access to them for their survival and they steer away from human activity.

Remember as you head back into this region that there is no dependable water supply, and there are few people to help you out in times of distress. Stay within your resources, and you should have no troubles. Needless to say, this is not a region you want to mess around in during the high temperatures of midsummer. Daytime highs are always in the 100s, and they often exceed 115 degrees. November to April is the best time to visit this hot, dry but fascinating corner of the state.

Directions: Take the Salome Road-Harquahala Road exit off Interstate 10 some 65 miles west of Phoenix. Head south about 15 miles on Harquahala Road to AT&T Frontage Road. Turn left and continue just under 10 miles to Palomas-Harquahala Road and follow it about 35 miles to Clanton Well. Turn left on Arlington-Clanton Well Road and follow it about 25 miles to the Eagletail Mountain Wilderness Area.

Note: These are general directions only. Do not use them without first obtaining a detailed map of the area and planning your trip well in advance.

Fee or Free: This is a free area.

Camping: You may camp anywhere in the area, but there are no improved campgrounds nearby.

Lodging: The closest lodging is in Phoenix, 65 miles to the east.

Contact: BLM Yuma Resource Area, 3150 Winsor Avenue, Yuma, AZ 85365; (602) 726-6300.

11

Red Mountain

North of Flagstaff

Want to see nesting golden eagles and peregrine falcons? Red Mountain is an interesting geological area where you have a good chance of doing just that during nesting season.

The mountain rises high above the surrounding scrub-covered desert as you head north along US 180 from Flagstaff. Steep slopes of red volcanic cinder surround the peak below the sheer cliffs where the raptors nest. Pinyon pine-juniper woodlands cover the broad reaches of surrounding plateau leading to the mountain, but large ponderosa pines rise above the narrow canyon that runs from the mountain to the highway.

The best time to try to spot the eagles and falcons is from May to July. Scan the ledges of Red Mountain's sheer cliffs, which offer the raptors excellent nesting sites, or over the surrounding country to see if they are soaring overhead in search of the many small animals that they feed on.

The trails here are minimal, but you can hike through the open forests as you attempt to get the best possible view of the cliffs. The Coconino National Forest has declared the cliffs off-limits to climbers, in order to protect the nesting raptors. Climbers who attempt to scale the cliffs will be prosecuted.

Elk are frequently seen along the road as the canyon begins to narrow near the parking area. For the best chance of seeing the elk, approach the area slowly and quietly in the early morning or late evening.

Come here during late spring and search the cliffs for telltale signs of the eagles' huge (often 10 feet across) stick nests. If you come after the eggs have hatched, you may get to watch the voracious youngsters fighting for the first bite as one of their parents returns to the nest with food.

Directions: Head north on US 180 from Flagstaff and continue for 31 miles to the marked turnoff to the Red Mountain Geologic Area. The parking area is just under a half mile from the highway.

Fee or Free: This is a free area.

Camping: Primitive camping is allowed in the national forest, but only away from the geologic area. There are no improved campgrounds nearby.

Lodging: There is plenty of lodging in Flagstaff.

Contact: Coconino National Forest, 2323 East Greenlaw Lane, Flagstaff, AZ 86001; (602) 527-3600.

San Francisco Peaks

In Coconino National Forest

Coconino National Forest extends for miles along the Colorado Plateau, and is part of one of the greatest ponderosa pine forests in the world. The high elevation of the forest lands ensures plenty of snow and rain to nourish the large stands of pines. Nowhere is there more precipitation than around the San Francisco Peaks, to the north of Flagstaff.

Humphreys Peak, at 12,633 feet, is the highest point in Arizona. Both summer and winter storms rise as they approach the barrier of Humphreys and the three nearby peaks—Agassiz, Doyle and Schultz— that comprise the San Francisco Peaks, dropping over 50 inches of water a year. This makes the region the wettest in a dry state, and visitors are drawn here in large numbers.

During summer, visitors come to hike and fish in the many lakes located in Coconino National Forest. In winter, they come to ski at the Fairfield Bowl, the oldest and largest ski area in Arizona.

A chairlift takes skiers in winter and sightseers in summer to the top of Agassiz Peak. This area has been closed to hiking, but you can take a four-mile trail from the ski bowl to the top of Humphreys Peak. Magnificent views reach out in all directions from the top of the peak, including great views of the North Rim of the Grand Canyon, which draw large numbers of hikers to the trail.

Other trails lead to the higher regions of each of the peaks, and the area is good backpacking country during Arizona summers when you want to escape from the heat of the lower elevations.

For those who don't want to exert themselves too much, a forest road leads to the Inner Basin, a spectacular high valley that sits in a bowl formed by the four peaks. This area is filled with much-photographed aspen groves and mountain meadows, which are covered with wildflowers in early summer. Only day-hiking is allowed in this fragile ecosystem.

Another popular nearby destination is the Lamar Haines Memorial Wildlife Area, an old homestead with trails that lead you through forests where songbirds are plentiful.

The San Francisco Peaks, which rise from surrounding desert country to alpine zones above treeline at the top, were where C. Hart Merriam formulated his concepts of "life zones" in the late 1800s. Six of the seven life zones designated by Merriam may be found on these slopes.

Directions: From Flagstaff, take US 180 north about eight miles. Turn northeast onto Forest Service Road 420, which leads to the south and east slopes of the peaks. Forest Service Road 146 heads off Forest Service Road 420 toward several good trailheads as it circles the peaks; it dead-ends near the Inner Basin. Or, from Flagstaff, head 12 miles north on US 180 to Forest Service Road 516. Forest Service Road 516 leads to the Lamar Haines Memorial Wildlife Area and the ski bowl.

Fee or Free: This is a free area, except for skiing and chairlift fees.

Camping: Backcountry camping is allowed, as is primitive camping in the national forest away from the recreation areas. The nearest improved campgrounds are on the road to Sunset Crater.

Contact: Coconino National Forest, 2323 East Greenlaw Lane, Flagstaff, AZ 86001; (602) 527-3600.

Sunset Crater & Wupatki National Monuments

Outside Flagstaff

While Sycamore Canyon is a true wilderness getaway where you are unlikely to encounter people in your travels, Sunset Crater and Wupatki national monuments are easily accessible getaways where the crowds become large during the height of tourist season. That doesn't make them any less worthwhile, though, for both the natural and human history of the monuments are awe-inspiring.

I return to the area time after time and never miss a chance to explore the cinder-covered lands that were dusted with volcanic debris less than a thousand years ago. My only disappointment is that I can no longer hike to the top of the crater.

The cinder cone was damaged by decades of hikers who crisscrossed it, wandering off-trail in search of an easier route to the top. In order to prevent further degradation, the park service has closed the trail to the top. Today, there is almost no sign that a trail ever led up the slopes, because the cinders have naturally moved downslope during weathering, covering up the old routes.

There are still plenty of trails, however, which lead through lava flows, across cinder-covered flats, and through the newly revegetated lands around Sunset Crater. The best of these is the Lava Flow Nature Trail, a self-guided hike that is routed through a variety of types of lava and by a lava tunnel.

The drive from Sunset Crater to the Wupatki ruins leads through rolling land that is slowly recovering from the eight-century-old eruption that completely covered the surrounding countryside with ash and cinders. This land was the home for native residents who farmed the countryside. After the volcano spread a thick layer of rich cinders and ash on the countryside, the local farmers enjoyed several centuries of productive farming that led to a population explosion.

You can see the remains of several large high-rise apartment buildings where the farmers lived in settlements of over 100 people. A short walk behind the monument's visitor center leads to the ruins of a large pueblo with almost-intact rooms, an amphitheater and a ball court where you can explore and compare the living conditions of the 13th and 14th centuries with those of today.

No one is quite sure why the residents of pueblos all across what is now northern Arizona and New Mexico deserted their developed communities some time in the late 14th century, but they did, and apparently in a very short time. Wupatki is just one of the sites they abandoned, but one that offers insight into the lives of an otherwise unknown people.

Although the two monuments combined cover over 100 square miles, no backcountry camping is allowed. You can hike across much of Sunset Crater National Monument without permits, but you must have a permit to explore the backcountry in Wupatki National Monument. These are available for free from rangers at the Wupatki Visitor Center.

Directions: Take US 89 north from Flagstaff for 15 miles to the turnoff to Sunset Crater. A 38-mile paved road winds through both monuments. The Sunset Crater Visitor Center is located about two miles from US 89 at the southern entrance to the monuments, and the Wupatki Visitor Center is 22 miles farther along the road. It is 14 miles south of the northern entrance.

Fee or Free: There is a $4-per-vehicle fee; you must pay at the visitor center.

Camping: The forest service operates a small campground with water and restrooms across from the Sunset Crater Visitor Center.

Lodging: There is abundant lodging in Flagstaff.

Contact: National Park Service, 2717 North Steves Boulevard, Suite 3, Flagstaff, AZ 86004; (602) 556-7134.

Bill Williams Mountain

South of Williams

For great views of the North Rim of the Grand Canyon to the north, the Verde Valley to the southeast, and the San Francisco Peaks to the northeast, I head for Bill Williams Mountain and an easy three-mile trail that leads to the top.

The trail begins at 6,900 feet and ends at the 9,260-foot peak. On the way up, it leads through pine forests before ending with a winding gravel path to the summit. This is a great day hike and an exhilarating break from driving along Interstate 40.

Bill Williams Peak is covered with snow during the winter—there is even a small ski area—so hiking is limited to spring through fall. Summer hiking poses no problem here since the elevation tempers the heat.

Spring is the best time to visit. The moisture from the snowmelt feeds a verdant growth of wildflowers as the spring sun warms the south-facing slopes of the peak. The small groves of aspen that grow beside open meadows near the trail are bright with new leaves at this time, and deer frequently browse on the fresh growth in early morning and late evening.

If you're in the area in winter, visit the small ski area here. When I say small, that's exactly what I mean. For those who have only visited huge, modern ski resorts where the only way up the slopes is by chairlift, a trip up the lift on Bill Williams Mountain is a nice surprise. Don't expect long lines or long stretches of downhill runs.

Poma lifts are simply improved rope tows. You hold a saucer-like seat between your legs, grab onto a metal bar, and glide on your skis as the rope pulls you up the slope. This antiquated equipment doesn't attract large crowds, but it's excellent for beginners or those who just want to take some short runs down a beautiful mountain.

Directions: Take exit 161 south off Interstate 40 about a mile west of Williams. Follow the old toll road to the trailhead.

Fee or Free: This is a free area.

Camping: There is unlimited camping in the national forest, but improved campgrounds are some distance away at Cataract, Kaibab and Dogtown lakes.

Lodging: There is lodging in Williams.

Contact: Kaibab National Forest, Williams Ranger District, Route 1, Box 142, Williams, AZ 86046; (602) 635-2633.

White Horse Lake

In Kaibab National Forest

South of Interstate 40 near Williams, White Horse Lake is a pleasant getaway among tall ponderosa pine where each spring you can catch stocked trout for the frying pan. It is a small, several-hundred-acre lake tucked away among the forests about 20 miles southeast of town.

Although this region defies descriptions of desert by having a decent amount of water and tall groves of pine, it is still part of the arid Southwest, just higher in elevation at about 7,000 feet. Summer thunderstorms and winter snowstorms drop plenty of moisture on the high meadows of the forests and the difference between the vegetation here and that found at lower elevations is dramatic.

The forest service maintains an improved campground with tables, fireplaces and restrooms near the lake, and along the lakeshore are housekeeping cabins, a small store selling groceries and fishing tackle, and a boat rental.

During midsummer, the campground and lake are crowded, at least by Arizona standards, but most of the year you can find a campsite easily, without worrying about someone catching you on their backcast.

If this site is a little too improved for your tastes, see the entry for Sycamore Canyon on page 81. One road to this rugged gorge takes off from the road from Williams to White Horse Lake.

Directions: Take Perkinsville Road south from Williams for eight miles to the intersection with White Horse Lake Road. Turn left at the intersection and continue another 10 miles to the lake.

Fee or Free: Day use is free; camping costs about $7 a night, on a first-come, first-served basis.

Lodging: There is lodging in Williams, as well as housekeeping cabins at the lake.

Contact: Kaibab National Forest, Williams Ranger District, Route 1, Box 434, Williams, AZ 86046; (602) 635-2633.

Sycamore Canyon

South of Interstate 40

I had been told that Sycamore Canyon would be worth any trouble I might encounter reaching it. Still, my first reaction as I viewed the wide expanse of the desolate red-rock canyon (after a 20-mile drive along dirt roads from Williams) was shock at the wild beauty of the place.

Although Oak Creek Canyon is the best known of the red-rock canyons that have been cut along the southern edge of the Colorado Plateau, Sycamore Canyon is just as beautiful, and much more isolated. This makes it an excellent destination for those who want to explore wild canyons where few people tread rather than fight for parking spaces at vista points along well-traveled highways.

Sycamore Canyon roughly parallels Oak Creek Canyon about 15 miles to the west, and is very similar to it topographically. The resemblance ends there, however. While Oak Creek Canyon is bisected by US 89A, is easily reached, and is a popular tourist destination, Sycamore Canyon can only be reached by minimally maintained dirt roads that run through Coconino and Prescott national forests. Consequently, it is visited by few people each year.

Deep gorges, high cliffs and spectacular geological formations carved out of red and white layered sedimen-

---

tary rocks provide the backdrop for hikes along the canyon floors. Hikers wander among riparian growth with tall stands of cottonwood, willow and sycamore lining the seasonal streams.

The canyon is over 20 miles long, and the widest point from rim to rim is about seven miles. The cliffs rise as much as 2,000 feet above the canyon floor in places.

Hiking is relatively easy as you follow the wide streambeds that cut through the canyon. The terrain is flat, and there are few obstacles. You can take sidetrips into some of the feeder canyons and return to the main path to continue your hike.

Be aware that summer temperatures frequently rise above 100 degrees and the streams provide no water during the dry season. There are a few springs in the canyon, but they are not dependable water sources. The best times to visit the canyon are spring and fall, when temperatures are lower and there is likely to be water in the streams.

You should always carry an adequate supply of water, however, as even during the wet seasons there is no dependable source of water in the canyon.

This is one of my favorite hikes in red-rock country. Many times I've enjoyed day and overnight hikes here, and only seldom have I encountered anyone else in the canyon.

Directions: From the north in the Coconino National Forest there are trailheads at Sycamore Pass, Turkey Butte and Red Hill, which lead to Sycamore Canyon. From the south, there is access to the canyon by Forest Service Road N in Tuzigoot National Monument.

The northern trailheads are only accessible over a maze of forest service roads; a current forest service map and planning are required to navigate the maze to the right trailhead. Any directions I could give here would only serve to confuse you unless you had a map in hand. The forest service will gladly mark the various routes to the canyon for you.

From the west, in Prescott National Forest, take Perkinsville Road south from Williams for eight miles and then go east on White Horse Lake Road for another eight miles to Forest Service Road 14, where a sign directs you to the canyon rim.

Fee or Free: This is a free area, but there is a charge for a forest service map. The forest service also publishes a leaflet and trail map for the wilderness area.

Camping: Primitive camping is permitted on national forest lands near the canyon; hike-in camping is allowed in all but a small portion of the canyon near the southern end.

Lodging: Plenty of lodging is available in Flagstaff, Prescott and the Oak Creek Canyon towns.

Contact: Coconino National Forest, 2323 East Greenlaw Lane, Flagstaff, AZ 86001; (602) 527-3600. Various ranger districts administer different sections of the canyon, and the forest headquarters can tell you who to contact for current road and backpacking conditions.

Oak Creek Canyon

West of Sedona

I really couldn't get by without at least mentioning Oak Creek Canyon. Everyone who goes to northern Arizona seems to find their way to this melange of tourists, beautiful red cliffs, scenic drives and New Age enthusiasts.

I personally prefer nearby Sycamore Canyon, but for those who have only a short time to explore the region, or who don't care to take wilderness trips into isolated areas, Oak Creek Canyon is an acceptable option. The drive is easy, there is plenty of civilization, and the scenery is breathtaking. The civilization part is what makes me want to avoid the area, but that is what attracts many others. Where else can you find such a combination?

US 89A begins in the ponderosa pine forests of the Colorado Plateau near Flagstaff, and then suddenly drops almost 2,000 feet into Oak Creek Canyon. The highway hugs tight to the stark, red canyon walls as it follows the twisting path of the creek winding down a narrow gorge. Multicolored mesas and buttes rise above the horizon in the distance as you drive down the canyon, and they become more visible as the canyon widens out after about

10 miles. The number of visible red, orange and gold buttes expands rapidly as the view widens with the canyon.

Before you reach Sedona you come to Slide Rock State Park. This is a small day-use park, and a good place to stop for a rest or snack. Young and old alike carouse on the natural waterslides formed in the small falls that flow over smooth red rocks in the creek. The highest of the falls is less than 10 feet high, and everyone enjoys sliding over the smooth passageways into the cool pools below.

The landscape around Sedona, a town of elegant resorts, pricey art galleries and New Age activities, becomes open, high desert as the canyon flattens out. Many visitors like to take in the views as they sit at outdoor restaurants and look out at the red-rock spires and cathedrals that surround the town.

One semi-wilderness stop near Sedona is Red Rock State Park. It sits along Oak Creek among tall stands of cottonwood, sycamore and willow. Birdlife is excellent here, with over 135 species reported. Bald eagles winter over in Red Rock, and black hawks nest in the spring. The park has a well-marked trail system that leads through the prime wildlife-viewing areas.

From Sedona, US 89A continues over a twisting path to the old, restored mining town of Jerome. From the steep slopes where Jerome hangs on for dear life, you can look back through the canyon. The drive (and US 89A) ends at Prescott to the south.

Directions: Take US 89A south from Flagstaff to Prescott. Red Rock State Park is three miles west of Sedona on US 89A. Turn onto Lower Red Rock Loop Road and go two miles to the park entrance.

Fee or Free: This is a free area, unless you count the pricey tourist stops around Sedona (where you often feel you are paying just to see the surrounding sights).

Camping: Undeveloped camping is available in national forest land to the east and west of the highway. There is a developed forest service campground at Mingus Mountain, just past Jerome.

Lodging: There is an excellent choice of lodging in Flagstaff, Sedona and Prescott.

Contact: Coconino National Forest, 2323 East Greenlaw Lane, Flagstaff, AZ 86001; (602) 527-3600. Red Rock State Park, HC02 Box 886, Sedona, AZ 86336; (602) 282-6907. Sedona Ranger District, P.O. Box 300, Sedona, AZ 86339; (602) 282-4119.

Mingus & Woodchute Mountains

Near Oak Creek Canyon

I discovered the lovely Mingus Mountain Campground after a visit to the historic mining town of Jerome, which is now a state historic park. The old town sits precariously on a mountainside overlooking the Verde Valley high up in the ponderosa pine forest of Arizona's Black Hills. It has long been a favorite photographic subject of mine.

After roaming around the picturesque community on one visit, where houses were slipping downhill at what seemed like an alarming rate, I began to search for a campsite. An open meadow in the forest would have been more than satisfactory to me, but the signs that pointed to the Mingus Mountain Campground along Forest Service Road 104 south of Jerome were enticing. The area seemed almost entirely unused, except for the old mines that were scattered along the slopes. I didn't expect to find a developed campground anywhere nearby.

I did find one, though, and one set at 7,600 feet in a ponderosa pine forest, with great vistas to the east and south over the Verde Valley. Today, this popular campground is the jumping-off point for wildlife viewing in the surrounding area. Turkey, band-tailed pigeons and Abert squirrels are seen in large numbers, as are mule deer.

Although this is an excellent site for wildlife viewing, the campground is seldom full. It is generally closed between December and March, due to snow and poor road conditions.

For more adventurous souls who wish to head into the wilderness rather than stay at an improved campground, the trailhead for the Woodchute Trail is near the junction of Forest Service Road 106 and US 89A. The seven-mile trail passes 7,834-foot Woodchute Mountain on its way into the Woodchute Wilderness.

Backpacking in this area is a treat. The trails are moderate as they follow the contours of the slopes. From Woodchute Mountain, you get excellent views of the Verde, Chino and Lonesome valleys, as well as the San Francisco Peaks.

Directions: From Cottonwood, take US 89A north about 16 miles to Forest Service Road 104. Turn south and continue about three miles to the campground. The Woodchute Trailhead is on Forest Service Road 106 about a quarter mile before the Forest Service Road 104 turnoff on the opposite side of the road.

Fee or Free: This is a free area, except for campground fees.

Camping: There is improved camping at Mingus Mountain Campground. Primitive and backcountry camping are allowed in national forest land.

Lodging: The nearest lodging is in Cottonwood and Prescott.

Contact: Prescott National Forest, 344 South Cortez Street, Prescott, AZ 86303; (602) 445-1762.

Forest Lakes of Coconino National Forest

Along the Mogollon Rim

It seems odd to discuss forest lakes in a book that is basically about deserts, but the high country of all the Southwest states includes a number of large forests at higher elevations where heavy snowfall occurs during winter. The melt from the snowpacks provides plenty of water for both natural and dammed lakes throughout the region.

A number of these lakes are found along the ponderosa forests of the Mogollon Rim to the south and east of Flagstaff. Set among tall pines in open meadows, they offer welcome relief from the hot summers of lower elevations. This makes them popular getaways for natives in the region. If you want a secluded wilderness experience, don't expect to find one at these lakes. What you will find at some of the less-developed lakes, though, is plenty of wildlife.

The lakes all sit at an elevation of about 7,000 feet, and are inaccessible during times of heavy winter snow. During late spring and early summer, the moisture from

---

the melting snowpack makes for great displays of wild-flowers in the meadows surrounding the lakes. Head for them as soon as you can while the blooms are out and the crowds have yet to arrive.

Mormon Lake is one of the most popular getaways near Flagstaff, and one of my favorites. It is the largest natural lake in Arizona when it is full, but it is quite shallow, with a maximum depth of about six feet. In dry years it is little more than a marsh.

Dry years make for few visitors because boating and fishing are severely restricted. That is when I most appreciate the lake and surrounding countryside. Wildlife watching is better with less human activity, when both large and small animals come great distances to the lake for water.

During the fall and spring migrations, there are always large flocks of migrating waterfowl at the lake, and during winter, when you can reach the lake, you are likely to spot a number of wintering bald eagles. They are joined by osprey, which hunt for fish in the shallow waters, and peregrine falcons, which feed upon the smaller waterfowl.

Almost year-round, you can see large numbers of elk, mule deer and pronghorn as they come to the lake's edges to drink in the early morning and evening.

A paved road leads around the lake, several forest service campgrounds are nearby, and it is only a short drive from Flagstaff. The drive around Lake Mormon is so popular that a viewing site, the Doug Morrison Overlook, has been built on the east side of the lake. It offers excellent views of the lake and the San Francisco Peaks.

Directions: Head south on Interstate 17 from Flagstaff to exit 339. Take Lake Mary Road (Forest Service Road 3) southeast for 21 miles to Mormon Lake. Forest Service Road 90 circles the lake.

Fee or Free: This is a free area, except for campground fees.

Camping: There are two forest service campgrounds on the west side of the lake.

Lodging: There is plenty of lodging in Flagstaff.

Contact: Coconino National Forest, 2323 East Greenlaw Lane, Flagstaff, AZ 86001; (602) 527-3600.

Apache Creek & Juniper Mesa Wilderness Areas

In Prescott National Forest

Want to hike through scenic country with plenty of rolling hills, steep escarpments and wide canyons? Want to roam for miles without running into any other hikers? Then head to the Apache Creek and Juniper Mesa wilderness areas at the north end of the Santa Maria Mountains. These two areas have all of the above, plus a pinyon pine-juniper forest that covers the slopes and tops of mesas. The elevations range from 5,200 to 7,050 feet, so hiking is easy even during midsummer when the temperatures are scorching at lower elevations.

Although there are not a lot of marked trails here, hiking is easy, and there is more water from small streams and springs than in most other wilderness areas in the state.

Since trails are few, and they really aren't necessary for hiking in this open country, you can begin your outing just about anywhere along the boundaries of the wilderness areas. Just head to the end of the forest service roads, park your vehicle, and head out into the canyons and rolling hills.

Few visitors venture into these isolated areas. The ones who do are mostly hunters, who come for the deer that roam here, as well as the antelope, turkey, quail and javelina. As recently as the late 1980s, fewer than a thousand visitors a year were reported in the Juniper Mesa Wilderness Area, and they still number in the low thousands for both areas. With over 7,500 acres in the Juniper Mesa Wilderness and 5,500 acres in the Apache Creek Wilderness, there is plenty of space for all who head here looking for a wilderness experience.

I have enjoyed hiking and camping in this backcountry a number of times, and am always amazed at the lack of companions. (Not that I am complaining, mind you.) A generally reliable supply of water, great views of canyons and mesas, plenty of wildlife and easy hiking make this a prime outdoor getaway.

Directions: Take Williamson Valley Road north from Prescott just over 20 miles to the small community of Simmons. About a mile past Simmons, Williamson Road dead-ends and Forest Service Road 6 continues toward the northwest. In about five miles, at the Mud Tank Wash, the road forks. Take Forest Service Road 6 to the left. Continue on it for 10 miles to the junction with Forest Service Road 95. Take a left on Forest Service Road 95 and follow it to the Walnut Creek Ranger Station.

From the ranger station, Forest Service Road 95F heads north to the boundary of the Juniper Mesa Wilderness Area and Forest Service Road 150 heads west toward the Apache Creek Wilderness Area. Within the first mile or so, forest service roads 150B and 150A head south to the boundary of the Apache Creek Wilderness Area.

Fee or Free: This is a free area.

Camping: Wilderness camping is allowed, but there are no improved campgrounds nearby.

Lodging: The nearest lodging is in Prescott.

Contact: Prescott National Forest, 344 South Cortez Street, Prescott, AZ 86303; (602) 445-1762.

Dead Horse Lake State Park

Along the Verde River

This state park set along the Verde River includes some of the best cottonwood-willow riparian forests in Arizona. I discovered it many years ago while my wife and I were going to school in Tempe. We were searching for good birdwatching spots away from the searing heat of the low desert and found this one.

Over 100 species of birds have been recorded in the park, and seven species of our only flying mammal, the bat, are regularly seen flitting in the evening sky in search of delectable insects. And insects there are, for the wetlands along the river and at nearby Tavasci Marsh are great breeding grounds for aquatic bugs. The bugs in turn lure birds who prey upon them.

Another feature of the 20-acre marsh are the active beaver ponds where wading birds congregate to feed in the shallow water.

This is a great place to camp overnight when you can walk among the riparian growth, searching for feeding birds. Beaver are also most active at night. Often you can hear their whistles and tail-splats, even if you don't catch a glimpse of the animals themselves. In the evenings during spring, summer and fall, the park offers interpretive programs at the campground.

The park's trails lead along the Verde River and around the wetlands of the marsh. Both are easily hiked and take you into areas with plenty of birds.

At 3,300 feet, the park is still pleasant during midsummer when the heat at lower elevations drives people to seek out cooler climes. I enjoy the park best during spring and fall, though, when there is more wildlife activity and the weather is a bit cooler.

Directions: From downtown Cottonwood, turn north on 5th Street off Main Street and cross the river to the park entrance. You can reach the marsh by continuing through the park 1.5 miles from the entrance.

Fee or Free: Day use costs $3 per vehicle; camping costs $8 to $11 per night.

Camping: The park has 45 campsites, which are on a first-come, first-served basis.

Lodging: The nearest lodging is in Cottonwood and Prescott.

Contact: Dead Horse Lake State Park, P.O. Box 144, Cottonwood, AZ 86326; (602) 634-5283.

Pine Mountain Wilderness Area

In Prescott National Forest

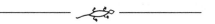

Prescott National Forest covers over 1,000,000 acres of desert, mountains and canyons in west-central Arizona between Seligman along Interstate 40 to the north and Interstate 17 north of Phoenix to the south. Ponderosa pine-covered peaks rise above 6,500 feet in the forest, an elevation which makes for good hiking even during the heat of summer. In winter, many of these peaks are covered with snow, and offer good cross-country skiing.

A number of wilderness areas have been designated in the forest, and most of these have well-marked and maintained trails that lead to mountain lakes and streams where fishing is good to excellent.

Several interesting areas lie within this grid. One of my favorites is the 11,450-acre Pine Mountain Wilderness. This little-visited area features 6,814-foot Pine Mountain, where there is a small island of tall ponderosa pine. It lies along the Verde Rim, offering magnificent views of the Verde River and surrounding desert.

Deep, rugged canyons below cut through pinyon- and juniper-covered mesas where you can get fine views of the Verde River as it runs toward the desert to the south. Deer, mountain lion, javelina and black bear are all found in the wilderness area, and birdwatching is fair.

The people who come here do so for the solitude found on the lightly used and maintained trails. I have seen signs of cougars and bears in the area, but have never witnessed the animals myself.

Summer hiking is feasible at this elevation, but days can still get quite warm. Be sure to take plenty of water when you can hike along the open trails.

Directions: Trailheads from Prescott National Forest are at Nelson Place Spring on Forest Service Road 68 and Hidden Spring on Forest Service Road 677A. Both head out from the Sycamore Ranger Station in Dugas. To reach Dugas, take Dugas Road (exit 268) southwest off Interstate 17 north of Cordes Junction.

Fee or Free: This is a free area.

Camping: Camping is allowed in the national forest and wilderness areas, but there are no improved campgrounds nearby.

Lodging: There is lodging in Williams and Prescott, as well as in Flagstaff and Phoenix a little farther away.

Contact: Prescott National Forest, 344 South Cortez Street, Prescott, AZ 86303; (602) 445-1762. The national forest publishes several brochures and maps on the wilderness areas.

23

Verde Hot Springs

Along the Verde River

Some would question why anyone would want to go to hot springs in a region where the temperatures regularly reach those of a sauna and where the humidity approaches that of a steam bath during the monsoon rains of late summer.

It's not for me to question the sanity of others. Remember, I like to travel in the low desert country of the Southwest during summer. Let's just say that there are several hot springs along the Verde River, and that some people like to soak in them.

Of the hot springs that I have visited, Verde is the easiest to reach and has the hottest water. Verde Hot Springs is on the site of a historic resort that burned down many years ago. The remains are clean, and sit high up on the west bank of the Verde River in high-desert country at about 2,800 feet.

Mineral waters flow out of several riverbank springs at about 104 degrees into several small, indoor soaking pools. A larger, outdoor cement pool is fed by a 98-degree spring. Below, near the river itself and only usable at low water, are several rock-walled soaking areas that were built after the resort burned.

About 50 feet upstream from the remains of the resort is a riverbank cave. Inside is a large cement pool filled from a 104-degree spring.

An amazing thing about this site is that there is almost no litter. (At least it was true the several times that I visited.) Those who venture into this isolated spring seem to have a vested interest in keeping it clean. Please join them in this effort if you visit.

Here's fair warning for those who are shy, or wish other people were: Local custom at Verde Hot Springs is clothing optional.

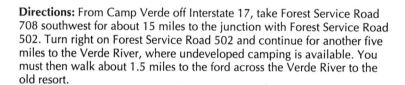

Directions: From Camp Verde off Interstate 17, take Forest Service Road 708 southwest for about 15 miles to the junction with Forest Service Road 502. Turn right on Forest Service Road 502 and continue for another five miles to the Verde River, where undeveloped camping is available. You must then walk about 1.5 miles to the ford across the Verde River to the old resort.

Fee or Free: This is a free area.

Camping: Camping is available along the Verde River on the north side; no camping is allowed on the south side of the river near the hot springs.

Lodging: The best chances for lodging are in Flagstaff.

Contact: Coconino National Forest, 2323 East Greenlaw Lane, Flagstaff, AZ 86001; (602) 527-3600.

The Senator Highway

From Prescott to Crown King

The word "highway" brings visions of paved roads leading through tame country where civilization reigns. While that may be true of most such designations, it certainly isn't true of the Senator Highway. This route, otherwise known as Forest Service Road 52, is unpaved and rough in spots as its curvy path leads through an area dotted with hills. It is also one of the premier drives in Arizona, however, running through an area of the Prescott National Forest that was once active with mining.

If you make this drive, be sure to take the short sidetrip to the top of Mount Union, which is reachable by car in good weather. One ranger called it "the best place in Arizona to appreciate its infinite space and comprehend its heritage." At 7,979 feet, Mount Union is the highest peak in the Bradshaw Mountains, and views from it include large sections of desert and mountain ranges that extend to the horizon in every direction.

As you drive through ponderosa pine forests, you occasionally come to open areas where you can pull over for views of the desert in the distance. You may even pass some serious mountain bikers who have discovered this road.

The goal for many who drive this byway is the old mining town of Crown King. Tourists keep this once-thriving community from becoming a ghost town by stopping through and spending a little money as they come to stay at the three nearby campgrounds around Horsethief Lake. The lake offers good, if not excellent fishing for bass, crappie, bluegill and a few rainbow trout.

A number of scenic trails lead out from the campgrounds. My favorite is the one that leads into the Castle Creek Wilderness Area, just to the south of Horsethief Lake; the trailhead is at the end of the forest service road at the boundary of the wilderness area. From here, you can hike into country that is more desolate than the developed recreation area around the lake. Keep your eyes peeled for old, abandoned mines, which dot the region.

Directions: Take the Senator Highway (Forest Service Road 52) south from Prescott into the Bradshaw Mountains. Crown King is a little over 25 miles in, traveling on curving, rough roads.

Fee or Free: This a free area, except for the forest service campgrounds, which range from $4 to $8 a night.

Camping: Three campgrounds near Horsethief Lake have almost 100 campsites. Lynx Lake and White Spur campgrounds take reservations for a fee; call (800) 280-2267.

Lodging: The closest lodging is in Prescott.

Contact: Prescott National Forest, 344 South Cortez Street, Prescott, AZ 86303; (602) 445-1762.

Agua Fria Canyon

Off Interstate 17, north of Phoenix

Lake Pleasant Regional Park lies to the west of Interstate 17 on the way to Flagstaff from Phoenix, and is the furthest from Phoenix of the large regional parks that is administered by the Maricopa County Department of Parks and Recreation. The lake was formed after the Agua Fria River was dammed early in the century. It has since become a popular boating and swimming destination for Phoenix residents.

Above Lake Pleasant, the Agua Fria River cuts through a 13-mile-long canyon out of the rugged area east of Black Mesa. Even when the lake and surrounding park are crowded with water-sports enthusiasts, the canyon above, which is undisturbed by roads, is quiet and a good place to hike in solitude.

The hanging flume of the 76-year-old Richbar Mine is strung along the northern side of the canyon. The ruins of the abandoned mine sprawl along the slopes above the river near the upper end of the canyon, and this makes a good starting point for hikes.

The hike to the mine from the parking area at the end of the access road is an easy day trek. For an overnight or longer hike, you can continue down the canyon to where it goes under the freeway.

While the remains of the old mine are interesting, it

is the stark beauty of the rugged river canyon that draws me to the region. The river has cut through an ancient lava flow and the high cliffs have eroded over time to form ledges and caves where raptors nest. Keep an eye on these as you hike along the river in late spring and you may see the large birds of prey feeding their young.

Temperatures in the canyon climb into the 100s regularly during the summer months. As with most areas at this elevation, the best time to visit is from November to April, when daytime temperatures are more conducive to hiking.

Directions: To reach the top end of the canyon, take the Badger Springs exit (exit 256) east off Interstate 17 and turn right at the first fork. Continue to Badger Creek. From here it is a three-mile hike to the mine.

To reach the bottom end of the canyon, take the Squaw Valley exit (exit 244) near Black Canyon City. Follow Squaw Valley Road east from Interstate 17 for a quarter mile. Turn left on Riverbend Road, and then take another left at the first fork. Continue for two more miles to the canyon.

Fee or Free: This is a free area.

Camping: You may camp on BLM land. The nearest improved campground is at Lake Pleasant Regional Park.

Lodging: There is abundant lodging in Phoenix.

Contact: BLM Phoenix Resource Area, 2015 West Deer Valley Road, Phoenix, AZ 85027; (602) 780-8090.

Phoenix's City & Regional Parks

In and around Phoenix

I generally steer clear of parks near major metropolitan areas. In my experience, they are frequently loud, raucous places where people head when they want to be outdoors but don't want to be too far from their next-door neighbors. This is just as true for the large parks in and around Phoenix as for those in any metropolitan area, but these parks have some qualities that compensate for the occasionally raucous crowds.

For one thing, the Phoenix area parks are huge. South Mountain Park, southwest of Phoenix, is one of the largest municipal parks in the world, with almost 15,000 acres. All the state parks in Arizona could be placed in it and have room left over. Yet it is not even the largest of over a dozen large and small city and county parks that Phoenix residents and visitors can escape to when they tire of the crowds in the city.

Large picnic areas and well-marked trails that lead along the slopes of South Mountain are scattered throughout the park, along the well-maintained paved roads. The trails, which lead through cactus forests, are pleasant for day hiking from early fall to late spring. In midsummer, you'll only want to venture out on trails before the sun rises in the morning and just before it sets in the evening. It is just too hot to hike in midday.

White Tank Mountain Regional Park, to the west of the city, is one of the large, minimally developed parks, and it is an excellent place to hike from early fall through late spring. The trails in White Tank Mountain Regional Park lead along the sides of the park mountains and have good views over Phoenix and the surrounding desert. They are also lightly used, considering their proximity to a major metropolitan area, and that makes wildlife viewing good. Birding is excellent here, and if you are quiet, you may spot some javelina and perhaps a bobcat as you hike in the early morning or late evening.

Papago Park, one of the smaller parks in the system near the eastern edge of Phoenix, includes the Desert Botanical Gardens and Phoenix Zoo, both of which include desert exhibits of interest to anyone who wants to explore in the hinterlands of the state. The botanical gardens, in particular, are excellent, offering good exhibits of the cactus that are common in the surrounding desert.

One note of interest about Phoenix-area parks: While city and regional parks in many parts of the country have defined hours (generally from dawn to dusk), which keep people out during the late evening, Phoenix's parks have hours that are appropriate to the climate. Most city parks in Phoenix are open from 5:30 a.m. until midnight. During summer, they are heavily used after dark when the temperatures drop to at least the 90s, which is mild in comparison to midday.

If you find yourself uncomfortably confined in Phoenix while on a trip to the Southwest, remember: There are thousands of acres of undeveloped parklands around the urban area with plenty of hiking trails for you to explore.

Contact: Maricopa County Parks and Recreation Department, 3475 West Durango Street, Phoenix, AZ 85009; (602) 506-2930.

Phon D. Sutton Recreation Area

Along the Verde and Salt Rivers, outside Mesa

The Verde and Salt rivers join together about 10 miles from downtown Mesa, a Phoenix suburb, and at their confluence stands a lush riparian habitat that rises in contrast to the arid desert that extends into the distance in all directions. This habitat, part of the Phon D. Sutton Recreation Area, is home to dozens of species of birds, including nesting bald eagles.

The tall cottonwoods and thick growths of willow that thrive along the banks of the rivers add a lush green color to the generally grey desert surroundings.

The trees here are among the few places anywhere in the Arizona desert where bald eagles nest, and their nests are protected by a buffer zone where visitors are not allowed to go.

Other birds found here on a regular basis include red-tailed and Harris hawks, osprey, cactus wren, phaineopepla and Gambel quail. All of these can be seen by simply walking along the Lower Salt River Nature Trail that leads through both desert and riparian habitats in the recreation area.

The flow of both rivers is controlled by upstream dams. Each has a relatively large flow year-round at the confluence, and this provides for an unusual desert environment.

Late fall to early spring is the best time to visit the area, and the wildflowers are spectacular in March and April after a winter of heavy rainfall.

Directions: Head north on the Bush Highway from the junction of US 60 and Powers Road in Mesa. Continue for 9.5 miles to the marked turnoff to the recreation area. Go north for another mile to the parking area.

Fee or Free: This is a free area.

Camping: Self-contained camp trailers and RVs can camp at the recreation area during the winter. There are numerous campgrounds in other national forest recreation areas along the Salt River, off the Bush Highway.

Lodging: There is plenty of lodging in the Phoenix area.

Contact: Tonto National Forest, 2324 East McDowell Road, Phoenix, AZ 85006; (602) 225-5200.

The Apache Trail

Along the Salt River, through the Superstition Mountains

The Apache Trail, or State Road 88 as it's formally known, is a dramatic, scenic drive through a wild region of volcanic debris and steep-cliffed canyons. The route was an ancient Native American shortcut through the Superstition Mountains; it closely follows the Salt River for many miles.

The 50-mile drive begins at Apache Junction just to the west of the Superstition Mountains and then turns to the northeast as it enters the foothills of the range. As the trail leads into the range, it follows the course of the Salt River. Soon it comes to a series of artificial lakes impounded behind dams along the once free-flowing river.

The first of these is Canyon Lake, where you can find a campground, picnic areas and boating facilities. There are even excursion boats that offer sightseeing tours. These tours take visitors into the smaller arms of the lake, along canyons where the exposed rock faces offer outstanding visual evidence of the turbulent geological history of the region.

At Canyon Lake, the road shifts to the south away from the Salt River. About 20 miles from Apache Junction, it comes to the small community of Tortilla Flat. The store, motel and restaurant here are the last services for 30 miles.

Tortilla Flat is also near the end of the paved road. Five miles past the town, the Apache Trail becomes a gravel road that winds up sharp switchbacks through a wild canyon. Here, layers of pink and tan, dotted with intrusions of quartz and feldspar, color the exposed faces of steep cliffs. This is Fish Creek Canyon, one of the most spectacular drives in Arizona.

The gravel road passes by the turnoff to Apache Lake, where you'll find small campgrounds that are less crowded than those at larger lakes, and continues to Roosevelt Lake, the largest reservoir in interior Arizona. The reservoir lies behind Roosevelt Dam, the world's largest masonry dam, and offers a wide variety of camping, fishing and boating activities.

I first came to these lakes in my younger days when I waterskied over their cool waters on hot summer days. For those who like waterskiing, fishing and developed campgrounds with all the amenities, these lakes are a great outdoor getaway. And for those who just want a scenic drive, the Apache Trail is unforgettable.

If you want to make a foray into the wilds of the Superstition Mountains, take the gravel road into First Water Creek about five miles out of Apache Junction. Hiking trails head out from the parking area near the creek. These trails are excellent for first-timers who are still leery of adventuring into truly wild desert country, and want to try their wings on a short sortie first.

Directions: Take US 60 east from Phoenix about 35 miles to the town of Apache Junction. Take State Road 88, the Apache Trail, northeast from there.

Fee or Free: This is a free area, but there are fees for camping and boating.

Camping: There are plenty of developed campgrounds in the area.

Lodging: Minimal lodging is available at Roosevelt, Tortilla Flat and Apache Junction. For more options, head to the Phoenix area.

Contact: Tonto National Forest, 2324 McDowell Road, Phoenix, AZ 85006; (602) 225-5200.

Lost Dutchman State Park

In Tonto National Forest & the Superstition Mountains

For years, the search for treasure in the mountains of Arizona has tantalized many. One legend purports that a large amount of gold and silver, which was lost while being transported by Spanish soldiers in the 16th century, is hidden in a canyon in the Chiricahua Mountains along the state's eastern border. Dozens of stories circulate about prospectors who supposedly had uncovered rich veins of gold, which they were never able to locate again.

None of these tales, however, can match the legend of the Lost Dutchman Gold Mine. This legendary mine, located in the Superstition Mountains, has been one of the most tantalizing mysteries of the Southwest since the late 1870s. At that time, "Dutchman" Jakob Walz was said to have shot two Mexican miners and taken over their mine.

This solitary prospector kept the location of his mine a secret, but he did show up in Phoenix periodically with bags of nuggets. He bragged of his strike as he spent his fortune in the saloons and gambling halls, but refused to reveal the whereabouts of the mine. Until he was on his death bed, nearly two decades later, that is...

With that revelation, he launched a quest that has never stopped. Even today, treasure hunters venture into the Superstition Mountains in search of a treasure that would be worth millions of dollars if it were found. Supposedly, it is somewhere near Weaver's Needle, the most recognizable landmark along the Apache Trail, the road that follows an ancient Native American trail. The Native Americans of the region supposedly knew of the mine and considered it a sacred site.

The legend has reached such proportions that it has been the subject of over 50 books and 800 magazine articles.

I have hiked in the area and have visited Lost Dutchman State Park, which is adjacent to the Superstition Wilderness, but I have never attempted to locate the mine. It's not that I'm afraid, mind you. It's just that I was in my teens when I read my first magazine article about the mine and it retains a hold on my mind. It told of bullet-pierced skulls, shots fired from nearby rocks at treasure hunters who felt they were close to the mine, and bounty seekers who were never heard from again after they set off to search for it.

Of course I know that the missing prospectors probably succumbed to the terrible heat of the region after wandering off the beaten path, and bullet-pierced skulls could be the remains of desperadoes fighting it out over their ill-gotten gains. Still, maybe, just maybe, there is something supernatural, if you will, about the mine. If there is, I don't want to have to deal with it in addition to the other hardships encountered while exploring the steep canyons of the region.

The 335-acre state park is an excellent jumping-off point for hikers and backpackers who wish to explore the Superstitions, for it is only a mile from the boundary of the Superstition Wilderness Area of Tonto National Forest. Several trails lead from the park into Superstition Wilderness Area.

This wilderness area is close to the spreading tentacles of Phoenix, the blob that ate Arizona, but its rugged terrain will never be eaten. It is more likely to eat, for this is one of those places that folks cocooned from the natural world by modern amenities such as air conditioning and piped water seldom venture into. At most, they stop by the park to picnic on their way to the reservoirs that have been impounded along the Salt River to the north.

For those who want to head into a rugged wilderness of true desert, there is no better place to begin. But beware: It is not a place to head to during midsummer, unless you are a camel. This is one of the hottest places in Arizona.

Directions: Take US 60 east from Phoenix to Apache Junction and turn northeast on State Road 88. The park is five miles northeast of Apache Junction.

Fee or Free: Day-use at Lost Dutchman State Park costs $3; camping is $8 per night.

Camping: There are 35 improved campsites at the park. You can wilderness camp in the national forest and wilderness area. All sites are first-come, first-served.

Lodging: There is abundant lodging in the Phoenix area, and more in Apache Junction.

Contact: Lost Dutchman State Park, 6109 North Apache Trail, Apache Junction, AZ 85219; (602) 982-4485. Tonto National Forest, 234 McDowell Road, Phoenix, AZ 85006; (602) 225-5200.

Mazatzal Wilderness & Pinal Mountains

In Tonto National Forest

Tonto National Forest is one of the most heavily visited national forests in the nation. While this may come as a shock to many, anyone who has spent even one summer in Phoenix will understand why. With over a dozen wilderness areas, 50-plus campgrounds and miles of forest service roads that lead into the backcountry, the forest is a great outdoor getaway for those who want to escape from the punishing heat that radiates from the asphalt carpet of the Phoenix metropolitan area.

One area of the forest that I have enjoyed over the years is a lightly visited wilderness area that lies just over an hour north of Phoenix. The Mazatzal Wilderness covers over 250,000 acres between the Verde River and the Tonto Basin, and ranges in elevation from 2,600 feet in the southwest corner to 7,903 feet at the top of Mazatzal Peak.

Although this area is easily accessible from Phoenix, it is much less crowded than the Superstition Wilderness

---

to the southeast. There is no rational explanation for this phenomenon, but many of the trails through both the lower and upper elevations near Mazatzal Peak are virtually unused. I have hiked in desert scrub during winter, pinyon pine and juniper forests and grasslands higher up as the temperatures began to rise, and the ponderosa forests at the higher elevations during the hot summer months, and seldom have I encountered other hikers or campers. And I can't understand why. Even the wild-flower displays in early spring don't seem to attract a great number of people.

A number of trailheads that lead into the wilderness area are located along State Road 87 as it runs north from Phoenix to Payson, and my favorite hike is the five-mile Barhardt Trail. This trail leads to the Mazatzal Divide Trail, which is a major north-south route through the wilderness area. To reach the top of Mazatzal Peak, you follow the Barhardt Trail to the Mazatzal Divide Trail, and from there follow the signs to the peak.

The canyons and ridges that you cross on this hike are some of the most beautiful of any in the forest, and you can enjoy them in solitude as you hike along the Barhardt Trail. As the trail ends at the Divide Trail, you can continue three miles for a view from the top of the peak, or you can return to your vehicle if your legs and lungs have had enough.

I prefer to make the climb to the peak slowly, and often plan on making it an overnight trip. If you choose to do this, remember that you should carry all the water you might need, since the streams in the region are not dependable water sources.

Another area in the forest that I like a lot is the Pinal Mountains near Globe. The tallest point in this 10-mile, forest-covered range is 7,812-foot Signal Peak.

This area has several particularly good campgrounds that offer excellent opportunities for day hikes into the backcountry. When I am in the mood for just camping and not interested in backpacking, this is one area in the national forest that I seek out. It is an easy drive from both Phoenix and Tucson, but it is not as crowded as one would imagine.

Late fall, when the air is crisp, the colors are out and the chance of snow in the higher elevations is inviting, is an especially invigorating time to camp here.

Directions: To reach the Barhardt Trail, go north on State Road 87 from Phoenix for 61 miles. Near mile 239, turn left onto Forest Service Road 419 and head five miles to the end of the road. Park and take the trail from the west side of the parking area. It helps to have a forest service map of the area, as well as a USGS topographical map.

The Pinal Mountains lie to the south of Globe and Miami off US 60. Several forest service roads cross this mountainous area, and you can obtain a forest service map that gives their locations, as well as the location of the campgrounds in the area.

Fee or Free: Day-use and camping are free.

Camping: There are several very good campgrounds here. One of the best is at Pioneer Pass on the banks of Upper Pinal Creek.

Lodging: There is lodging in Miami and Globe. The Phoenix area also has plenty of lodging.

Contact: Tonto National Forest, 2324 McDowell Road, Phoenix, AZ 85006; (602) 225-5200.

Boyce Thompson Southwestern Arboretum

Between Florence Junction and Superior

Butterflies and hummingbirds flock to the flowering plants of 35-acre Boyce Thompson Southwestern Arboretum much of the year, and there is something new and interesting every season. In spring, you can enjoy profuse cactus blooms, while fall brings berries that add to the annual display of red and gold leaves in shaded areas.

This historic site, now administered as a unit of the Arizona state parks, was founded in the early 1920s by William Thompson who wanted to create a beautiful as well as useful desert garden where desert plants could be studied in depth. Thompson named the arboretum for his son.

Today, visitors will find a picturesque visitor center built of local stone, which offers displays and information about the arboretum. Beyond the visitor center are trails that wind among hundreds of cacti, succulents and other water-efficient plants.

This site is a perfect place to learn about desert

plants before you venture into the wilderness. Its manicured trails lead you through exhibits where you can look at, without worrying about getting stung by, the prickly tentacles of desert plants.

Directions: The arboretum is located off US 60 about 10 miles east of Florence Junction and five miles west of Superior.

Fee or Free: There is an entrance fee of $4, $2 for children.

Camping: There is a large private campground at Queen Valley and a public campground at Oak Flat Recreation Area.

Lodging: Lodging is available in Superior, Apache Junction, Florence and Miami.

Contact: Boyce Thompson Southwestern Arboretum, 37615 East Highway 60, P.O. Box AB, Superior, AZ 85273; (602) 689-2811 or (602) 689-2723.

Homolovi Ruins State Park

Near Winslow

Want to learn more about the people who lived in northern Arizona in ancient times? Then head for Homolovi Ruins State Park just north of Interstate 40 near Winslow. Excavated sites, ruins and an interpretive center all help you understand more about the Anasazi Indians who pre-dated the Navajo and Hopi in this region.

The ruins here were a pueblo of about 250 rooms, which covered almost two acres and housed some 300 people during the 15th century. Most of what remains are low-standing walls, but a few excavations have dug below the surface to expose the floor of some homes, complete with fire pits. Excavations of these ruins began in the early 1900s, but the area wasn't established as an official state park until 1986. The excavations continue today at this 960-acre site.

The washes and cliffs in this region are some of the most colorful in Arizona—a mix of reds, pinks, blues and grays—and one area nearby is called the Little Painted Desert for its layered formations.

For those who want to work as well as learn, volunteer opportunities for helping on the excavations are sometimes open. Call or write the park to learn more. There are developed camping and picnic facilities where you can stay for extended periods while you investigate early Native American life along the Little Colorado River.

Directions: From Winslow, head about three miles west on Interstate 40. Follow the signs to the park.

Fee or Free: This is a $3-per-vehicle fee to enter the park. Camping costs $8-$13.

Camping: There is a campground at the park.

Lodging: There is plenty of lodging in nearby Winslow.

Contact: Homolovi Ruins State Park, HC 63, Box 5, Winslow, AZ 86047; (602) 289-4106.

Petrified Forest National Park

In northeast Arizona, along Interstate 40

My first memories of the Petrified Forest and Painted Desert region come from a cross-country trip my family took when I was a teenager in the mid-1950s. We had missed a side trip to the Grand Canyon because two airliners had collided in midair above the canyon and crashed to the ground nearby. All roads were closed to the canyon from the south because of the investigation of the crash.

Since I was typical teenager, I was sure any trip was going to turn out just like the planned trip to the Grand Canyon did—a bust. So, with that mindset, I prepared myself for the Painted Desert the next day. I was so sure that it, too, would be a bust that I wasn't paying attention and didn't even notice the colors before we reached the turnout on US 66, which then ran right by the desert.

There was no way I could miss the desert, though. It had rained early that morning, and the sun was just pushing its way through a cloud bank in the east to highlight the brilliant reds of the hills. It was truly a painted desert that morning, one that even woke up a sleepy, pessimistic teen.

To this day, I don't know if my memory is true to the colors that I saw that day, although my parents also claim to have seen those most vivid colors in the hills of mud, sand and clay. What I do know is that I have spent many days walking around in the Painted Desert and Petrified Forest area, and have never seen the colors quite so vivid since. Many years later, I lived less than 25 miles from the Painted Desert as the crow (or raven in that region) flies, and while I saw great days, none matched that first sight in my memory.

Several years ago, some 35 years after my first visit to the area, I took my son Kevin on a tour of the Southwest. The day we visited the Painted Desert in what is now Petrified Forest National Park was almost a replica of my first visit. It had rained early in the day, the clouds filtered the morning sun, and the colors were vibrant. Not as vibrant as on my first visit, mind you, but vibrant nevertheless.

I hope that in Kevin's eyes and memory the colors from his first visit stay as vivid as they did for me. Maybe he saw what I did—how the coloration can change before your eyes, from an almost blank canvas with muted colors outlined in soft curves to a startlingly brilliant study in reds.

The Painted Desert is only one small portion of the park, though, and the number of short trails that lead through colorful logs of petrified wood introduce visitors to a natural phenomenon that is not found in such profusion anywhere else in the world.

The 27-mile scenic drive through the park takes you to the Painted Desert to the north of Interstate 40, and then heads south as it crosses under the highway to the area richest in petrified logs. This drive is only an introduction to what appears to be an empty and inhospitable region, though, and those who want to hike into the backcountry and camp on the east side of a particularly colorful group of rounded hills, in order to catch the dew reflecting on them in the sunrise, can do so by picking up a free backcountry permit from the rangers.

This is a waterless badlands region, and you must pack your own water in, but otherwise it is prime backpacking country. The grades are easy, the hiking is unhindered by large obstacles, and you can see for miles in any direction. Waking up to watch the breaking of day as the first rays of sunlight reach the multicolored hills is unbeatable.

Directions: The north entrance to the park is off Interstate 40 about 25 miles east of Holbrook. The south entrance is off US 180 about 15 miles southeast of Holbrook.

Fee or Free: Entry to the park costs $5 per car.

Camping: Only backcountry camping is allowed in the park, and there are no improved campgrounds nearby.

Lodging: There is lodging in Holbrook, as well as Winslow to the east and Gallup, New Mexico, to the west.

Contact: Petrified Forest National Park, P.O. Box 2217, AZ 86028; (602) 524-6228.

Fool Hollow Lake & the Mogollon Rim Drive

In Apache-Sitgreaves National Forest

As you drive west on State Road 260 from Show Low toward Payson, you closely follow the curving path of the Mogollon Rim, a 100-mile-long cliff. This is one of the most scenic drives in this section of the state. The meandering route takes you through tall ponderosa pine forests and open grasslands. This is prime wildlife-viewing country, and Fool Hollow Lake, the center of the Fool Hollow Recreation Area, sits just north of the rim and attracts a wide variety of birds and mammals to its shore.

The U.S. Forest Service, Arizona State Parks and the city of Show Low jointly manage Fool Hollow Recreation Area as a full-service recreation area with all the amenities. There are 134 developed campsites for those who want to enjoy nature in comfort. The 500-acre lake is deep and cool, which makes it perfect for trout fishing. Trout are planted in the lake each spring, and the catch tends to be fair to good throughout most of the summer.

If you prefer camping at more primitive sites, pay a visit to Fool Hollow, then continue to drive along State Road 260 toward Payson as it winds through the largest stand of ponderosa pine in the world. The route continuously drops in elevations as it follows the Mogollon Rim. At several spots, there are outstanding vistas to the south over the high desert, which stretches for miles a thousand feet or more below the sheer cliffs of the rim.

Look for any of the improved gravel roads that lead away from the rim and head for small lakes such as Woods Canyon Lake and Blue Ridge Reservoir in the Apache-Sitgreaves National Forest to the north. Camping is excellent in the open understory of the forest along these roads, and only a few people take advantage of it. I just drive off the road into a flat area surrounded by groves of trees, where I am out of sight to anyone who might to drive by.

Directions: Take State Road 260 west from Show Low for just over two miles to Fool Hollow Recreation Area. The drive along the rim from Show Low to Payson is a little over 100 miles.

Fee or Free: Day use costs $5 per vehicle; camping costs $10-$15.

Camping: There is an improved campground at Fool Hollow and plenty of primitive camping in the national forest.

Lodging: There is lodging in Show Low and Payson.

Contact: Apache-Sitgreaves National Forest, P.O. Box 640, Springerville, AZ 85938; (602) 333-4301. Fool Hollow Lake Recreation Area, P.O. Box 2588, Show Low, AZ 85901; (602) 537-3680.

Allen Severson Memorial Wildlife Area & Jacques Marsh

In the White Mountains

As I search for outdoor getaways, I generally avoid artificial sites such as reservoirs and cultivated parks. There are two such sites in the White Mountains, however, that I highly recommend.

In the 1970s, several small communities in the White Mountains developed an innovative approach to disposing of their wastewater effluent. They joined with Apache-Sitgreaves National Forest to create new, artificial wetlands. Show Low was the first community to do so, creating a 370-acre marsh known locally as Pintail Lake (officially called the Allen Severson Memorial Wildlife Area), in the midst of a pinyon pine and juniper forest off Route 77, about five miles north of town.

Today, not only do wildlife congregate there, but

waterfowl and wading birds are abundant at the marsh year-round as well. Visitors find it an excellent spot to sight many bird species not commonly seen in great numbers in the pinyon pine-juniper country. These include pintail, cinnamon teal, yellow-headed blackbird, great blue heron and belted kingfisher.

In 1978, the communities of Pinetop and Lakeside followed Show Low's example and constructed their own marsh to treat and dispose of wastewater effluent. The result was 93-acre Jacques Marsh, which is set in a large, open meadow surrounded by pine forest and features 18 waterfowl nesting islands. Waterfowl, at times exceeding 1,500 in number and including over a half-dozen varieties of ducks, reside here year-round.

An added bonus at Jacques Marsh is the large number of elk that come here for water. In winter, the herd numbers over 250. You can generally see at least a portion of the herd near sunrise and sunset during the cooler months of fall and winter.

Directions: For the Allen Severson Memorial Wildlife Area, take Route 77 north from Show Low for four miles to the signs for Pintail Lake. Turn east and continue for one-third of a mile to the parking area.

For Jacques Marsh, take Porter Mountain Road off State Road 260 in Lakeside. Stay on Juniper Drive for 1.5 miles, then turn left at the sign for the marsh and continue for just over a half mile to the parking area.

Fee or Free: These are free areas; nearby campground fees vary.

Camping: There are a number of improved forest service campgrounds in the area. To reserve a campground, call (800) 280-CAMP.

Lodging: There is lodging in Show Low.

Contact: Apache-Sitgreaves National Forest, P.O. Box 640, Springerville, AZ 85938; (602) 333-4301.

White Mountains

In eastern-central Arizona

High peaks, meadows with vibrant fields of colorful wildflowers, and mountain lakes all make the White Mountains, which extend along the border between Arizona and New Mexico, a choice destination during midsummer when many regions of the Southwest are roasting. And the snow-covered peaks of the range that rise to over 11,500 feet offer great prospects for winter-sports enthusiasts.

The White Mountain Apache and Fort Apache Indian reservations cover a large part of the range to the south of Show Low, and the eastern peaks and meadows are in Apache-Sitgreaves National Forest. Springerville, which sits at the junction of US 60 and US 180-191, is the nearest population center, and most visitors to the region pass through it on their way to the mountains.

Whenever I visit the White Mountains, I like to head for Mount Baldy, which is the highest peak in the region at 11,590 feet. Still, I have never climbed to the top. It is located on reservation lands and is not accessible to the public. Instead, I aim for the excellent 14-mile loop of the Mount Baldy Trail, which leads along the West Fork of the Little Colorado River through parts of the Mount Baldy Wilderness Area near the base of the mountain. From late May, after the snowpack has disappeared, to October, when the first winter storms appear, wildlife is abundant in the region. I often see beaver, elk, deer, wild turkey and blue grouse as I hike along the river.

Another of my favorite destinations in the region is Escudilla Mountain. This 10,877-foot peak is one of the more accessible summits in the region, and you don't have to work to reach the top. A road that you can drive on loops around the peak and Terry Flat, a meadow alongside the road, at over 9,000 feet where old-growth stands of Engelmann spruce and Douglas fir are home to an astonishing number of birds. The wildflower displays are outstanding in July and August.

For those who prefer lakes to peaks, there is no shortage of getaways here. Big Lake, about 20 miles south of Springerville, has long been a favorite spot of mine during early summer when the birds are nesting and the elk, pronghorn and deer are active in the early morning and evening. Nearby Salt House Marsh and Mexican Hay Lake are two of the best high-mountain marshlands in Arizona, and both have plenty of wildlife.

The 575-acre Big Lake, about 20 miles south of Springerville, has well-developed facilities, including a visitor center and store. The ponderosa forest grows to the edge of this clear blue mountain lake, and fishing is excellent among the many nooks and crannies of the ragged shoreline.

Luna Lake, much smaller at 75 acres, is another high-mountain lake where waterfowl nest and muskrats and beaver thrive in the surrounding marshes. Fishing is good, and the lake's undulating, cove-lined shore makes for a pleasant hike.

These are just a few of my favorite spots in the White Mountain region. As you travel here, you are sure to discover your own favorite sites that are as remarkable for their lack of visitors as they are for their abundance of beauty.

Directions: Mount Baldy rises to the west of Eager. Go 19 miles on State Road 260, and then south for nine miles on State Road 273 to the Little

Colorado River. The trailhead is after a half mile on Forest Service Road 113J.

To reach Escudilla Mountain and Terry Flat, head north of Alpine on US 180 for 5.5 miles to Terry Flat-Hulsey Lake Road (Forest Service Road 56). Go about six miles to the beginning of the six-mile loop around Terry Flat.

For Big Lake, take Water Canyon Road (Forest Service Road 285) from Eager. Continue for about 20 miles and follow the signs to Big Lake.

To reach Luna Lake, take US 180 east from Alpine for four miles to the lake.

Fee or Free: These are free areas; campground fees vary.

Campgrounds: There are plenty of forest service campgrounds in the region. To reserve, call (800) 280-CAMP.

Lodging: There is some lodging in Springerville, but your best chances are in Show Low and Holbrook.

Contact: Apache-Sitgreaves National Forest, P.O. Box 640, Springerville, AZ 85938; (602) 333-4301.

Chapter 3

Southern Arizona

Maps 7, 8, 9

Map 7

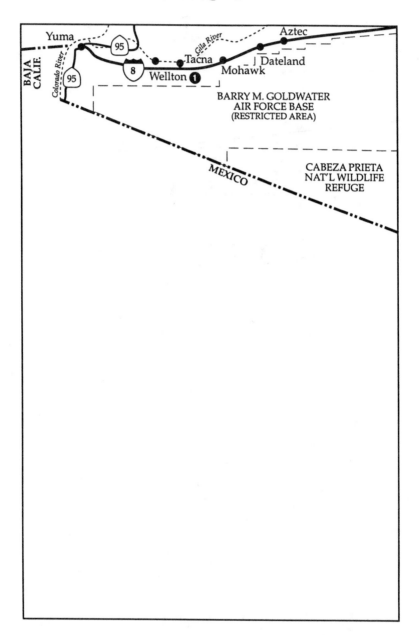

Map 8

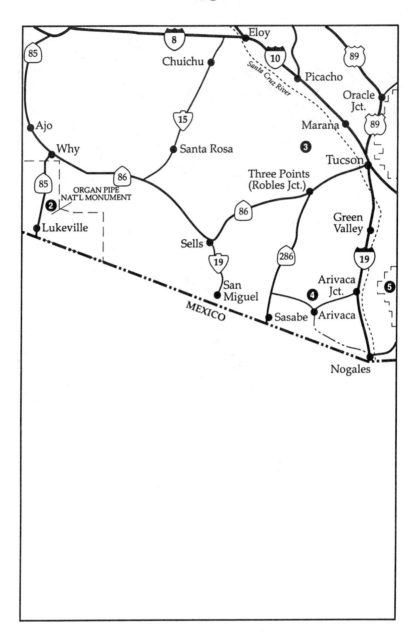

Map 9

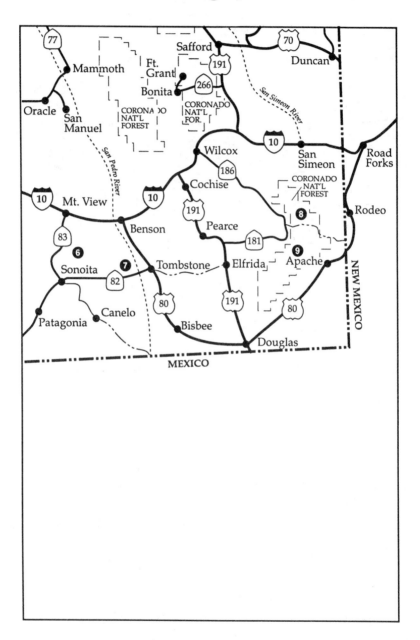

Mohawk Sand Dunes & Mohawk Mountains

Along Interstate 8, east of Yuma

Although Arizona is noted for its desert, it is not noted for one feature that people frequently associate with deserts: sand dunes. These desert phenomena are found only in the far southwestern corner of the state, and most are not easily accessible.

As you drive along Interstate 8 between Gila Bend and Yuma, you cross a desolate, dry wasteland which the early Spanish explorers called *el despladado* (uninhabited land). Passing mile after mile of nothing, you'll probably find the Spanish name fitting. The mood that emanates from the vast desert is one of loneliness, or more accurately, aloneness. Mountains tower above the flat plains, always in the distance, but little else rises above the low-lying desert scrub.

That is until you come to Mohawk Sand Dunes, the largest and most accessible dunes in the state. They are

---

south of Interstate 8 (a few miles of low dunes extend north to the Gila River), just west of the Mohawk Mountains about halfway between Gila Bend and Yuma.

Of all the desert lands of Arizona, this is the most barren and least inhabited. Even the Sand Papago natives (poor cousins to the more prosperous Papago to the east), who not only lived but prospered on some of the most desolate land in the region, could not survive here. (They tried and failed, before disappearing as a tribe altogether early in this century.)

Today, you'll find few settlements as you drive the lonely stretch of highway. When you pass an exit, it looks like the road leads to nowhere. And that is exactly where you'll head when you take the Tacna exit off Interstate 8 some 50 miles west of Yuma—nowhere. Or rather to what most people think of as nowhere, for you will soon be in the middle of the Mohawk Sand Dunes, a field of sand about 18 miles long and from one to three miles wide. No one lives here, and only a few people visit.

I wandered into this vast sandbox one day almost as an afterthought. Lured by the promise of dunes, I took the exit and followed the road back to the east for about eight to ten miles as it paralleled Interstate 8. At the north end of the dunes, I parked and climbed the nearest ridge. The sand continued south as far as the eye could see, then even farther.

I wanted to explore more, but I was stopped by a sign stating that the dunes were a restricted area, and that I would have to get permission from the military before entering the region.

The military? That's right. The dunes sit in the middle of the Barry Goldwater Air Force Range where both the Marines and Air Force practice bombing runs from nearby bases.

This makes for mind-numbing moments when jets roar low overhead unexpectedly. It also means that you have to obtain a permit before you enter the area. You must write or call Marine Range Maintenance for a visitor information packet. Among its contents are a handout on Explosive Safety Awareness and a disclaimer called a

Hold Harmless Agreement. These are to protect visitors and the Air Force from problems stemming from careless handling of any unexploded armaments that visitors might run across on treks through the dunes.

If you truly want to experience what it is like to wander in the midst of a desolate dune system, obtain your permit and return to the north end of the dunes. From here, continue along the service road another mile to a fork. Turn right and continue in toward the center of the dunes. At 11 miles is a second fork where you take another right.

This road takes you toward the southern end of the dunes where few people venture. At 24 miles from the Tacna exit, you pass the turnoff to Game Tanks (tanks are waterholes in the desert). About 50 yards beyond the turnoff to Game Tanks is another turnoff to the right. Take this cutoff to Tule Wells Road for about a mile to the middle of the Mohawk Sand Dunes.

Park anywhere, set up camp, and take exploratory treks into the dunes, making sure you can return to your vehicle easily. Look around. Realize that you are alone— probably as alone as you ever will be. About the only people who come to this section of Arizona are the military, drug runners and scared illegal immigrants. Of these, only the military will help you if you become lost or incapacitated.

When I take trips to areas such as this, I try to make them coincide with a full moon. I like to set up camp, fix dinner early, and have everything ready for nighttime by the time the sun drops over the horizon. There is no real darkness. As the full moon rises in the east, it casts a soft light over the nearby mountains and dunes. The distant mountains are only a dark outline against the early evening sky.

The light of the full moon does hinder stargazing, which is another favorite desert activity, but nothing beats taking a walk into the dunes under the light of the full moon. Just don't get too carried away and venture so far from your vehicle that you can't find your way back.

———————— ————————

Directions: The Tacna exit (exit 42) is 86 miles west of Gila Bend and 50 miles east of Yuma on Interstate 8. The above directions are meant for information only. You should plot out your trip on a detailed USGS topographical map of the region before entering the dunes area. If you have any questions, talk to the information officer at Luke Air Force Base when you obtain your permit.

Fee of Free: This is a free area.

Camping: You may camp anywhere in and around the dunes, but there are no improved campsites nearby.

Lodging: There is plenty of lodging in Gila Bend and Yuma.

Contact: Station Operation and Maintenance Squadron, MCAS, Box 99220, Yuma, AZ 85369-9220; attention Range Permit Officer; (602) 341-3402.

2

Organ Pipe National Monument

In southwest Arizona

The far southwest corner of Arizona is a no-man's-land where coyotes outnumber people—only those who are prepared to survive in the most extreme conditions should venture here. This section of the Sonoran Desert stretches from the Colorado River on the west, at the border of Arizona and California, to the Baboquivari Mountains to the east. Its most frequent human visitors are illegal immigrants attempting to enter the U.S. across unguarded borders and drug runners using the lightly traveled, little-maintained desert roads to transport illegal substances into the country.

Two large tracts of this wild and untamed land have been set aside as public parkland and wildlife refuge. (An even larger tract is restricted to visitors, since it is used as a gunnery range by the Air Force and the Marines.)

Of the accessible areas, the easiest to reach is Organ Pipe National Monument. This large park was once the home range of the most famous desert rat of them all, Edward Abbey. Abbey's books chronicled his desert wanderings and curmudgeonly character, but they were also stories of the desert at its best.

While Abbey's writings are hard to define—not exactly natural history, not exactly travel literature—they are essential for anyone who wants to gain insight into the region around Lukeville, Arizona. This small community is a border-crossing town, and gateway to the popular Mexican coastal village of Puerto Penasco. It was also Abbey's home for many years.

It was from here that he ventured into the backcountry of Organ Pipe National Monument and Cabeza Prieta National Wildlife Refuge, and you can do the same. The monument's headquarters and visitor center are located off State Road 85, about five miles north of Lukeville. You can obtain information about the monument and wildlife refuge, as well as about the natural history of the region, from the rangers there.

For those who want to explore by car, but camp in leisure and comfort, the campground at the visitor center offers over 200 pads for RVs. Be aware that snowbirds flock here in their RVs during the peak of the winter season. If you camp here in winter, expect close neighbors who are more interested in the warm winter sun than in the natural world that lies just over the hills from the campground.

If you want, you can explore the parklands' vast expanses of cactus forests on three maintained roads, which are marked as self-guided tours. The closest of these to the visitor center is the 21-mile Ajo Mountain Drive. It begins just across the highway from the visitor center and takes you to Arch and Estes canyons in the foothills of the Ajo Range, which separates the monument from the Tohono O'Odham Indian Reservation.

Along these roads, you drive through large fields of organ pipe, saguaro and cholla cacti. The saguaro, with their trademark arms reaching out from a central stalk, rise high above most other cacti. Only the organ pipe comes close, reaching up to 15 feet. The organ pipe cacti are distinguished by their multiple large stalks that rise from the ground. They really do look like organ pipes as they bunch together in varying heights.

Watch out for the cholla, which look like miniature saguaro. They are said to jump out and grab unsuspecting hikers. Although they don't really jump, their spines are extremely sharp and do have small barbs at the end, which make them difficult to extract if you get stuck.

The rugged land in the monument is part of the Basin and Range Province where flat valleys separate small mountain ranges. Since the annual rainfall here is less than 10 inches (most of which falls in midsummer and mid-winter), the region is covered by desert scrub.

To get a better feel of the isolation of the region, take the 53-mile Puerto Blanco Drive that leads far into the outback of the monument to the west. A good stopping place along the way is an unusual oasis at Quitobaquito Springs, just a few miles north of the Mexican border. The road skirts the Puerto Blanco Mountains as it heads past the abandoned Golden Bell Mine and Bonita Well on its way south.

The oasis is one of the few spots in the monument where wildlife can depend on finding water year-round. The spring feeds a small pond where both birds and mammals come to drink, and an endangered subspecies of desert pupfish lives in the shallow waters.

A number of birds that come to the spring are colorful additions to the drab landscape. The satin black phainopela and bright red vermillion flycatchers dart among the green growth around the springs. Kildeer, quail and roadrunners can be seen on the ground beneath the desert scrub surrounding the water.

Throughout the park, you are likely to see larger mammals, such as coyote, deer, javelina and bobcat, but only in the late evening as they seek food in the cool of darkness.

Several miles north of the oasis, a rough, unmaintained road heads north toward Pozo Nuevo and Bates Well before leading more than 50 miles into the wilds of Cabeza Prieta National Wildlife Refuge. This road is only for those who want to camp in the true back-country of this primitive region, and should not be under-taken without plenty of planning. In fact, you must obtain a permit to enter the wildlife refuge since it is part of a gunnery range.

If you do want to camp in the backcountry of the monument, you must acquire a permit from the rangers at the visitor center. This is to ensure that the rangers know of your trip, when you expect to return, and where you are likely to be camping.

Although few people take advantage of this opportunity to explore this desolate country, delving into the backcountry is the best way to see Organ Pipe. The wildlife is abundant and there is solitude for anyone who ventures here. This does not necessarily mean quiet, though, since much of the monument is frequently flown over by low-flying jets on training runs from nearby Luke Air Force Base.

Directions: Organ Pipe National Monument is located on both sides of State Road 85 for over 20 miles north from the Mexican border. The visitor center is five miles north of the border on State Road 85.

Fee or Free: Day use costs $4; camping is $8 per night, first-come, first-served.

Camping: There is a large, highly developed campground near the visitor center, or you can obtain permits from the rangers for backcountry camping.

Lodging: Lukeville has limited lodging, and there is more across the border in Sonoita.

Contact: Organ Pipe National Monument, Route 1, Box 100, Ajo, AZ 85321; (602) 387-6849. Although the monument does not administer the wildlife refuge, you can obtain visitor information from monument head-quarters, as well as information about how to obtain permits to enter it.

3

Giant Saguaros

In Saguaro National Park, near Tucson

Of all desert plants and animals, none is more closely identified with the Sonoran Desert than the giant saguaro. Rising over 80 feet and living as long as 200 years, these sentinels of the desert cover thousands of acres around Tucson and throughout southern Arizona. They provide food and shelter for dozens of animals, from gila woodpeckers to javelinas.

Near Tucson, three large tracts of saguaro forests have been set aside as preserves. The 83,576-acre Saguaro National Park, with two separate sections, the Rincon Mountain Unit east of Tucson, and the Tucson Mountain Unit to the west, protect pristine regions where humans have had little impact. Adjoining the Tucson Mountain Unit west of Tucson is the 11,000-acre Tucson Mountain Park. It is the largest regional or county park in the area, as well as home to more stands of giant saguaro than any other regional or county park.

When I am in the Tucson area, I head straight for the park, and in it, for one of the top zoos in the world, the Arizona-Sonora Desert Museum. This zoo, arboretum and museum includes the best desert exhibits in the Southwest, and has been rated one of the top 10 zoos in the world for the past several decades. One special feature of the zoo is its aviary, where you can walk among the

---

vegetation and see the birds up close. Other open exhibits include large cats common to the desert, javelina and a wide selection of reptiles and insects.

If you haven't had any luck in spotting desert wildlife, you can at least see what they look like up close here, and the setting is spectacular—along a slope of tall saguaros with views over a desert plain and a rugged mountain range to the west.

Although you are close to Tucson (development has reached almost to the edge of Tucson Mountain Park), this is true, undisturbed desert, and the saguaros are astounding.

Joseph Woods Krutch, the well-read critic and author, built his desert home near this area in the late 1950s. It was here where he wrote his glowing reports of desert living. While more homes have been built between the city and the monument and the zoo has become a major tourist attraction, in the past several decades, little else has changed since Krutch wrote his highly influential essays.

Hikers will want to head to the Rincon Mountain unit of Saguaro National Park. Here there are well-maintained and marked trails that lead up into the rugged hills among tall stands of saguaro.

Directions: Take Speedway Boulevard west from Tucson and follow the signs for about 10 miles to Tucson Mountain Park, and about 13 miles to the Arizona-Sonora Desert Museum and Saguaro National Park.

Fee or Free: To enter the park costs $4 per vehicle or $2 per person. The museum costs $7.95 for adults.

Camping: Tucson Mountain Park has a large hike-in (5.6 miles) campground. Pick up a free permit at the visitor center, available until noon on the day you wish to camp there. There is also a developed campground in the park.

Contact: Tucson Mountain Park, 1204 West Silverlake Road, Tucson, AZ 85713; (602) 882-2690. Saguaro National Park, 3693 South Old Spanish Trail, Tucson, AZ 85730; (602) 296-8576. Arizona-Sonora Desert Museum, 2021 North Kinney Road, Tucson, AZ 85743; (602) 883-1380.

Buenos Aires National Wildlife Refuge

Southwest of Tucson

I wasn't sure the sidetrip to the Buenos Aires National Wildlife Refuge was worth the effort the first time that I visited. State Road 286 from Robles Junction to Sasabe passed through some of the most impressive expanses of grassland I had ever crossed in Arizona, but there seemed to be no access to the refuge.

There were fences along both sides of the highway, and small white signs with "CLOSED" written in large, dark letters on them. Even after I stopped, walked up to the fence to take some pictures, and listened to see if I could hear the call of the masked bobwhite or Montezuma quail, both of which are found at the refuge, I thought the refuge was closed.

It was only by accident that I read one of the signs more closely and realized that the refuge was closed to dove hunting by the Arizona Department of Fish and Game, and that all the green gates that I had passed led

---

to unmaintained dirt roads that crisscrossed the wide expanses of the refuge. After that, there were no doubts that the trip was worth the effort.

Between 1865 and 1985, the 115,000 acres of grassland of the refuge in Alter Valley were used for cattle ranching. Before the early white settlers came to the region, masked bobwhite, pronghorn, wolves, black bear and jaguar roamed the grasslands and surrounding mountain ranges. All were exterminated by ranchers, and only the pronghorn and masked bobwhite (a type of quail) have been reintroduced into the region.

It was to protect the masked bobwhite that the refuge was established in 1985. Masked bobwhite had been discovered in the region in 1884 just south of Sasabe along the Mexican border. Their range extended from Alter Valley several hundred miles south into Mexico. By the early 20th century, bobwhite were gone from the U.S., and by 1949 none of the birds were known to survive in Mexico. Two brothers from Tucson discovered a small population of the birds in 1964 and began an effort to reintroduce them onto the lands of the Buenos Aires Ranch in the 1970s. The effort was successful in wet years when there was plenty of lush vegetation, but in dry years the cattle ate all of the grasses that the quail needed for survival.

The U.S. Fish and Wildlife Service decided that the only way to ensure the survival of this rare bird was to purchase a large chunk of the ranch and control grazing, which they did in 1985. Today, about 1,500 birds are released into the wild each year on the largest expanse of ungrazed grasslands in Arizona, and between a quarter and a half of these survive the winter. Birds will continue to be released until the refuge has at least 500 breeding pairs of masked bobwhite, which should be a self-sustaining population.

From the wildlife-viewing area along Arivaca Creek and Arivaca Cienega, off Arivaca Road on the eastern edge of the refuge, to the 10-mile Antelope Drive from Sasabe to the refuge headquarters, this is a magnificent trip.

There is even wilderness camping at designated sites

throughout the refuge, which are used primarily by hunters during hunting season. What more could you ask for? You'll find wide-open spaces with mule and white-tailed deer, javelina, desert tortoise, coyote and bobcat. Even coatimundi, ring-tailed cat and cougar live in this diverse natural system, and the views from along both the backcountry roads and several backcountry trails are exceptional.

On our first night at the refuge, we followed the backcountry road directly across State Road 286 from the entrance to the refuge headquarters for about a half mile to a marked, primitive campsite. We didn't even make it all the way to the site before we were out of the truck and taking in the vista. Ahead of us lay the wide expanse of a wash. Beyond it, the skyline was dominated by the gray hues of distant peaks. To our right were the flat grass-lands of the refuge surrounded by even more peaks. Far to our left, lights from an isolated ranch were only pin-points at the base of a low mountain range.

An early-summer storm front passed through as we set up camp, and the distant mountains were alternately in shadow and light. Coyotes began to howl, not in the distance, but close enough so we could easily distinguish individual calls. The stars sparkled in the clear desert air between the passing clouds as dusk turned to night. And we were the only campers around. We could not have asked for, or found, a more perfect evening.

This little-known, little-visited site is bound to become more popular, so go now, before it does. Enjoy southern Arizona as the early explorers to the region did. You can even imagine that you hear wolves howling along with the coyote.

Directions: Buenos Aires National Wildlife Refuge is located about 50 miles southwest of Tucson in the Alter Valley. To reach it, take State Road 86 west from Tucson 15 miles to Robles Junction, then take State Road 286 south for 46 miles toward Sasabe. Or take Interstate 19 south from Tucson 33 miles to Arivaca Junction, then take Arivaca Road 20 miles west to Arivaca and the refuge.

Fee or Free: This is a free area.

Camping: Primitive camping is allowed at designated sites in the refuge.

Lodging: There is lodging in Green Valley and other towns along Interstate 19 between Tucson and Nogales.

Contact: Buenos Aires National Wildlife Refuge, P.O. Box 109, Sasabe, AZ 85633; (602) 823-4251.

5

Madera Canyon

In the Santa Rita Mountains

The Santa Rita Mountains rise from the surrounding desert in southeastern Arizona, offering an escape from the enervating summer heat for residents and visitors alike. These visitors aren't all human, though. Elegant trogons (brilliantly colored tropical birds) and buff-collared nightjars (nocturnal birds) also use the canyons of the mountain as a retreat from the heat of the low-lying desert.

Madera Canyon is just one of the many canyons that has been sliced by roaring water from summer storms through the steep slopes of the Santa Rita Mountains. Like many other sites near Tucson, it is extremely popular. A different crowd heads for Madera Canyon, though, because it is one of the premier birding spots in all of North America. Five to seven species of hummingbirds are common here, and gray-breasted jays, acorn woodpeckers, and various nuthatches are all easily seen as you hike along the creeks.

And don't forget the elegant trogons and buff-collared nightjars. Of the more than 200 bird species included on the birding checklist furnished by Coronado National Forest, the one that draws birders from as far as Australia and Europe is the elegant trogon. This parrot-

---

like bird comes to Madera Canyon and several sites in southeastern Arizona to mate and nest each spring.

On a recent trip to Madera Canyon, I sat in the courtyard of the Santa Rita Lodge, where feeders attract both a wide variety of birds and a corresponding number of birders, who often take the easy way out as they attempt to increase the birds on their life list. Here I met a couple from Switzerland, two Brits, a number of Canadians and a lone birder from Australia, as well as birders from all over the U.S., all of whom had made the long trek to southeastern Arizona in search of the elusive trogon.

For non-birders—and many do come to Madera Canyon—there are numerous hiking trails and a good developed campground with private sites in a forest at Bog Springs.

Don't expect to find many non-birders at the Santa Rita Lodge, though. It is so popular with avian enthusiasts that its 15 cabins are filled almost year-round by birdwatchers.

Directions: Take exit 63 off Interstate 19 at Green Valley, south of Tucson. Continue east past Continental School and head east on Forest Service Road 62 for nine miles, to the junction with Forest Service Road 70. Take Forest Service Road 70 south to its end in Madera Canyon.

Fee or Free: This is a free area; the campground costs $5 per night.

Camping: There is a good campground at Bog Springs.

Lodging: Santa Rita Lodge is a comfortable lodge with individual cabins set near a creek and trails radiating out from them, but you must make reservations early. There is plenty of lodging in Green Valley and Tucson.

Contact: Coronado National Forest, Federal Building, 300 West Congress, Tucson, AZ 85701; (602) 670-4552.

6

Empire-Cienega Resource Conservation Area

In grasslands north of Sonoita

The pronghorn buck and two doe stood silently as I crept over the roadside embankment for a closer shot. As I lifted my camera, I saw movement from the buck and feared that I had moved too quickly. Instead of bolting, though, he simply walked a step or two to reposition himself in a better pose. At least that's how it seemed to me as I pressed the shutter release.

Even after I had taken several shots and walked even closer, the three simply kept their distance as they browsed on the low-lying scrub brush of the grasslands. They wouldn't allow me to get too close, but they weren't afraid either. When I mentioned this to the BLM ranger at the unit headquarters, he wasn't surprised.

"Yeah, some of those bucks are real show-offs," he said. "Not many people come here, but the pronghorn

---

know that no harm is going to come to them."

In the Empire-Cienega Resource Conservation Area, the pronghorn, as well as plenty of deer and plenty of birds, live on over 45,000 acres of prime grassland and riparian habitat. The BLM acquired this land in 1988 when plans for developing the area were well underway. If the development had occurred, the pronghorn would have been driven out, but now they stand by the road as you take their picture, and gray hawks nest in the tall cottonwoods along the creeks where vacation homes were planned.

A friend and I explored this lightly visited area one May recently. We were thoroughly impressed with the tall stands of grass that covered the vast area, almost six feet high in some areas, and ate lunch under one of the largest cottonwood trees I have ever seen. Although we didn't see it, a record Emory oak—which is 43 feet tall, over 20 feet in circumference, and has a 63-foot crown spread—stands in one of the secluded canyons of the conservation area.

Birders in particular come to the area for a chance to spot gray owls, warblers and the green jays that nest along the creek. No paved roads cross the area, and wildlife is easily spotted as you drive along the roads, hike across open countryside, or stroll through riparian growth along year-round Cienega Creek.

Directions: One entrance to the Empire-Cienega Conservation Area is off State Road 83 seven miles north of Sonoita. Another is five miles east of Sonoita off State Road 82.

Fee or Free: This is a free area.

Camping: Camping is allowed anywhere in the area, except where otherwise posted. No camping is allowed within a quarter mile of water or stock tanks.

Lodging: The best lodging is available in Tucson, 45 miles to the northwest.

Contact: BLM Tucson Resource Area, 12661 East Broadway Boulevard, Tucson, AZ 85748; (602) 722-4289.

⑦

San Pedro River

Near the Mexican border, west of Bisbee

———————— ⟡ ————————

A green ribbon 40 miles long and five miles wide runs north through the desert from Mexico, in the country to the east of the Huachuca Mountains, to near Interstate 10 in Arizona, providing a sanctuary for hundreds of species of birds that migrate north from Mexico during spring. This ribbon is the lush riparian forest of cottonwood and willow that grows along the banks and floodplains of the San Pedro River.

Here is a birder's heaven that competes with the more publicized sites found in the canyons of the Sky Islands in southeastern Arizona. From the Mexican border to just south of Interstate 10, once-private lands have been acquired to form the San Pedro Riparian National Conservation Area. Cottonwood and willow dominate the ecosystem along the San Pedro for 40 miles north of the border, and these are home to an unbelievable number of birds.

Raptors abound here, nesting in the high trees and soaring above the surrounding desert in search of prey. Gray hawks, crested caracara and Mississippi kite are among the 35 species of raptors that have been spotted along the river, and another 379 different species of birds have been recorded here. Over 100 species actively nest

---

in the riparian forests along the river.

Although State Road 82 and several roads near Sierra Vista cross the river, I try to search out a new backroad from the barren desert to the river each time I visit the area, and then backpack into isolated sites in the conservation area. Once here, I spend my days wandering up and downstream in search of birds, setting up camp whenever I feel the urge. Sometimes I stay in one spot for several days, while other times I move out after a single night. It all depends upon how the birding is going.

Although few people head here for the scenery, it is a pleasant spot to set up camp and take easy day hikes up and down the river. Some pools in the river are even deep enough for swimming on hot days.

Directions: Access to the river is easiest at Land Corral south of St. David off US 80, at Fairbanks off State Road 82 (where the BLM headquarters is located), off State Road 90 as it crosses the river, off Hereford Road north of State Road 92, and off State Road 92 as it crosses the river. All of these are west of US 80 between Benson and Bisbee.

Fee or Free: This is a free area.

Camping: Primitive backcountry camping is allowed within the conservation area.

Lodging: There is lodging in Sierra Vista and Bisbee.

Contact: BLM San Pedro Riparian National Conservation Area, 1763 Paseo San Luis, Sierra Vista, AZ 85635; (602) 458-3559.

Chiricahua National Monument

In Coronado National Forest

Birding and hiking are the main attractions to the Chiricahuas, but to visit an outstanding geological site in Arizona, head to the northeast corner of the range for one of the least-known national monuments in the country. Here, the outlandish and unearthly rock formations of Chiricahua National Monument rise from a canyon carved among an exposed volcanic field.

Wind and water have eroded ancient lava beds into strange and unique forms over eons. A drive to Massai Point through a canyon with spires that tower high above the monument's only road offers one of the best geological tours that I have ever taken.

The views from the point are fantastic in the truest sense of the word, for the rock formations appear to be fantasy shapes rather than what you would expect to see from natural erosion. More than 20 miles of hiking trails lead through the formations, and few hikers use them.

For a visual delight, hike along the trail that winds

through the formations in Rhyolite Canyon at dusk when the low light of the setting sun casts shadows on the worn boulders and cliffs, enhancing their already fantastical features.

The Chiricahua Apache, under the leadership of Cochise and Geronimo, hid from the U.S. Calvary in these badlands in the later years of the battles between the Indians and the army. As you wind in and out of the canyons and mazes along the trails, you can almost feel the ghosts of those who fought to preserve a way of life that the stronger newcomers would not allow.

While the Grand Canyon and Canyon de Chelly are better known, I would choose to visit this area if I only had one place in Arizona where I could go to explore geological formations and enjoy them in solitude.

Directions: Take Interstate 10 east from Tucson to Wilcox. Take State Road 186 southeast to the junction with State Road 181. Turn east on State Road 181 and continue to the monument entrance.

Fee or Free: Day use costs $4 per vehicle; camping costs $7 per night.

Camping: There is a campground in the monument. Primitive camping is allowed in the national forest outside the monument.

Lodging: There is some lodging in Wilcox, but the best bet is Tucson.

Contact: Chiricahua National Monument, Dos Cabezas Route Box 6500, Wilcox, AZ 85643; (602) 824-3560.

9

Birding in the Chiricahua Mountains

In Coronado National Forest

Cave Creek and Rustler Park are names so familiar to birders in America and around the world that you don't have to add any other address. Birders know these as true meccas for anyone who wants to add rare and unusual birds, such as the elegant trogon and Montezuma quail, to their life lists.

For those who don't know, Cave Creek and Rustler Park are prime birding locations in the Chiricahua Mountains along the eastern border of Arizona. The Chiricahuas are Sky Islands and among the top five birding destinations in the country. Vagrants that range north from their traditional grounds in Mexico, migrants that use these cool rest stops on their way farther north during the spring and fall, and several species that are found nowhere else west of Texas—are all part of the magnet that attracts thousands of birders to the region each year.

But birds are not the only attraction to the region. Trails lead out from forest service campgrounds into high country where the nights are cold and the days cool, and you can camp near lakes and streams where fish are found, although not in large numbers.

While Cave Creek and Rustler Park are the two most famous locations in the eastern Chiricahua Mountains, excellent birding and camping also may be found at Rucker Canyon and Turkey Creek on the western side of the range.

All have excellent birding year-round, but many of the migrants nest in the canyons in late spring. This makes birding more special at that time.

The 400-square-mile Chiricahua Range is a long way from any population center. Once you leave the prime birding locations, you are often alone in the campgrounds, and certainly on most trails.

The campgrounds in Cave Creek Canyon are located along the creek and set among tall cottonwood and sycamore. All have isolated campsites where you have considerable privacy from nearby campers. Red cliffs dotted with numerous caves rise above the canyon and adventurous sorts can bushwack up the lower slopes to reach them.

Rustler Park Campground surrounds an alpine meadow above 8,000 feet in a ponderosa pine forest. Trails lead higher into the mountains where you can get great views of the peaks to the east.

For solitude and quiet enjoyment of open pine forests, creeks lined with sycamore and cottonwood, and cliffs dotted with dozens of caves, the Chiricahuas are among the best getaways in the state.

Directions: To reach Cave Creek and Rustler Park, take Interstate 10 east about 150 miles from Tucson to the small town of Road Forks just over the line in New Mexico. From there, take State Road 80 south about 30 miles to Rodeo, and then Portal Road east about seven miles to the small community of Portal. A ranger station is located just outside Portal.

For Turkey Creek, take Interstate 10 east about 85 miles from Tucson to

Wilcox. At Wilcox, take State Road 186 31 miles southeast to State Road 181. Head south about 10 miles on State Road 181 to Turkey Creek Road. Turn east and continue about six miles to the Turkey Creek Ranger Station.

For Rucker Canyon, continue south about eight miles on State Road 181 until it ends at Kuykendall Cutoff Road. Continue five miles on Kuykendall Cutoff to Rucker Canyon Road. Turn east and continue 13 miles to Rucker Canyon.

It is best to have a Coronado National Forest map to refer to on the way to the campsites.

Fee or Free: This is a free area; campground fees are $5-$6.

Camping: There are campgrounds at Cave Creek, Rustler Park, Rucker Canyon and Turkey Creek. Primitive camping is allowed in most areas of the national forest.

Lodging: You'll find some lodging in Wilcox, but little elsewhere.

Contact: Coronado National Forest, Federal Building, 300 West Congress, Tucson, AZ 85701; (602) 670-4552.

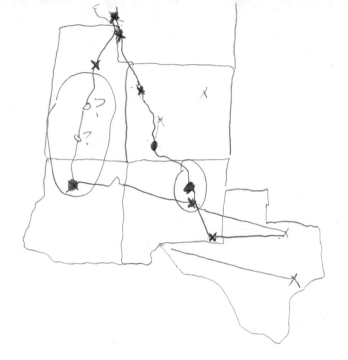

New Mexico

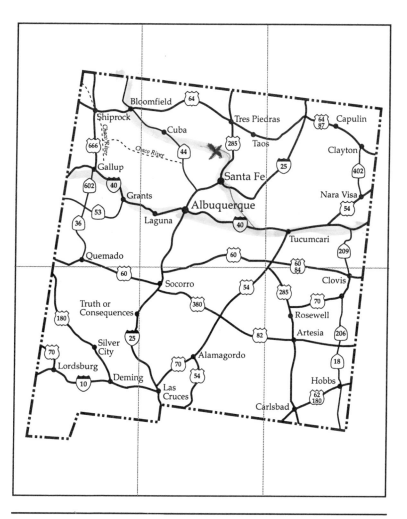

Introduction to New Mexico

Many people see Arizona and New Mexico as twin states with little difference between them. In fact, there are great differences between the two. Arizona is primarily a desert state, with large chunks of it taken up by sections of the Mojave, Sonoran and Great Basin deserts. Only the Sky Island, San Francisco Peaks and White Mountain regions rise to high elevations where there is significant rainfall.

New Mexico, on the other hand, only has small portions of the Chihuahuan and Great Basin deserts within its boundaries, and major portions of the state have significant rainfall. Most of these areas are in the higher elevations of the Rocky Mountains. Two subranges of the Rockies, the Sangre de Cristo and the San Juan, cover most of northern New Mexico, and their 13,000-foot peaks are covered with snow year-round.

The eastern third of the state consists of gently sloping rangeland that is considered part of the Great Plains, and many of the Native American tribes that roamed the plains, such as the Kiowa and Comanche, ranged into what is now New Mexico.

Even the plains of eastern New Mexico are high, with elevations ranging from 6,000 feet in the west to about 4,000 feet at the Texas border.

Since almost half the state is mountainous, many outdoor getaways in New Mexico include mountain-related activities.

New Mexico also has much more land of recent volcanic origin than Arizona, as well as many more caves. In fact, the state is the best in the West for spelunkers, with many little-explored caves on BLM land in the state's southeastern corner near the celebrated Carlsbad Caverns. To explore the most interesting volcanic fields, head to El Malpais National Monument and Valley of Fires Recreation Area.

About a third of New Mexico is federal land, most of which is in the western two-thirds of the state. Here, you find large tracts of roadless lands where you can hike for miles across heavily forested mountain slopes.

New Mexico is proud of its state park system, and rightly so. I haven't included many of these in this guide, however, as most are very heavily developed and offer little in the way of outdoor getaways where you can explore far from crowds and civilization. I have included several archaeological sites, however, which are located in isolated areas where you can hike and camp away from the hordes.

If you are primarily interested in viewing wildlife, head to Bosque del Apache, Guadalupe Canyon or Maxwell wildlife refuges. The best place in New Mexico to go river rafting is on the Rio Grande or the Chama River. And if you just want great backpacking, make your way to Gila National Forest in the southwest corner of the state.

Chapter 4

Northern New Mexico

Maps 10, 11, 12

Map 10

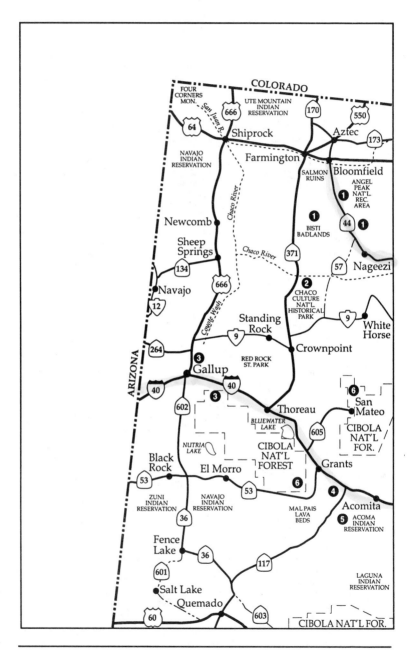

Map 11

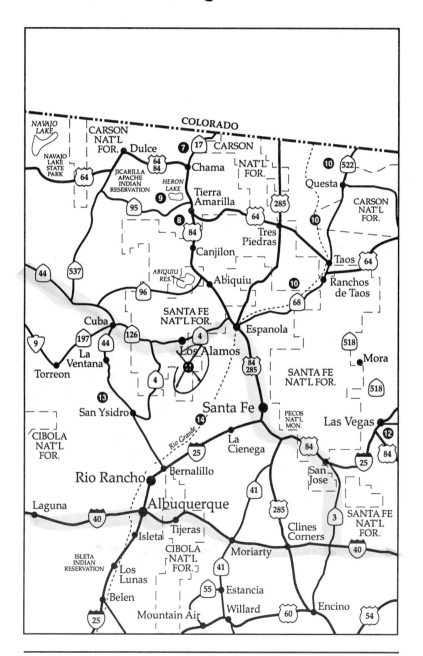

Map 12

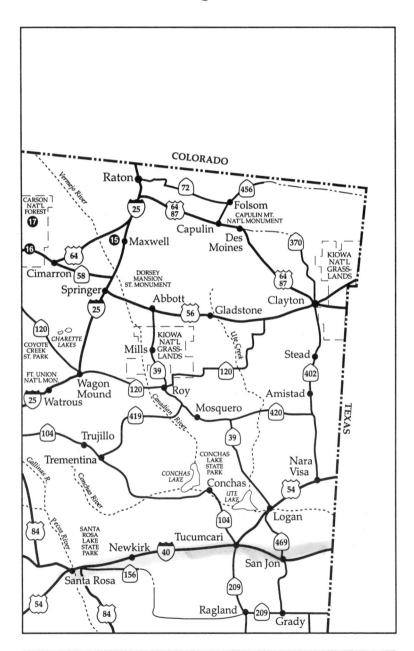

New Mexico Badlands

In the northwest corner of New Mexico

Everyone is familiar with the badlands of South Dakota, some with the badlands of North Dakota, but few with the badlands of New Mexico, and that is too bad. In the far northwest corner of New Mexico are some of the premier badland formations in the country, and they are also among the least visited. Even those within the Angel Peak National Recreation Area, in the eastern portion of the badlands, are seldom visited. I have camped in the campgrounds in the recreation area and been entirely alone—with not one other campsite occupied. That's not what you expect at a national recreation area.

This lack of visitors seems natural to those who can't readily appreciate the beauty of the treeless, desolate country. Some people just don't want to camp where there is no water, no shade and no campfire talks. For those of us who like the desolation and openness of desert lands, there couldn't be a better place to camp during spring and fall. And for those of us who are *really* into the desert, even the cold, windy days of winter and the hot, still days of summer aren't really objectionable.

Angel Peak is named for the odd-shaped rock formation that towers above the surrounding countryside, but the weathered and colorful formations below are the real attraction here. A combination of the Grand Canyon and the Painted Desert, the weathered slopes of the 10,000-acre recreation area are filled with hues of red and lavender, which change colors as the light changes. During early mornings, late evenings and overcast days, the hues deepen to dark tones, but the same colors look washed out in the midday sun. Grays and oranges are interspersed with the reds and lavenders. After a summer rain, the slopes are a vibrant palette of colors.

Neither of the two campgrounds at the recreation area have water and only a few sites have any shade, but they do offer level campsites with tables and pit toilets. Trails lead into the barren canyons, and summer evening walks are especially pleasant. Keep an eye out for fossils as you walk along. This area was once an inland sea, and it is rich in fossils from that era now. Do not collect any petrified wood, fossils or artifacts, though: it is strictly prohibited by federal law.

A short distance away, the Bureau of Land Management has set aside 30,000 acres of badlands in two areas. They are much like those at Angel Peak National Recreation Area, and they are even less crowded. Bisti Wilderness, a spectacular region in the southwest part of the badlands, filled with spires and formations known locally as "hoodoos," is more rugged than Angel Peak National Recreation Area. There are no formal trails or roads within the wilderness, no camping permits are required, and no open fires are permitted, even if you can find enough dead wood to build one. Unfortunately, there is also no water available.

De-Na-Zin Wilderness, which adjoins Bisti, is very similar, but with fewer spires. Both are prime walking lands, however. You can wander among the canyons and mesas forever without seeing another soul. You won't even see much wildlife. Desert cottontails, jackrabbit and coyote, along with the ever-present raven, are about it. There are occasional raptors that nest in De-Na-Zin, and the BLM closes the area to protect them during some nesting seasons.

If you plan to do a lot of wandering, you should be proficient with compass- and map-reading. It is easy to get lost as you explore the twists and turns of the canyons and washes. You should also be aware of distant clouds that may drop rain, even if they are far from you. Rain, even from a distance, can turn into dangerous flash floods that roar down narrow washes with little warning.

Another warning to those who like badlands: The three areas mentioned here are protected by federal law, but the surrounding lands aren't. And this puts them in danger, for beneath the surface here lies one of the largest deposits of coal in the West. Strip miners have long fought for permission to mine the coal, but so far they have been foiled in their attempts.

Directions: Angel Peak National Recreation Area is about 15 miles south of Bloomfield off State Road 44. A mile in along the dirt road that traverses the recreation area, you will find a small picnic area and lookout. The campgrounds are four and seven miles from the main road. The last one is the biggest and has the best sites. You should be able to travel the road with a passenger car, but be careful after a heavy rain. It can get slippery.

De-Na-Zin Wilderness is farther south along Highway 44. El Huerfano Trading Post is about 30 miles south of Bloomfield. Head southwest from the trading post on County Road 7500 for 11 miles to the parking area. The road is similar to the one to Angel Peak. Although generally good, it can become slippery after rain.

Bisti Wilderness lies about 40 miles south of Farmington and 46 miles north of Crown Point on Highway 371. Watch for signs (the BLM claims to have placed them), and follow a gravel road that locals call Old State Highway 371 past the Bisti Trading Post to the undeveloped parking area.

Fee or Free: This is a free area.

Camping: There is an improved campground at Angel Peak; primitive camping is allowed on BLM land.

Lodging: Lodging is available in Bloomfield and Farmington.

Contact: BLM Farmington District Office, 1235 La Plata Highway, Farmington, NM 87401; (505) 599-8900.

Chaco Culture National Historic Park

In western New Mexico

In U.S. history, there have been few instances of entire communities pulling up the stakes and leaving behind ghost towns without any indication of what drove the people away. During the great gold- and silver-mining eras, people did move out of small, temporary towns as the ore gave out, and we see signs of these abandoned settlements all across the West. Most of these were never intended to be permanent communities, however, where residents had made a strong commitment to living in the area for extended periods.

At Chaco Culture National Historic Park are the remains of a ghost town where it appears that all the residents just up and moved after almost 400 years of settlement. The residents of the towns at Chaco Canyon were farmers—people who had a connection with the land. They were also builders who constructed the first high-rise apartment buildings in the country.

Long before the first Europeans set foot on North American soil, the residents of Pueblo Bonito built apartment buildings that rose three and four stories high and housed over 1,500 residents. You can roam around inside and admire this red-rock structure. It is only one of over a dozen similar settlements that archaeologists have uncovered in the Chaco Canyon region.

A mass exodus occurred in settlements over vast areas of the Southwest, from the Grand Canyon in the west to Chaco Canyon in the east, and up to Mesa Verde in Colorado. Little is known about why these early communities were deserted. Excavation of the ruins has provided no solid evidence.

Many ruins from that period have been excavated, but none compare, in my mind, with those that are found on the floor of Chaco Canyon. They are well worth visiting, and getting there can be an adventure in itself. The park is located about midway between Grants along Interstate 40 to the south and Farmington on US 64 to the north. Between these two population centers, there is little but open expanses of land. Access is via dirt or gravel roads only. The nearest town to the park is 60 miles away, although there are trading posts at Crown Point and several other reservation crossroads.

This remote park sits among mesas, washes and canyons where few people venture, and it is easy to find solitude on long hikes to the top of mesas through desert scrub. If the park were not so remote and inaccessible, I am convinced it would be as crowded as most other national parks in the region. The views from the mesas look out over the ruins along the canyon floor and the remains of the irrigation systems constructed by the Anasazi Indians a thousand years ago along the top of the mesa and on its slopes.

Several trails lead into the backcountry to unexcavated sites, but backcountry camping is not allowed. Check at the visitor center for trail maps and information about these sites.

I like to divide my time between hiking and exploring the excavated ruins, which the park service does an excellent job of explaining in their brochures. During summer visits, I like to explore the ruins in the morning, rest in camp during the heat of the afternoon, and hike at dusk. In cooler periods during spring and fall, hiking is best during midday when the low sun warms the slopes.

The park is set at an elevation of 6,200 feet and the climate is one of extremes. Nights are cool to cold, even during summer, except after extremely hot days. It can be downright frigid during fall and spring. The roads to the park are often closed by snow during winter.

My wife and I visited Chaco Canyon one spring not long after we met, and she soon realized she didn't have as good a sleeping bag as she had thought. She had recently moved west from Chicago and had little knowledge of how cold it got at night at higher elevations. During our first night at the park, the temperatures dropped into the low teens and the wind chill was even worse. We survived only by cuddling up in the rear of a small cave near our campsite.

The best way to visit the park is to stay for several days, or even a full week. This gives you time to both explore the ruins and to hike along the mesas.

Directions: From the south, take State Road 371 north from Thoreau on Interstate 40 to Crown Point. Continue two miles past Crown Point, then turn right onto a dirt road and follow the signs for 20 miles to the park. From the north, head south on State Road 44 from Bloomfield for 30 miles to State Road 57. Turn right and continue along the well-marked road for about 25 miles to the park.

Fee or Free: Entrance to the park costs $4 per car; camping at the developed park campground costs $8 per night.

Camping: There is a 46-unit free campground near the park visitor center.

Lodging: The best chances for lodging are in Bloomfield, Farmington, Gallup and Grants.

Contact: Chaco Culture National Historic Park, Star Route 4, Box 6500, Bloomfield, NM 87413; (505) 786-7014.

❸

Red Rock State Park & McGaffrey Recreation Area

Off Interstate 40, near Gallup

If you're heading to or from Albuquerque on Interstate 40, Red Rock State Park and McGaffrey Recreation Area, about 10 miles apart on opposite sides of the highway, make excellent places to pull over, get out of the car and stretch your legs. You might even decide to pitch a tent and stay overnight.

Three miles east of Gallup and about a mile north of Interstate 40, the highly developed, 640-acre Red Rock State Park is where the Gallup Inter-Tribal Ceremonial is held each August. These festivities include outdoor and indoor marketplaces where over 1,000 Native American artists sell their wares, two nights of competitive drumming and dancing involving the top Indian dancers from North and Central America, and three nights of noncompetitive dancing. There is also a rodeo and plenty of traditional Native American food. Stop at the information booth at the park for more details on the festivities.

During the rest of the year, the park is a pleasant

place to stop and take a hike among juniper and pinyon pine, beneath the towering red cliffs that have been carved into exotic shapes by centuries of wind and rain. Because the park is fairly small, you can explore it and check out the little museum, too, in less than one day.

A little farther east and to the south of Interstate 40 is the McGaffrey Recreation Area of Cibola National Forest. McGaffrey Lake is the centerpiece of this area, but there are plenty of hiking trails that lead you through ponderosa pine forests to the top of a mesa. The best of these is the Strawberry Patch Trail, which leads to a forest service lookout tower. You have wonderful panoramic views of the desert to the east from here.

Deep, 500-acre McGaffrey Lake sits in a high meadow hidden among ponderosa pine. Fishing is good most of the year, and locals come for the trout planted here by the Department of Fish and Game. On a short visit, you may want to take advantage of the cool shade near the shore for an outdoor picnic.

Directions: Red Rock State Park is three miles east of Gallup and one mile north of Interstate 40. McGaffrey Recreation Area is 15 miles east of Gallup on Interstate 40 and 10 miles south on State Road 400.

Fee or Free: Day use at Red Rock is free; camping costs $8-$12 per night. Day use at McGaffrey costs $5; camping costs $7-$10; call (800) 280-CAMP to reserve a site.

Camping: There are campgrounds at both parks.

Lodging: There is plenty of lodging in Gallup.

Contact: Red Rock State Park, P.O. Box 328, Church Rock, NM 87311; (505) 722-3839. McGaffrey Recreation Area, Cibola National Forest, 1800 Lobo Canyon Road, Grants, NM 87020; (505) 287-8833.

④

El Malpais
National
Monument

Off Interstate 40, west of Albuquerque

Either I lived near active volcanoes in a previous life or I am going to return as a volcanologist in my next one. I just can't get enough of cinder cones, lava flows and other signs of volcanic activity. Therefore it shouldn't be surprising that one place I never miss when I visit northern New Mexico is El Malpais—The Badlands—near Grants off Interstate 40.

Almost 400,000 acres of forbidding landscape with lava flows, cinder cones, spatter cones, ice caves and lava tubes hide forests of pine and aspen and large areas of open grassland in a huge valley where molten lava flowed as recently as 1,000 years ago. Today, you can walk peacefully among the rugged remains of those ancient flows, but the natural beauty of this quiet place cannot hide the awesome destructive power of volcanoes.

The BLM has set aside several large tracts of the badlands. One is the 114,000-acre El Malpais National Monument. Another is the 262,000-acre El Malpais National Conservation Area that surrounds the monu-

---

ment. Within the conservation area, two wilderness areas have been designated, West Malpais and Cebolla. West Malpais is primarily open prairie, with a 6,000-acre *kipuka*—an island of grassland surrounded by lava flows. Cebolla is more rugged and home to hawks and eagles that nest on the cliff faces of the mesas and hills.

I generally set up a base camp near one of the many dirt roads that meander through the conservation area and spend days hiking among the lava flows, looking for depressions where small forests of pinyon pine and juniper have risen from the windblown debris.

Each of these has its own microclimate, and a wide variety of plants and animals can be found in them. I also search for exposed lava tubes (there is one which is 17 miles long in the monument) and caves where ice stays year-round.

The area can be very hot during midsummer and bitter cold in winter, but the weather is mild during spring and fall. Beware: There is no water within the monument or conservation area and you must take plenty to keep your thirst quenched.

For those who only wish to look but not explore, there are several drives that take you to overlooks where you can get a feel for what it must be like to hike through the rugged terrain. State Road 117 closely follows the entire eastern edge of the lava beds, while State Road 53 follows the upper half of the western edge.

Directions: Drive five miles east of Grants along Interstate 40, then take State Road 117 south. In less than five miles, you will see various sites to the west of the highway. Several dirt roads lead you into the monument.

Fee or Free: This is a free area.

Camping: Wilderness camping is permitted in the conservation and wilderness areas. Remember that there is no water available.

Lodging: Lodging is available in Grants, Gallup or Albuquerque.

Contact: BLM Grants Field Station, 620 East Santa Fe Avenue, Grants, NM 87020; (505) 285-5406.

5

Rimrock Area

Off Interstate 40, west of Albuquerque

As State Road 117 heads south from Interstate 40, the land to the east of the road rises in stark contrast to the rugged lava beds to the west. Sculptured sandstone bluffs stand to the east of the road and continue to reach higher levels along a strip between two and six miles wide until they reach Cebolita Mesa. It is here that the Acoma Indians have lived for over 1,000 years in their mesa-top pueblo.

Although the sandstone bluffs and accompanying canyons are not as dramatic as the badlands to the west, they are more inviting to those who want to hike among a region with diverse landforms, flora and fauna. Canyons and draws, where water occasionally roars through the washes with powerful surges after particularly heavy summer storms, offer level hiking routes, and the vistas from atop the sandstone mesas reach to the lava fields to the west.

Primitive roads lead into the region at Cebolla, Sand and Armijo canyons, and you can set up base camps on the adjoining BLM lands, from which you can venture into the lonely lands. Remember, there is no dependable water supply in this region, so you must bring your own.

The flora here is limited to that found in high desert, such as greasewood, rabbit brush and some pinyon pine

---

and juniper. Among the plants, you may see jackrabbits, jays and plenty of ravens, which come to scavenge the roadkill and unsuspecting rodents.

After you have finished exploring the desolate lands of the Rimrock area, you may want to head for the village of Acoma. This is one of the oldest continuously settled villages in the country, and the Native American residents present ceremonial dances during late summer. The tribe has a visitor center and guides conduct tours through the ancient pueblo. Contact the New Mexico Commerce and Industry Department at (505) 827-4011 for information about the dances at Acoma and at other pueblos in the state.

Directions: Take State Road 117 south from Interstate 40 about five miles east of Grants and continue for about 15 miles. Dirt roads lead into the area at intervals.

Fee or Free: This is a free area.

Camping: Primitive camping is allowed on BLM lands.

Lodging: Some lodging is available in Grants, but the best bets are Gallup and Albuquerque.

Contact: BLM Albuquerque District, Rio Puerco Resource Area, 435 Montano Road Northeast, Albuquerque, NM 87107; (505) 761-8700.

6

Mount Taylor & Paxton Cone

In Cibola National Forest

Cibola National Forest covers more than a million acres of land in various districts around New Mexico, and one of my favorite areas includes the two units in the Mount Taylor Ranger District near Grants. To the north of Interstate 40 are the San Mateo Mountains and 11,301-foot Mount Taylor, an extinct volcano that is sacred to the Navajo.

In the open forests of the San Mateo Mountains, there is no great need for formal trails. The open understory of ponderosa and Engelmann spruce makes for easy hiking, and you can go just about anywhere you want throughout this range, which is bisected by the Continental Divide.

Hiking and camping around Mount Taylor are made especially easy by a paved road that comes within four miles of the peak and a dirt road that continues almost to the top. If you want to hike a little farther, you can take the three-mile trail from Forest Service Road 501 to the summit. Fewer than 500 hikers a year use this trail, so you are unlikely to encounter anyone else on your trek.

Other roads, both designated forest service roads and primitive tracks made by the repeated use of hunters, crisscross the forest and lead to excellent hiking country.

Fifteen miles south of Interstate 40 in the Zuni Mountains, and about 40 miles from Mount Taylor, is another reminder of the violent natural history of the region. Paxton Cone is a 1,000-foot-high cinder cone created by volcanic activity between 10,000 and 40,000 years ago when an eruption sent a river of lava down Zuni Canyon. Cinder fell around the opening from which the lava flowed, building a large cone.

Today ponderosa pine and Douglas fir grow on the slopes of this cone, and a hike to the top is an easy, 1.5-mile round-trip trek. Since I can no longer hike to the top of Sunset Crater near Flagstaff, I frequently travel to the Cibola to wander up the cinder slopes of Paxton Cone.

From the top, the view includes expanses of ponderosa pine forests, the lava fields of El Malpais and the mesa of the Acoma.

Directions: The northern unit of Cibola National Forest near Mount Taylor is accessible from Interstate 40 by heading north on State Road 605 to San Mateo. From there, you can follow forest service roads into the high country. For other routes to Mount Taylor, contact the forest service for a map of the forest.

To reach Paxton Cone, take State Road 53 south from Grants through Zuni Canyon for a little over 10 miles to the dirt road that leads to the cone. A sign on State Road 53 points you in the right direction.

Fee or Free: This is a free area.

Camping: There are a number of forest service campgrounds with tables, fire rings and pit toilets scattered throughout the forest, but you can make a primitive camp anywhere.

Lodging: There is some lodging in Grants, but more in Gallup and Albuquerque.

Contact: Cibola National Forest, Mount Taylor Ranger District, 1800 Lobo Canyon Road, Grants, NM 87020; (505) 287-8833.

7

Edward Sargent Fish & Wildlife Management Area

Near the Colorado border

The 32-square-mile Edward Sargent Fish and Wildlife Management Area is a well-kept secret that was once owned by The Nature Conservancy. Though the management area's objective is to make for a better elk range, and elk hunting is allowed in season, the rolling land, covered with high aspen meadows, forested slopes and streams with low-lying riparian growth, is great hiking country.

With an elevation of about 8,000 feet, the management area has mild summers and frigid winters. The best time to visit is in the fall after the first frosts have hit and the elk are bugling for their harems from the cover of red and gold oak and aspen forests.

Wildflowers cover the meadows in late spring after the snow has melted, and many desert birds, including grouse, quail and raptors, nest in this little-visited habitat.

Alder-lined streams cut through the area, and I like to head for one of them for the fine cutthroat and rainbow trout fishing. Several of these streams are within easy hiking of the parking area at the end of the road at the management-area boundary.

Although hikers and backpackers outnumber hunters in the area, you may want to call ahead to find out if there is an open season when you are planning to visit.

Directions: Head north on Pine Street in Chama. The management area extends from Chama along State Road 17 to the Colorado border. Only the road northwest from Chama is open to vehicles. To reach the interior of this area, you must either hike or ride horseback.

Fee or Free: This is a free area.

Camping: Primitive camping is allowed near the entrance. Hike-in camping is allowed, except during hunting season.

Lodging: There is some lodging in Chama, but the best prospects are in Santa Fe to the south.

Contact: Department of Fish and Game, P.O. Box 25112, Santa Fe, NM 87503; (505) 827-7899.

Rio Chama Wild & Scenic River

South of Tierra Amarilla

There are several ways to travel along the Rio Chama River from Heron Lake to Abiquiu Reservoir some 35 miles downstream. Most people like to raft through some of the best whitewater in New Mexico, but I like to hike along the bottom of the gorge.

Most folks who travel along the flat grazing land that the river cuts through are surprised at the abundant wildlife and great scenery along the bottom of the 900-foot-deep canyon. A constant water supply and green riparian growth along the river, alongside the red, brown and orange rocks of the sloping cliffs, provide both a lush habitat for birds and mammals and truly brilliant colors at sunrise and sunset.

On most hikes through desert country, you have to worry about water and heat, but on this one you have a ready supply of water from Rio Chama. Even during the hottest days of midsummer, the temperatures seldom rise above 90 degrees.

Hiking is great here year-round. Spring brings new growth on the trees along the river and bright wildflowers

---

on the open slopes. Summer has nesting birds and young animals exploring the world for the first time. And fall is a burst of color as the leaves turn yellow and gold. Even winter has its moments. As the first snows fall, you can hike along a snowless, protected gorge with white patches on the cliffs above.

For those who wish to float down the Rio Chama, the best spot to put-in is at El Vado. Most people take a two-day trip to Abiqui. This stretch takes you through Class I, II and III waters. For more information on float trips, contact the New Mexico State Parks at (800) 451-2541 for their publication *New Mexico Whitewater, a Guide to River Trips*. This guide includes information about outfitters and rafting trips for everyone from novices to experts.

Directions: The best access to the canyon is below Heron Lake. Head west on BLM 1023 about two miles south of Tierra Amarilla. This dirt road has numerous branches that reach the east rim of the canyon. Check with the BLM office in Taos about road conditions before you head out.

Fee or Free: This is a free area.

Camping: There is primitive camping on BLM land above the canyon and hike-in camping in the canyon itself.

Lodging: The best bet for lodging is Santa Fe to the south.

Contact: BLM Taos Resource Area, 224 Cruz Alta Road, Taos, NM 87571; (505) 758-8851.

9

Heron Lake State Park

West of Tierra Amarilla

I didn't know Heron Lake was a reservoir the first time that I visited. As I approached the lake, it appeared to be natural and there were no sounds of motor boats and waterskiing on the water. That made it most pleasant indeed. It was only after exploring around the area that I realized how unusual this "no-wake" reservoir was in the Southwest.

New Mexico State Parks has resisted efforts to allow fast and loud water sports on the 5,000-plus-acre lake, as almost all other reservoirs in the region do. Instead, they insist that Heron Lake remain a low-key, low-noise escape for those who want to head for water without having the quiet and solitude of Heron Lake State Park shattered by noises from loud motors.

Pine forests surrounding the lake are open and easy to hike in. (For more on the excellent hiking in the river gorge below the dam, see the story on the Rio Chama Wild and Scenic River on page 185. Heron Lake is a dammed section of the Rio Chama.)

Hikers can head through the open forests to the surrounding slopes where several sagebrush meadows

---

offer great views of the lake. The best hiking, though, is along the Rio Chama Trail, below the dam. This trail leads through the rugged river canyon for 5.5 miles to El Vado State Park. The trailhead is off a marked spur road near the park entrance at the dam.

The irregular shoreline of the lake includes many small coves where you can swim in seclusion or fish for bass.

If you are looking for a casual rest stop rather than a full-day outing, there are several scenic overlooks along the shore of the lake off State Road 95 that are ideal for a quick picnic stop.

Directions: Head west on State Road 95 from Tierra Amarilla for 11 miles to the park entrance.

Fee or Free: Day use costs $3; camping is $7, first-come, first-served.

Camping: Both developed and primitive camping are available in the park.

Lodging: The best bet is in Santa Fe to the south.

Contact: Heron Lake State Park, P.O. Box 159, Los Ojos, NM 87551; (505) 588-7470.

Rio Grande River & Gorge

In north-central New Mexico

The climb down the 200 feet of the sloping walls of the Rio Grande River Gorge just south of the Colorado border is an easy one. This access leads to the beginning of a 48-mile stretch of river, protected under the Wild and Scenic Rivers Act, which is one of the most popular rafting areas in the Southwest.

The Rio Grande winds in goosenecks through a gorge cut from layer upon layer of sedimentary rock deposited by ancient seas. The relentless cutting of the water through the region helped make this gorge into a miniature version of Colorado's Grand Canyon.

This smaller, more intimate canyon varies from a depth of about 200 feet deep at the Colorado border to over 800 feet at the confluence of the Rio Grande and the Red River. Although this section of the river is more popular as a rafting site, it also offers excellent hiking along the floor of the gorge next to the river.

The slope of the canyon walls are gentle enough that you can climb down them to the river in many places. Access is especially easy from the east rim of the gorge

---

and the road that runs alongside the lip for almost 10 miles.

Most hikers prefer to take day-hikes from the campgrounds and overlooks along the road; trailheads lead down into the gorge from all of them. Others like to backpack along the gorge and spend their days lazing by the river, dipping into the cool water as the mid-afternoon sun heats up the narrow gorge.

As the gorge widens downstream from the Taos Junction Bridge near the end of the protected area, the 1,341-acre Rio Grande Gorge State Park sits beside the river. Here you can camp as you explore both upstream and down, or just enjoy swimming in the cool waters during the warm summer months.

The most popular section of the river for rafting is the Lower Box that begins at the John Dunn Bridge Recreation Site and extends 16 miles to the Taos Junction Bridge. The section includes Class I to IV rapids and ends at the boundary of the state park.

For those who like their water warmer, several hot springs are located above Taos along State Road 522 and west of the small community of Arroyo Hondo. The best of these is Black Rock Hot Springs, a natural mineral pool that flows up through the bottom of a rock pool on the west bank of the Rio Grande. The water stays at about 97 degrees, except when the river rises high enough to inundate the pool.

I prefer to head for the hot springs when I am hiking in the area during late fall and winter. As the air temperature drops and snow begins to cover the ground, the rising steam from the springs condenses into clouds around the pools. After a strenuous hike or cross-country ski outing, the warm water heals the body as well as the soul.

In winter, cross-country skiing is good to excellent along the level country above the river and also near Rio Grande Gorge State Park.

Directions: To reach the Rio Grande Wild River National Recreation Area, go north on State Road 522 for three miles from Questa and then west on State Road 378 for just over five miles. Other roads head west from scenic State Road 522 to the river as you head south.

To reach Black Rock Hot Springs, head west on the paved road from Arroyo Hondo for about a mile to its end. Take a right on a gravel road as it crosses the river. Park at the end of the first switchback on the west side of the river and hike down to the springs.

For Rio Grande Gorge State Park, continue south on State Road 68 from Taos for 16 miles to the signs for the park; it's on the west side of the river.

Fee or Free: Most areas are free, but there is a day-use fee at the state park.

Camping: There is primitive camping along the river at selected sites, and plenty of campsites in the park.

Lodging: The best bets for lodging are in Taos and Santa Fe.

Contact: BLM Taos Resource Area, 224 Cruz Alta Road, Taos, NM 87571; (505) 758-8851. Rio Grande Gorge State Park, P.O. Box 215, Penasco, NM 87553; (505) 751-3551.

Bandelier National Monument

In Santa Fe National Forest

Bandelier National Monument has dozens of out-standing ancient cliff dwellings on the slopes of the Pajarito Plateau that are accessible by car, but it also has over 30,000 acres of backcountry that are open to hikers.

And it is the latter that I head for when I visit Bandelier. There is nothing more exciting to me than to happen upon a ruin or cliff dwelling unexpectedly while hiking through steep-walled canyons, some 600 to 800 feet deep, whose streams drain into the Rio Grande in White Rock Canyon. About 70 miles of trails lead into the backcountry where these ruins and cliff dwellings are found, and several designated backcountry campgrounds are located along the trails.

Summer hiking can be warm in the monument, but the nights are cool. During summer, I like to hike in the early morning, rest with a siesta under a tree during the heat of midday and early afternoon, and then hike to the next campsite in the early evening. Fall and spring are also great times to hike in the monument, when the daytime temperatures are pleasant. Nights can be cool to cold, however, and winters are unpredictable. During some winters there is very little snow and hiking is good, but others get enough snow to cross-country ski along the mesa tops.

The main ruins at the monument are well worth a day visit, if you don't have time for an overnight or more, and some of the short trails lead into canyons where you can enjoy a midday picnic before heading on.

The ruins of the monument are multi-story, stone pueblos built between 1200 and 1600 A.D. by the Anasazi Indians. The ruins in Fijoles Canyon near the visitor center include Tyounyi Pueblo, Long House, a talus ruin, Ceremonial Cave and Rainbow House a half mile down the canyon. Tyounyi is the largest and most fully excavated site. This masonry pueblo had 250 ground-floor rooms and three *kivas*, or ceremonial rooms.

The self-guided, one-mile Ruins Trail leads from the visitor center past Tyounyi to the Ceremonial Cave, which is 150 feet above the stream. Two ladders, totaling 100 feet, lead up to the cave, which has a small, restored *kiva*.

Other trails, which can take from two hours to two days, lead into the backcountry to other pueblo ruins, such as Yapashi, the Stone Lions, Painted Cave and San Miguel. There are many other smaller, unnamed sites along the trails as well.

For complete information on these trails, pick up the brochure "A Hiker's Guide to Bandelier National Monument" at the visitor center.

Directions: Take State Road 501 south from Los Alamos to the junction with State Road 4. From the junction, follow the signs eight miles to the park entrance.

Fee or Free: There is a $5 entrance fee, which is good for one week.

Camping: There are improved campgrounds in the monument, plus designated backcountry campsites.

Lodging: There is plenty of lodging in Los Alamos and Santa Fe.

Contact: Bandelier National Monument, HCR 1, Box 1, Suite 15, Los Alamos, NM 87544; (505) 672-3861.

Las Vegas National Wildlife Refuge

East of Santa Fe

This is great raptor country. Just driving along the interpretive loop drive in the Las Vegas National Wildlife Refuge, you may see harriers gliding over the grasslands, kestrels hovering overhead, and redtails and roughlegs sitting on top of tall cottonwoods. If you are lucky, you may even see a prairie falcon swooping down from on high to gather up a careless ground squirrel. And these are just a few of almost a dozen raptors that you can see at the refuge throughout the year.

In general, this is a birder's paradise. Sandhill cranes, Canada geese, snow geese and thousands of ducks all winter over here. In spring, songbirds such as rock and canyon wrens, mountain and western bluebirds, green-tailed towhees, and several species of humming-birds have all been sighted.

Water birds, waterfowl, songbirds, raptors, small mammals and wildflowers all combine to make this refuge a visual delight, especially as you look across the acres of

---

prairie grasslands toward the Sangre de Cristo Mountains to the west.

The two-mile round-trip nature trail that follows the meandering, green Gallinas Creek is one of the most spectacular I have ever hiked in a wildlife refuge. It leads between granite and sandstone cliffs where prairie falcons nest and cliff swallows flit in and out of their mud nests. Soon you are over 200 feet above the creek, enjoying outstanding views of the refuge. While it's steep in spots, it is worth the effort.

Summer here can be quite warm, and winter frequently has slashing winds that permeate even the most protective winter wear. Fall and spring are the outstanding times to visit as the spring wildflowers and fall leaves provide spots of color to the prairie country.

Directions: Take State Road 104 east from Las Vegas for two miles to State Road 281. Turn south and continue four miles to the refuge entrance.

Fee of Free: This is a free area.

Camping: Developed campgrounds are available at Storrie Lake State Park. There are primitive campsites at the McAllister State Waterfowl Area. Both are within 25 miles of the refuge.

Lodging: Good lodging is available in Las Vegas.

Contact: Las Vegas National Wildlife Refuge, Route 1, Box 399, Las Vegas, NM 87701; (505) 425-3581.

Cabezon Peak Wilderness Study Area

Near the Zia and Jemez Indian reservations

Cabezon Peak is a 7,775-foot-high volcanic plug that rises over 2,000 feet above the surrounding valley and dominates the skyline. Points of geological interest and outstanding vistas of mountains and prairie make this a favorite getaway for hikers, climbers and backpackers. The surrounding wilderness study area extends for several miles on every side of the peak. Views from the top reach to the Great Plains to the east and the Rockies to the west.

A hike to the top of the peak leads along a lightly marked, primitive trail, but that hasn't kept hikers from around the world from making the climb. If you want to see who made the climb and where they came from, flip through the visitor book near the peak—some of the addresses are sure to amaze you.

From the trailhead, it is only two to four hours to climb to the top, and everyone from beginning hikers to serious climbers seems to enjoy this moderate trek.

There is no dependable water supply, but backcountry camping away from the main trail is pleasant, even though few people take advantage of the opportunity.

Directions: Take State Road 44 north from San Ysidro for 19 miles. Look for the sign to Cabezon and turn left on a dirt road. Continue for about 15 miles to Cabezon.

Fee or Free: This is a free area.

Camping: Primitive and backcountry camping are allowed in the wilderness study area.

Lodging: The best bet for lodging is Albuquerque.

Contact: BLM Rio Puerco Resource Area, 435 Montano Road Northeast, Albuquerque, NM 87107; (505) 761-8700.

Tent Rocks

Near the Cochiti Indian Reservation

Fellow writer Michael Hodgson and I seem to have the same feeling about this site. How can anything so interesting and so close to major population areas be so little known? Like my colleague, though, I am not complaining. I have enjoyed coming to Tent Rocks since the mid-1960s, and I have almost never seen another person when I've visited.

This wonderland between Albuquerque and Santa Fe is a badlands formation with huge tent-shaped hills that rise from 40 to 90 feet above the surrounding washes. These look like very large tepees, and are tempting to climb. Don't. They are comprised of soft material that is slowly eroding, and anyone climbing on them only speeds up the process.

Although there are no marked trails, hiking is easy as you wind among the formations on level ground. Notice the regular shape of the tents and how erosion is slowly changing the area. In another millennium or so, these will all have disappeared and the area will have the same flat regularity as that surrounding it.

Mountain bikers also enjoy riding among the tents. For tips on where and when to cycle, the BLM has a small booklet entitled "Bike Excursions in Tent Rocks," as well as a map that shows hiking trails.

I like to hike here after a light snow has fallen. The tops of the tents are capped with white snow that stands out against the red formations.

This 4,200-acre area is close to the Cochiti Pueblo, which is well worth a visit after you have finished exploring the tents. Several times during the year, the Cochiti tribe holds ceremonial dances that are open to the public. You can learn more about these and dances at other pueblos by contacting the New Mexico Commerce and Industry Department at (505) 827-4011.

Directions: Take Forest Service Road 266 north off State Road 22, east of the Cochiti Pueblo. The turnoff is marked by a brightly colored water tower.

Fee or Free: This is a free area.

Camping: Primitive camping is allowed on BLM lands, but please be mindful of reservation boundaries nearby. You should not camp on Native American lands without permission.

Lodging: There is plenty of lodging in Albuquerque and Santa Fe.

Contact: BLM Rio Puerco Resource Area, 435 Montano Road Northeast, Albuquerque, NM 87107; (505) 761-8700.

Maxwell National Wildlife Refuge

Off Interstate 25, west of Maxwell

No matter when you visit, something's always happening at Maxwell National Wildlife Refuge.

From fall through winter, bald eagles feed on rainbow trout and carrion from the flocks of over 10,000 Canada geese and 12,000 ducks that died while wintering over at the refuge. Black-tailed prairie dogs frisk in a "town" of over 50 acres, and burrowing owls nest in the abandoned holes they leave behind.

During spring mating season, bufflehead drakes spread their white crown feathers and bob up and down in a courtship dance, while hundreds of Wilson's phalaropes whirl around to stir up prey in the water.

Above all this, raptors soar on thermals as they search for food among the unsuspecting small birds and mammals that reside in the refuge's flat grassland and flooded marsh.

At only 3,600 acres, Maxwell is small as wildlife refuges in the Southwest go, but the variety of wildlife activity that occurs year-round attracts a steady flow of birders and photographers. Maybe it's more of a steady trickle, as it always seems like the visitors are few when I visit.

Among the many water birds seen at the refuge are five species of grebes, and even white pelicans stop over for a rest during the fall migration.

Birds are not the only animals that thrive in the refuge habitat. Coyotes live here in large numbers, and once I even spotted a long-tailed weasel in its white winter coat scurrying across the snow.

During fall migration, I often camp near the ponds where the Canada geese and ducks feed, and fall asleep in the cold nights to the cackling noises of the waterfowl as they seek their proper place in the flock before they, too, settle into sleep.

While there are no set hiking trails, you can hike around the refuge. The only catch is that you must obtain a free permit from the refuge's headquarters to do so. This is to insure that hikers don't wander into particularly sensitive areas or unwittingly disturb nesting species.

Directions: From Maxwell on Interstate 25 south of Raton, take State Road 445 for just under a mile to State Road 505. The entrance is 2.5 miles west on State Road 505.

Fee or Free: This is a free area.

Camping: Primitive camping is allowed on the refuge.

Lodging: The best bets for lodging are Raton to the north and Las Vegas to the south.

Contact: Maxwell National Wildlife Refuge, P.O. Box 276, Maxwell, NM 87728; (505) 375-2331.

Colin Neblett Wildlife Area & Cimarron Canyon State Park

In Carson National Forest

I have never been through Cimarron Canyon State Park on a weekend when the campgrounds were not full. The canyon of the Cimarron River, which runs through the Colin Neblett Wildlife Area, is spectacular with tall pines and crenulated granite palisades towering far above the trees. Both hunting and fishing are good to excellent in the wildlife area, which is the largest (33,116 acres) and most popular state wildlife area in New Mexico.

Most of the crowds are made up of people who come to the area to hunt and fish, and this is reflected in the fact that, although the campgrounds in the state park along the highway are free, at least one person in each vehicle must have a valid New Mexico hunting or fishing license.

Elevations rise over 12,000 feet in the mountainous backcountry, where you'll find well-maintained and little-used hiking trails. Trailheads are marked along the road, water is plentiful in the forests, and summer temperatures are moderate. These factors combine to make backpacking here a great experience with beautiful scenery and plenty of solitude.

I particularly like to take the trail up Clear Creek, where there are several eight- to 10-foot-high waterfalls. These are exceptional in late spring and early summer after the snowmelt has filled streams with cold rushing water.

Few visitors other than hunters venture into the backcountry, however. The deep canyons here are home to black bear, mountain lion, deer, elk, turkey and grouse, all of which are pursued by hunters in open season. Call the wildlife management area for information on hunting seasons, especially if you want to avoid visiting in the midst of a turkey (or any other kind of) shoot.

Birding is good in the riparian growth along the river, and the sheer granite cliffs are great for photography buffs. You can expect to find a wide variety of songbirds among the area's cottonwood and aspen, as well as in the ponderosa pine and juniper on the higher slopes.

Directions: The wildlife area and all of the campgrounds are located along the 25-mile stretch of US 64 between Cimarron and Eagle Nest.

Fee or Free: This is a free area.

Camping: Camping is allowed in designated sites along the highway.

Lodging: The best bets for lodging are in Cimarron and Taos.

Contact: Colin Neblett Wildlife Area, P.O. Box 136, Cimarron, NM 87714; (505) 376-2682. Cimarron Canyon State Park, P.O. Box 147, Ute Park, NM 87749; (505) 377-6271.

Elliott S. Barker Wildlife Area & Valle Vidal

In Carson National Forest

Few people come to the 100,000-plus-acre Elliott S. Barker Wildlife Area and Valle Vidal unit of Carson National Forest. That's not a complaint, mind you. It just means that we lucky ones who do venture out here can enjoy some of the best scenery in this section of the state without any crowds.

The large canyon of Ponil Creek cuts through a long, high mesa, and birds and large mammals such as deer, elk and bear abound in its many small side canyons. While sagebrush and other high-desert scrub covers much of the lower reaches of the 5,415-acre wildlife area, ponderosa pine and juniper cover its higher elevations and the lands outside it in Valle Vidal.

Mountain lions feed on the deer and elk in winter when the snow is heavy, and some hunters also come to pursue them as well. During spring and summer, there is plenty of nesting activity, for songbirds are plentiful in the area. Turkey, dusky grouse, band-tailed pigeon, magpie, raven and hawk also thrive in the area's forests and sagebrush.

Valle Vidal, which lies just to the north of the wildlife area, is a 100,000-acre tract of land given to the U.S. Forest Service by the Pennzoil Corporation a number of years ago. Access to this area is limited to foot and horseback. You can get here from the wildlife area along Middle Ponil Creek.

The reason that few people come to this area is because there are no developed campgrounds, and that is just fine with me. I just set up a primitive camp in the lower end of the canyon along the creek, and enjoy my good luck at having found such a beautiful and little-used getaway.

A word of warning: Although the road into the wildlife area through the sometimes narrow canyon is well maintained, heavy storms frequently deposit large boulders and tons of mud on it. This debris can make the road impassable, so you should always check with the wildlife area or forest service about road conditions before entering the area.

Directions: Just west of Cimarron, take State Road 204 northwest for 14 miles to the wildlife area.

Fee or Free: This is a free area.

Camping: Primitive camping is allowed only in the lower third of the canyon floor in the wildlife area. You may hike in and camp anywhere in the national forest.

Lodging: The best bets for lodging are Cimarron and Taos.

Contact: Elliott S. Barker Wildlife Area, P.O. Box 136, Cimarron, NM 87714; (505) 376-2682. Carson National Forest, P.O. Box 558, 112 Cruz Alta Road, Taos, NM 87571; (505) 758-6200.

Chapter 5

------------- ~🦅~ -------------

Southern New Mexico

Maps 13, 14, 15

Map 13

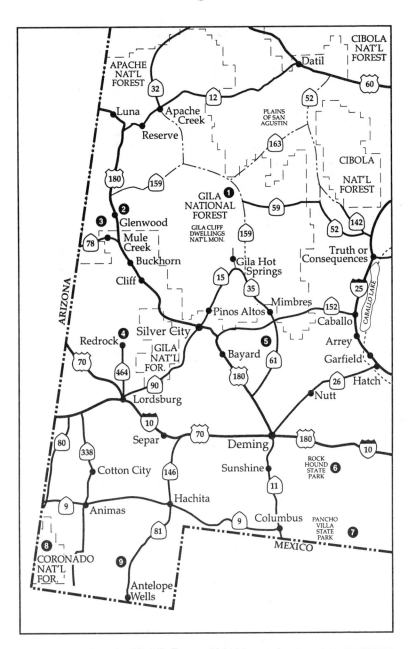

Map 14

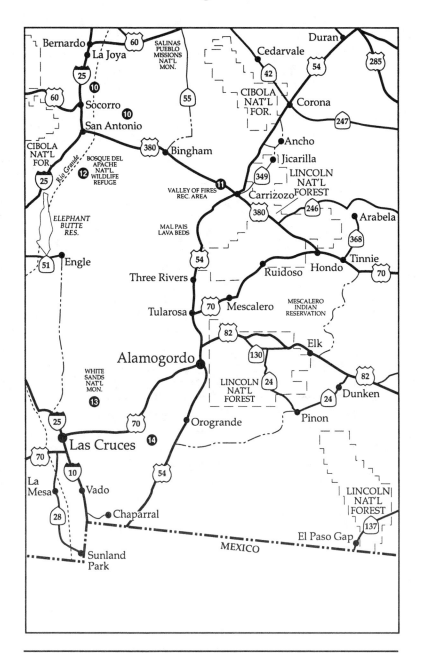

Map 15

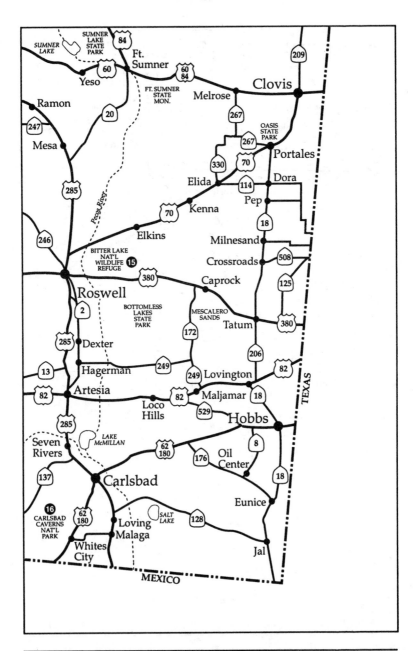

Gila National Forest

In southwest New Mexico

The over three million acres of Gila National Forest make it by far the largest national forest in New Mexico, as well as one of the largest in the nation. Even more impressive is that almost all of its lands are contained in one large block.

Although large, the forest is lightly used, especially in comparison to others like Tonto National Forest in Arizona, which is located near several large metropolitan areas. This makes for relatively few campgrounds (only about 20, with less than 300 total campsites) and trails (about 1,000 miles of maintained trails).

The forest is so huge that it would take a whole book just to write about the places to explore, but you really can't go wrong anywhere in the region. One of the great things about this area, almost unheard of in the South-west, is that there is plenty of water. Streams and rivers that flow year-round, and lakes filled by snowmelt, pro-vide dependable water supplies to backpackers.

Since there are no huge campgrounds in the forest or big-ticket attractions to draw large numbers of visitors to any one spot, people tend to disperse over wide areas. Most people who visit Gila come to hike, birdwatch,

---

backpack, hunt, fish or simply camp.

Visitors are also kept dispersed by the fact that about one-third of the forest is designated wilderness, and the only ways to explore those areas are on foot or horseback. You may spend weeks in these areas of the national forest and never see another person.

The exception is in the 560,000-acre Gila Wilderness Area, strewn with mountain streams and ponderosa pine forests. In 1924, it became the first wilderness area in any national forest in the country to be given special protection. Because it is the oldest, it is also the most talked about and well-known wilderness area, and it attracts most of the backpackers who come to the forest. If you choose it as your destination, you are likely to have company.

The other wilderness areas, such as the 200,000-acre Aldo Leopold and 30,000-acre Blue Range, are just as beautiful as Gila and much less visited. All three have excellent hiking trails, including a portion of the Continental Divide National Scenic Trail, which runs along the ridgeline in the Aldo Leopold Wilderness Area. The most popular trails enter the Gila Wilderness Area from the Gila Visitor Center just north of Silver City.

Although there are no roads in the wilderness areas, the roads through the rest of the national forest are especially scenic as they lead through tall ponderosa pine forests, by mountain lakes and above deep canyons. I sometimes head for Gila just to drive along the back-country roads and car camp in the open forests wherever the mood strikes me.

If you do camp or backpack in the region during summer, however, be sure to bring rain protection and a good tent. Thunderstorms appear almost like clockwork during summer afternoons and the heavy rains with huge drops can rip through flimsy rainflies.

Directions: Gila National Forest covers much of southwest New Mexico and there is access from many directions. The best way to plan a trip is to obtain a forest service map of the forest before you head for the region. From Silver City, Route 15 heads north into the middle of the forest, to Gila Wilderness Area.

Fee or Free: This is a free area.

Camping: Although there are only a few improved forest service campgrounds, you can primitive camp almost anywhere in the national forest.

Lodging: The best bets for lodging are Silver City to the south and Truth or Consequences to the east.

Contact: Gila National Forest, 3005 East Camino del Bosque, Silver City, NM 88061; (505) 538-2771.

2

Whitewater Canyon & The Catwalk

In Gila National Forest

The small resort town of Glenwood on the west side of Gila National Forest is a base for backpackers and fishermen who are heading into the Gila Wilderness Area, but I like it because of another nearby attraction.

Whitewater Canyon is a steep, narrow box canyon which has had a long and varied history. Geronimo once used it as a hideout, and later there was heavy mining activity in the canyon.

During that period, a water pipe was built along the side of the canyon to a mill at the mouth. The first pipe was four inches in diameter, and strung along the canyon wall above high water levels.

After some time, the pipe began to corrode. In order to repair it, miners crawled along the pipe itself to reach the spots that needed mending. The pipe became known as the Catwalk and miners continued to crawl along it until it was replaced with a larger, 18-inch pipe that they could walk on. The pipe remained in place after the mining activity in the area ceased in 1913, but it was no longer used.

Locals remembered its history, though. In 1961, the U.S. Forest Service replaced the pipe with a true catwalk that is wide enough for a person to comfortably walk along. Today, whitewater roars by underneath as visitors walk suspended against the rock face of the cliff up to the head of the canyon.

The Catwalk itself is only about a 30-minute round-trip hike, but the trail continues up into the canyon as it crosses the creek on a series of wooden, metal and suspension bridges.

This trek cannot be topped as a day outing when you want to stretch your legs but don't want to get too ambitious. As I move along the Catwalk, I drift back in time and imagine myself as one of the early miners. At the upper reaches of Whitewater Canyon, I can even sense the feeling of protection the area must have given to Geronimo and his desperate band.

Directions: Take Catwalk Road east out of Glenwood on the north side of town and follow the signs for a little over five miles to the parking area near the Catwalk.

Fee or Free: This is a free area.

Camping: There are no improved campgrounds nearby but you can primitive camp on national forest land outside town.

Lodging: The best bet for lodging is Silver City to the south.

Contact: Gila National Forest, 2610 North Silver Street, Silver City, NM 88061; (505) 538-2771.

❸

San Francisco River Hot Springs

Near the Arizona border in southwest New Mexico

Some people come to the San Francisco River as it flows to the west of Glenwood for its whitewater rafting action, while others come to swim in the still, deep pools found between the roaring rapids. Still others make the trip to enjoy two hot springs that flow from the river's banks.

Coming from Glenwood, the first of the hot springs are the San Francisco Hot Springs. Mineral water flows from the ground at 110 degrees into rock and mud pools built by volunteers. The second are Bubble Hot Springs, which are about another half-mile downstream. These are truly impressive springs, with the 50- by 100-foot pool at the base of a spectacular cliff held in place by a sand dam deposited by a major flood a number of years ago. The pool even skims and cleans itself as it flows over the dam.

The 96- and 102-degree water throughout the five-foot-deep pool is constantly heated as 106-degree water seeps up through the sandy bottom.

After a week backpacking trip in Gila National Forest, a trip to the hot springs is almost mandatory. The deep pool provides plenty of room to float, and the hot water soothes sore muscles as it removes the caked-on grime.

While the hot springs are well known, they are also little used. When I visited Bubble Hot Springs, the pool was completely empty. There were two other couples at San Francisco Hot Springs, but that couldn't be considered crowded by any standards, let alone free-outdoor-mineral-soak standards.

Just so you know: Both of these springs have been "clothing optional" the times that I have soaked here, although the U.S. Forest Service has a "Clothing Required" sign near San Francisco Hot Springs.

Directions: From Glenwood, continue south on US 180 to the small community of Pleasanton. Continue two more miles to the signs to San Francisco Hot Springs on the right. Turn right and follow the gravel road as it crosses two creek beds, then park in the parking area. San Francisco Hot Springs are only about 10 yards from the parking area.

Bubble Hot Springs are about a half mile farther downstream. The trail crosses the river several times before reaching the large pool.

Fee or Free: This is a free area.

Camping: Primitive camping is allowed on the river side of the parking area on national forest land. The land on the other side of the parking area under the trees is privately owned land.

Lodging: The best bet is in Silver City to the south.

Contact: Gila National Forest, 2610 North Silver Street, Silver City, NM 88061; (505) 538-2771.

4

Lower Box of the Gila River

In southwestern New Mexico

Large rock formations and steep canyons line the banks of the Gila River as it leaves Gila National Forest to the south. There, side canyons cut through as tributary streams feed the river. Even during times of low water, the groundwater beneath the dry streambeds provides nourishment to willow and cottonwood where songbirds nest in large numbers.

The expansive, five-mile-long canyon of the Gila offers easy hiking. Water levels are low during most of the year, and the "hoodoos" (the local term for strange rock formations) and rock columns that rise from the canyon floor add a magical quality to the landscape. Exploration of the side canyons is easy as you follow the dry or slow-moving streams up toward the highlands.

Here you are most likely to encounter the abundant wildlife of the region. Find a water hole during dry times, sit behind a natural blind, and wait for the animals to come to drink as dusk approaches. You may see raccoon, bobcat, coyote, rabbit or deer as you wait for dark to take hold.

On nights of the full moon, dark never quite takes hold. Then you can hike along the side-canyon floors back to the main canyon where the hoodoos and rock columns take on a unique identity. They appear to be alive as the shadows cast by the moonlight slowly move over the large formations, and nocturnal birds such as owls and bats, their constant companions in the New Mexico deserts, dart and glide in and around the columns.

During fall, the hiking changes as the nights turn cold and the trees of the riparian forest turn golden. Then migrating birds, mostly waterfowl, also congregate along the river as they head south for warmer climes.

Directions: The best entry point is at the Red Rock Bridge on State Road 464 about 25 miles north of Lordsburg.

Fee or Free: This is a free area.

Camping: Primitive camping is allowed anywhere in the area on BLM land.

Lodging: The best bets for lodging are Lordsburg, Deming and Silver City.

Contact: BLM Las Cruces District Office, 1800 Marquess Street, Las Cruces, NM 88005; (505) 525-4300.

5

City of Rocks State Park

Near Silver City

Stonehenge in the desert? No, just the remains of rhyolite outcroppings from ancient volcanic activity. Although the rocks, some of which reach as high as 60 feet, appear to be some prehistoric site built by humans, they have only been eroded into weird shapes by wind, water and extreme temperature changes over millions of years. What makes the formations appear to be unnatural is the fact that they are confined to a 40-acre field in the midst of the desert.

This unnatural appearance is what has undoubtedly drawn humans to the formations for at least 1,000 years. Today, the rocks form the centerpiece of a park and campground, but Native Americans also camped here 500 to 1,000 years ago and used some of the flat rocks as mortar stones where they ground corn. You can see rounded depressions left by this activity as you wander among the large stones.

The site may also have been used for religious activities by the early residents of the region. During unusual lighting conditions, such as during a summer thunderstorm near dusk, when lightning flashes highlight the rocks against the dark clouds, or when the shadows cast by a full moon among the rocks take on the shape of devils and demons, you can understand how people could have attached mystical meanings to the rocks.

While I saw plenty of youngsters scrambling over the rocks while I was here, I saw no technical climbers. Some of the higher rocks are good for novice climbers, though.

Directions: Heading northwest on US 180 from Deming, drive 24 miles to State Road 61. Head northeast on State Road 61 about eight miles to the park.

Fee or Free: Day use costs $3; camping costs $7, first come, first served.

Camping: The park has an improved campground with a cactus garden.

Lodging: There is lodging in both Deming and Silver City.

Contact: City of Rocks State Park, P.O. Box 50, Faywood, NM 88034; (505) 536-2800.

6

Rock Hound State Park & the Florida Mountains

Southeast of Deming

The Florida Mountains, a rugged, jagged range with many steep canyons, some with near-vertical walls, rise for several thousand feet above the desert to the southeast of Deming.

While wildlife is abundant in this desert range—including the exotic Persian ibex, which was released here in the 1970s and seems to be thriving—more people come to the region to look for rocks than for animals.

A unique state park is located at the base of the range. Rock Hound State Park is one of the few parks in the country that actually encourages visitors to look for and collect rocks. Geodes, jasper, rhyolite and agate are just a few of the rocks and stones that you can find here as you dig in the recently tilled soil—that's right, tilled by the park rangers to help rock hounds in their endeavors.

I was amazed the first time I visited this park to see dozens of people rummaging through freshly tilled soil and coming up with excellent samples of jasper, agate, carnelia and pitchstone. Even in areas where you can collect these semiprecious stones, you generally have to dig on your own for them. Here, the state park does the hard work. As you walk around the tilled areas, it is almost like picking up potatoes from the garden.

If you like to search for rocks, and also like to meet with other rock hounds, head for the park in March when the Deming Gem and Mineral Society (P.O. Box 1459, Deming, NM 88031) sponsors an annual Rockhound Roundup. Over 500 participants from some 40 states enjoy taking guided rock tours and attending rock-judging seminars.

Directions: Take State Road 11 south from Deming for five miles to the road to the park. Turn east and follow the signs to the parking area and campground.

Fee or Free: Day use costs $3; camping runs $6 to $7.

Camping: There is an improved campground at the park, and you can primitive camp on BLM land outside the park.

Lodging: There is lodging in Deming.

Contact: Rock Hound State Park, P.O. Box 1064, Deming, NM 88029; (505) 546-6182. For state park information, contact the BLM Las Cruces District Office, 1800 Marquess Street, Las Cruces, NM 88005; (505) 525-4300.

7

Volcanic Areas of the Potrillo Mountains

In south-central New Mexico

To the south of the Florida Mountains along the Mexican border lie several hundred square miles of wild, uninhabitable land where raptors rule. This hot volcanic field known as the Potrillo Mountains includes almost 50 volcanic cones that range between 1,000 and 3,000 feet in diameter. In addition, there are lava flows, sand dunes and plenty of rodents to feed the large raptor population.

This wild land has few improved roads, but locals have developed many tracks with their four-wheel-drive vehicles. These lead into interesting regions, but they can also lead into trouble of the where-the-heck-are-we variety. Before heading out into this hostile area, check with the BLM and locals about road conditions and hazards.

In the midst of the range are two interesting features, one of which is a national landmark. Kilbourne Hole National Natural Landmark is technically a "maar," or a crater formed by a gas explosion. And a large hole it is, with a maximum width of two miles and a maximum depth of 450 feet. These geological features are rare, and this is one of the largest in the country. You can hike around inside it; you feel like you're walking in a big, black bowl. The nearest comparison to this hole that I have seen is Meteor Crater in northern Arizona, but that large hole is located in the middle of a large flat desert.

Another interesting area is Indian Basin, where you sometimes encounter flocks of ducks in the midst of the lava field. They stop over for a rest on their fall migration when the basin temporarily fills with water.

Directions: Contact the BLM for a map of the region and talk to locals in Deming and Columbus before venturing out into this desolate and rugged land.

Fee or Free: This is a free area.

Camping: Primitive camping is allowed anywhere on BLM lands.

Lodging: The best bet for lodging is Deming.

Contact: BLM Las Cruces District Office, 1800 Marquess Street, Las Cruces, NM 88005; (505) 525-4300.

8

Birding in Guadalupe Canyon

In the far southwest corner of New Mexico

Serious birders will go to the ends of the earth to get a new bird for their life list, or to see a rare bird that they have only seen once or twice. It is nothing for them, therefore, to travel to the far ends of New Mexico to an isolated section of the Mexican border in the Guadalupe Mountains. In fact, the region is in such a far corner of New Mexico that you can't even reach it from the state. You have to come at it from Douglas, Arizona.

Shallow Guadalupe Canyon—it never reaches over 600 feet deep—is along the southern border of Coronado National Forest, and the BLM has declared it an outstanding natural area for its birding habitat.

For those who truly want solitude, the region is one of the best getaways in the Southwest. And if you get tired of the desert landscape in the canyon, you can hike to nearby Bunk Robinson Peak in the Peloncillo Mountains where the views cover large areas of New Mexico, Arizona, and Sonora and Chihuahua in Mexico.

The streams in the canyon and feeder side canyons flow intermittently during late summer and early fall after the summer thunderstorms, but there are no reliable water sources. With the summer storms, however, come flash floods—floods that can be devastating if you are not on your toes.

Avoid camping in the flats of the canyon floors, and listen for distant roaring when hiking in narrow areas. Floods don't have to follow downpours nearby. They frequently come from distant storms that drop vast amounts of water into the upper reaches of the drainage area. You may not even have been aware of a storm that sends thundering rivers of water down narrow canyons, picking up speed and power as they join together in the larger canyons below.

Although the solitude is great and the hiking is good, most people head for Guadalupe Canyon for the birding. Almost 160 species have been recorded in the canyon, and many of these are rarely seen in the U.S. Guadalupe Canyon is the far northern range of many of these species, including the buff-collared nightjar, thick-billed kingbird, fan-tailed warbler and elegant trogon. The birding is so good here that many birders think this region falls only slightly below Madera Canyon and Cave Creek in Arizona for quality, although it is not nearly as accessible.

Spring and fall are the busiest times in the canyon for migrating birds. High heat in summer keeps bird activity low, and winter is cold in the canyon, keeping both people and birds away.

Directions: Follow Geronimo Trail east from Douglas, Arizona for about 25 miles to Guadalupe Canyon Road. Take a right and continue to the New Mexico state line. Just past the state line, take a forest service road north for two miles to the canyon. Note: The entire route from Douglas is on improved dirt road.

Fee or Free: This is a free area.

Camping: You may camp anywhere on BLM or national forest lands, but do not camp in washes or on canyon floors. Flash floods are a real danger in this area.

Lodging: The best bet for lodging is Douglas, Arizona.

Contact: BLM Las Cruces District Office, 1800 Marquess Street, Las Cruces, NM 88005; (505) 525-4300.

Big Hatchet Wildlife Area

In the southwest corner of New Mexico

Isolated and almost inaccessible, Big Hatchet is a refuge for wildlife ranging from coyotes, ring-tailed cats and mountain lions to javelinas. All of them can be seen if you set up watch at dawn and dusk in the wildlife area, but the centerpiece of the refuge, the reason for its existence, is a herd of about 100 desert bighorn sheep, which the refuge was created to protect in 1926.

Over the years, the population of the herd has fluctuated with weather and disease, but it seems to be holding steady after long years of protection.

For good views of the herd, plan for an extended stay at the refuge. A day visit just isn't worth the effort. By the time you reach the area, set up camp and locate signs of the sheep, it will be sunset and too dark to see.

Since the sheep are most active in early morning and late evening, plan on hiking around the refuge at dusk and dawn, then resting during midday when all things great and small escape from the bright sun and heat.

There are no developed hiking trails or campgrounds in the region, but a hike to the top of Big Hatchet Peak along deer trails ends with one of the best views in this part of the state. This is also a good place to start your search for the elusive sheep. Depending on where you start, expect this to be a five- to six-mile round-trip hike.

A good pair of binoculars or a spotting scope are a necessity if you want close-up views of the sheep, and cameras are generally useless with anything less than a 1000mm lens.

Directions: The wildlife area is almost completely surrounded by private lands with locked gates; the best way to reach it is from the northeast side. Take State Road 81 south off Hachita for about a mile to where the paved road turns west. If you reach Hatchet Gap on the paved road, you have gone too far. Take the dirt road at the bend to the east until it ends near the Mexican border. The wildlife area is to the west of the road.

Fee or Free: This is a free area.

Camping: Primitive camping is allowed anywhere on BLM lands.

Lodging: The best bets for lodging are Deming and Lordsburg to the northeast and northwest.

Contact: BLM Las Cruces District Office, 1800 Marquess Street, Las Cruces, NM 88005; (505) 525-4300.

Presilla & Sierra de las Canas

On the Rio Grande

Two miles east of downtown Socorro, across the Rio Grande, red and white sandstone hills rise more than 1,000 feet above the river. Box canyons and red sand dunes are scattered throughout the hills. When the river is low, residents of Socorro simply walk across the riverbed to some of the large arroyos in the Presilla unit of the BLM's 28,600-acre Sierra de las Canas Management Area where they take day hikes and picnics in wild country.

I like to head for the Arroyo del Tajo, a canyon which extends east into the Presilla just south of Socorro. Here, in the Tinajas Natural Area of Critical Environmental Concern—a Bureau of Reclamation designation to protect a historic site—the rock faces still boast an array of pictographs, which were first painted thousands of years ago.

The Presilla unit's proximity to downtown Socorro has a drawback, however—since it's easy to reach, it's heavily used. If you want solitude and true wilderness, you'll have to head just a bit farther from downtown into the Sierra de las Canas area.

It is an area worth exploring. Deep gorges with multicolored layers of rock along their steep walls cut through this rugged desert range, which in many ways reminds me of a smaller version of the Grand Canyon.

The region is most definitely Chihuahuan Desert in vegetation and in climate, however. It's not a place to visit in midsummer, unless you are a real desert fanatic. The temperatures reach 100 degrees on most days, and there is no relief provided by shade or water activities. The desert scrub includes creosote bush, cholla, datil yucca, desert willow, ocotillo and honey mesquite.

Hiking through the canyons of the Sierra de las Canas is great the rest of the year, as even winter in the Chihuahuan is mild. The sun shines steadily all day, every day, and the stars of the night skies twinkle in the clear, cool evenings.

Directions: Presilla is just across the Rio Grande from downtown Socorro. Sierra de las Canas is about 45 minutes east of Socorro along Quebradas Road. Park along the road or at the canyon mouth and hike in; there is no parking lot or trailhead.

Fee or Free: These are free areas.

Camping: Primitive camping is allowed on BLM land in Sierra de las Canas.

Lodging: There is adequate lodging in Socorro.

Contact: BLM Socorro Resource Area, 198 Neill Avenue, Socorro, NM 87801; (505) 835-0412.

Valley of Fires Recreation Area

West of Carrizozo on US 380

A thousand years ago, the Carrizozo Lava Flow began covering a 50-mile region along what is now US 54 with a thick layer of red-hot molten rock. The flow, one of the youngest in the U.S., reaches a width of over five miles in places and a depth of more than 70 feet.

Little was known about this 200-square-mile badlands until recently as both Native Americans and early European explorers avoided the rugged terrain. In recent years, wildlife biologists have become interested in the plants and animals that survive in such adverse conditions, and have discovered a wide array of wildlife flourishing here.

It is difficult to traverse the sharp, jagged lava for any long stretches, and almost no one attempts to backpack in the region. But you can hike and camp in the 463-acre Valley of Fires Recreation Area, which has a campground and marked nature trails and lies near the northern end of the lava beds.

Here you can make a base camp and take day trips to the various access points of the vast lava flow. You, too, can search for the wildlife that survives in the arid fields where daytime temperatures in midsummer can exceed 150 degrees at ground level.

Although the area does not have the dramatic formations found in El Malpaís National Monument farther north, it is nevertheless an interesting place to explore the results of geologically recent volcanic action. Because it is recent, the lava flow has not eroded as much and few plants have set root here.

A modest wildlife population, chiefly small mammals such as ground squirrels, mice and rabbits, along with plenty of reptiles, lives among the plants that have taken root in the crevices where windblown sand has collected. The primary birds in the area are ravens and raptors, which eat the rodents.

The best way to explore the interior of the lava flow is along the many jeep trails that run along its edge. A nature trail leads three-quarters of a mile from the recreation area's campground through a nearby lava field.

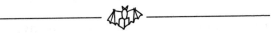

Directions: The recreation area's visitor center and bookstore are four miles west of Carrizozo on US 380.

Fee or Free: This is a fee area.

Camping: There is a developed campground in the recreation area. Day use is $5 per vehicle; camping costs $7 per night.

Lodging: Socorro to the west and Roswell to the east are your best bets for lodging.

Contact: Valley of Fires Recreation Area, P.O. Box 871, Carrizozo, NM 88301; (505) 648-2241. BLM Roswell Resource Area, P.O. Box 1857, Roswell, NM 88202; (505) 624-1790.

Bosque del Apache National Wildlife Refuge

South of Socorro along the Rio Grande

Greater sandhill cranes never came as close to extinction as their close cousins, the whooping cranes, but as their nesting grounds in the north were disturbed and turned into agricultural fields in the early part of the century, their population plummeted. One attempt to bolster their dipping numbers was to ensure that their winter feeding grounds remained protected. Bosque del Apache National Wildlife Refuge, established in 1939, was one of the first refuges set aside in the attempt to help rescue the endangered greater sandhill cranes from the fate suffered by whooping cranes.

There were fewer than 1,000 cranes using this flyway in those years, and a measure of the success of the efforts of those early conservationists is the more than 12,000 cranes that now fly into the refuge each winter with their raucous calls and joyous dances.

These days, they are even joined by a dozen or so whooping cranes. In the 1970s, the U.S. Fish and Wildlife

Agency made an attempt to have sandhill cranes raise young whooping cranes at their Idaho nesting grounds. They have had partial success, and are continuing their program in hopes of establishing a new flock of this endangered bird.

The cranes are just a few of the hundreds of thousands of waterfowl and wading birds that winter over in this desert refuge, which the Rio Grande meanders through on its way south to the Gulf of Mexico.

A 15-mile loop leads along levees around the ponds where the wintering flocks are thickest, but I like to hike the short hiking trails that lead along some of the levees and the three longer trails that take you into the upland areas of the refuge. Everyone who comes here can get out of their vehicles and close to the raucous sounds that come from the waterfowl as they establish their feeding territories.

The refuge is open year-round, but the best time to see the birds is during the winter months. That is also the best hiking weather, although it does get cold at the refuge during mid-winter when the winds bite through even heavy coats and wool pants.

Directions: Take Interstate 25 south for about 18 miles from Socorro and follow the freeway exit signs to the refuge.

Fee or Free: There is a $2 fee for the loop tour; access to the visitor center is free.

Camping: There are no public campgrounds nearby, but the private Bosque Birdwatchers Park offers campsites near the refuge. You can primitive camp on BLM land away from the refuge.

Lodging: The best bet for lodging is Socorro.

Contact: Bosque del Apache National Wildlife Refuge, P.O. Box 1246, Socorro, NM 87801; (505) 835-1828.

White Sands National Monument

Near Alamogordo

Southwest of Alamogordo off US 70 is some of the strangest land you will ever encounter. Pure white dunes form a stark-white rolling ocean that contrasts with the clear, blue sky above. Notice that I didn't say sand dunes, however. These dunes are comprised of extremely fine gypsum that has eroded from the San Andres Mountains to the west.

White Sands National Monument is enormous—228 square miles—and always surprising. I like to just walk among the dunes here, not knowing what to expect as I reach the top of each one. I may see a single yucca plant that has survived the harsh environment. I could stumble upon a large, flat area with very small dunes or encounter a dune that reaches as much as 60 feet above the surrounding land. Whatever I find here, I know it will be different from just about any other place I have ever explored.

There is one primitive backcountry campsite and I like to stay there during a full moon—you can almost read without a lantern by the moonlight reflecting off the dunes. For those who do not want to camp out, the park is open until midnight during full moons in the summer months.

To get a sense of the vastness of the monument, take the 16-mile loop drive that leads through its various regions. Then, to have a good time, get out of the car and begin to hike around the dunes.

It has been said that White Sands National Monument is the place to be a kid, because it invites child's play no matter what age you are. Tumble down steep slopes that are as white as snow, but soft and warm, as the gypsum brushes against your skin. Gather up great heaps of gypsum and let the fine white grains sift through your fingers. Run and jump over ridges that drop off precipitously, but don't worry about breaking your neck— just plop into the soft dune and slide to the bottom.

Sounds like fun, doesn't it? That's what White Sands is all about.

Directions: Take US 70 southwest from Alamogordo for about 16 miles to the marked monument turnoff. The monument visitor center is eight miles west from US 70.

Fee or Free: Entrance to the area costs $4 per car.

Camping: There is one primitive backcountry campsite. To camp there, you must obtain a free permit from the visitor center.

Lodging: The best bets for lodging are Alamogordo and Las Cruces.

Contact: White Sands National Monument, P.O. Box 1086, Holloman Air Force Base, NM 88330; (505) 479-6124.

Organ Mountains Recreation Area

East of Las Cruces

Towering mountains, huge boulder fields, miles of hiking and backpacking trails, and plenty of climbing opportunities (from easy to extremely difficult technical climbs) are all within easy reach of US 70 in the 35,000 acres of the Organ Mountains.

They rise to the east of Las Cruces, offering some of the best true desert experiences in New Mexico. The BLM has designated a number of recreation areas in the region where you can set up a base camp and explore by car or foot deep into rugged and remote country.

The high spires and peaks that rise to over 9,000 feet are quartz monzonite, a very hard rock face with many cracks and crevices that is attractive to technical climbers. They are also of interest to photographers who obtain great color shots of the cliffs and peaks as the rays of the setting sun highlight the pink of the quartz in the peaks and slopes.

The Baylor Pass Recreation Trail runs for six miles from the Aguirre Springs Campground, and is a good mountain biking (as well as hiking) trail. For those who

---

don't want to compete with mountain bikes, there is the 4.5-mile loop of the Pine Tree Trail that also begins at the campground.

Another area from which to explore the backcountry is Dripping Springs. There is no campground here, but there is a large picnic area with tables and shade.

The campground and the developed trails near it are frequently crowded during midsummer, and the BLM has set a limit on the number of visitors that are allowed into the area. When that number is reached, no more cars are allowed to enter. Away from the campground the crowds are smaller, and you can hike on dirt roads through the site.

Directions: Take US 70 east about 19 miles from Las Cruces and watch for signs to the Organ Mountains Recreation Area.

Fee or Free: This is a free area.

Camping: There is a developed campground at Aguirre Springs, and backcountry camping on BLM lands.

Lodging: You'll find lodging in Las Cruces and Alamogordo.

Contact: BLM Las Cruces District Office, 1800 Marquess Street, Las Cruces, NM 88005; (505) 525-4300.

Bitter Lake National Wildlife Refuge

Near Roswell

Bitter Lake is too alkaline for human or cattle consumption, so ranches were never developed around it, but it is apparently fine for the thousands of waterfowl and wading birds that collect here each winter.

Up to 20,000 lesser sandhill cranes winter along the shores of the natural lake, and you can view them and the other winter residents as you drive along the eight-mile auto-tour loop.

The 100th meridian is the general cutoff between eastern and western bird species of North America, and Bitter Lake is a good birding site because it lies near that line and attracts birds from both sides. It also attracts birds that live in both high and low elevations.

This is the only place in New Mexico where you can find the endangered interior least terns. They share nesting sites with another threatened species, the snowy plover. One spring when I was visiting, I not only saw both of these species nesting, but I also saw also avocets and black-necked stilts.

The nesting site is so important that the Air Force attempts to keep low-flying planes from crossing the refuge during nesting season, because the shadows of the aircraft may be mistaken for birds of prey and frighten nesting birds.

Near the refuge, black-tailed prairie dogs have hundreds of burrows, which are often shared with burrowing owls. Colorful ferruginous hawks come to the refuge in winter to hunt for prey.

Larger mammals, such as coyote, badgers and bobcats are common in the refuge, but I have only seen coyote. The other two are secretive and generally don't venture out and about during daylight hours.

Fall through late spring are the best times to visit the refuge. Summers are quite hot and few birds are present.

Directions: Take US 380 (Second Street) east from Roswell for about three miles to the signs directing you to the refuge. It is eight miles to the refuge headquarters from the highway.

Fee of Free: This is a free area.

Camping: State park campgrounds are to the south at Bottomless Lakes.

Lodging: Good lodging is available in Roswell.

Contact: Bitter Lake National Wildlife Refuge, P.O. Box 7, Roswell, NM 88202; (505) 622-6755.

Carlsbad Caverns National Park

In southeastern New Mexico

The 47,765-acre Carlsbad Caverns National Park, home of one of the most famous cave complexes in the world, lies in the Guadalupe Mountains of southeastern New Mexico, and attracts tourists from around the world. Most of these come only to take the national park tours of the main cave and then leave for the next tourist attraction.

Visitors to Carlsbad who expect rugged spelunking are in for a surprise. Paved trails and electric lights make the stroll through the caves easy. An elevator from the visitor center takes you down 750 feet below the surface to the beginning of a 1.5-mile walk through the chambers and tight passageways to the Big Chamber where water action has left a fantastic display of stalagmites and stalactites.

It's impressive, and not a bad introduction to limestone caving, but don't get back in your car just yet. Those in the know stay to explore the over 45,000 acres of backcountry that are part of the park, and to watch the bat flights out of the cave each evening at dusk. They also head for the much-less-visited New Cave where the park

---

service also leads tours. These are without the benefit of electric lights and elevators, however, and give you the feel of true spelunking, although there is nothing at all dangerous about them.

This region was once a huge limestone reef, and the caves formed as the limestone slowly eroded over millions of years as water seeped through cracks. Underground caverns formed as the more soluble rocks were eaten away, and these now lie beneath large tracts of land in the mountain range.

On the surface, most of the park's terrain is rocky ridges and rugged canyons. Although there are no developed campsites in the park, there is almost unlimited hike-in camping in the backcountry. You only need to obtain a free permit from the visitor center and head into the rugged wilderness.

Remember, there is no dependable water supply in the region and you must carry your own. If you happen across a cave on your hikes, you should explore it with caution, but only if you have experience spelunking—do not enter if you are a novice. Report any finds to the rangers, in case you have made a new discovery.

Outside the park, the BLM manages over 150 caves from its Carlsbad office. About 20 of these caves are gated and locked with access only by permit. The rest are open for exploration.

Of all outdoor activities, spelunking is one of the most dangerous. For that reason, the BLM only gives directions and access to caves when they are assured those seeking directions are experienced cave explorers who are not likely to harm themselves or the cave environments, which are home to a number of rare and endangered species, including several species of bats.

If you are an experienced spelunker and wish to explore this region for caves, contact the BLM office for information.

Directions: Take US 62/180 south for 20 miles from Carlsbad to the park. Contact the BLM for information about directions to other caves.

Fee or Free: Entrance to the caves costs $5.

Camping: There is no car camping in the park, although backcountry camping permits are available. You may primitive camp on BLM lands outside the park.

Lodging: There is adequate lodging in Carlsbad.

Contact: Carlsbad Caverns National Park, 3225 National Parks Highway, Carlsbad, NM 88220; (505) 785-2232. BLM Carlsbad Resource Area, 101 East Mermod Street, P.O. Box 1778, Carlsbad, NM 88220; (505) 887-6544.

Nevada

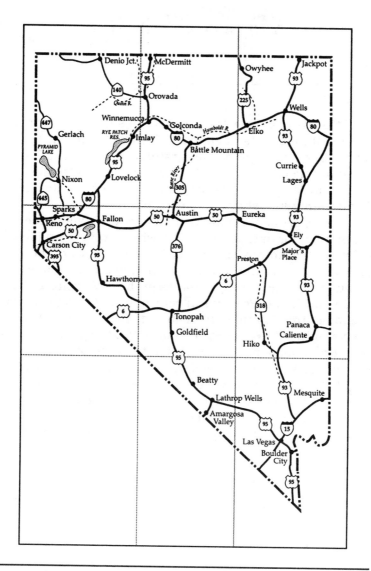

Introduction to Nevada

Nevada is a state of extremes. No state has more of its land in public domain, most of which is administered by the BLM. No state has less rainfall. Only Alaska has fewer people per square mile. And no state has more mountain ranges—at last count geologists identified no fewer than 236 distinct ranges within the state.

These elements combine to make Nevada a prime destination for outdoor getaways where you are unlikely to encounter hordes of visitors. From stretches of the Mojave Desert in the southwestern corner of the state, through the many ranges that form the low basins of the Basin and Range Province in central Nevada, to the small section of the Columbia Plateau in the northeastern corner of the state, you can enjoy great, unspoiled wilderness excursions in the driest climate in the country.

While all of Nevada is dry, the amount of heat and cold that you must tolerate varies greatly as you move through the state. The southern portions have horrendous highs that often exceed 115 degrees during midsummer, and moderate winters where only the nights dip below freezing with any regularity.

In the higher elevations to the north, you can expect summer temperatures to be more moderate, but winter lows often dip into the teens and below as the mountain tops are covered with snow.

By far the largest amount of land, about 75 percent

of the state, is in the Basin and Range Province. This geological formation is notable for its many mountain ranges that rise above level valleys, all except one of which run north and south. These give the state an appearance of corduroy from the air, and on the ground they provide you with places to go that are visited by few others.

Some of the best outdoor activities in Nevada are wildlife viewing in the Sheldon, Desert and Ruby Lake wildlife refuges; caving in the Goshute Mountains; and backpacking in the dramatic Ruby Mountains and the Jarbridge Wilderness.

Chapter 6

Northern Nevada

Maps 16, 17, 18

Map 16

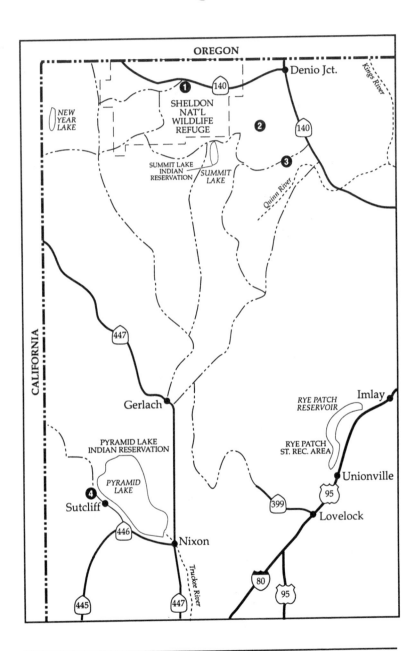

Northern Nevada (maps on pages 252-254)

Map 17

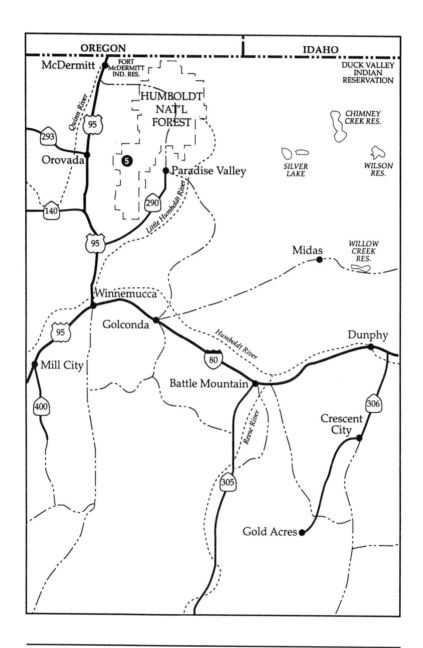

Map 18

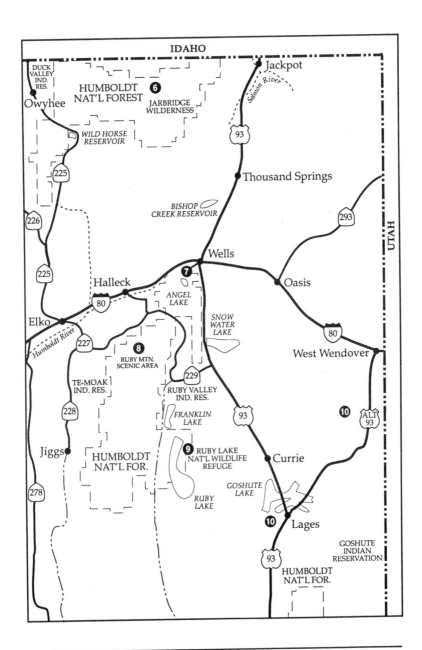

Sheldon National Wildlife Refuge

In the far northwest corner of Nevada

If you were soaring with a golden eagle over the Sheldon National Wildlife Refuge, you would see upwards of 8,000 pronghorn spread out in small herds in the 500,000-plus acres of sagebrush country in this remote northwestern corner of Nevada. You won't see quite so many on your drive into the refuge, but you will see herds as they roam over a ruggedly beautiful desert landscape where the rolling sagebrush country is broken by out-crops of rimrock and deep gorges.

This is the country where you look up as often as you look around. Up high you may see golden eagles soaring overhead in search of a jackrabbit, or a prairie falcon preparing to swoop toward the ground at over 150 miles an hour to snatch a vole or mouse from its hiding place among the sagebrush.

As captivating as these large raptors are, I head to Sheldon to see swift, graceful pronghorn, the fastest mammals in North America. As you drive through the refuge, a small group of six to eight frequently follows along the road beside your car for some distance before suddenly, without warning, spurting ahead and crossing in front of you. While I know to expect this, I seldom find myself prepared for their rapid escape and I am always stunned by their speed—they have been known to travel at up to 40 miles per hour for six miles.

Although they are spread throughout the refuge most of the year, pronghorn can generally be seen in small numbers around Swan Lake, the major lake in the refuge, in the spring and summer. They collect by the hundreds at Big Springs and Gooch Tables in the winter.

Precipitation is heavier in the wildlife refuge than anywhere else in Nevada, and the 20 inches that fall each year feed the springs and lakes scattered throughout the refuge. Many of these are near the more than 50 miles of gravel roads that wind through a variety of habitats.

Over 175 bird species, a large number by Nevada standards, can be seen in the refuge. Around the low-lying brush, look for sage grouse, quail and chukars. Around the canyons, scan overhead for eagles, falcons and kestrels. Waterfowl such as Canada geese, mallards, gadwalls and other ducks may be seen at Dufurrena Ponds, Catnip Reservoir and Bad Springs—various water holes around the refuge. For songbirds such as Say's Phoebe and green-tailed towhees, look near the riparian growth along the streams and around Dufurrena Ponds.

An unusual feature of the refuge is the fact that rockhounds are allowed to look, but not dig or blast, for opals and sunstones on the refuge lands. You are permitted to take home seven pounds of these semi-precious stones per visit.

The entire refuge is open to backpackers and horseback riders, and 19 primitive campsites are scattered throughout the backcountry.

Directions: From Denio Junction near the Oregon border, take Route 140 west for 25 miles to the refuge entrance sign. Turn south and continue one mile on a gravel road to the Dufurrena Field Station. To find the lakes and water holes, ask for a map at the refuge headquarters.

Fee or Free: This is a free area.

Camping: Primitive camping is allowed on refuge lands, at 19 primitive campsites and at the developed Virgin Valley Campground, one mile past the field station.

Lodging: The best bet for lodging is in Winnemucca, 100 miles south.

Contact: Sheldon National Wildlife Refuge, P.O. Box 111, Room 308, U.S. Post Office Building, Lakeview, OR 97630; (503) 947-3315.

❷

Blue Lakes & the Pine Forest Mountains

Just south of the Oregon border

Glaciers in Nevada? Not today, but there were during the Ice Age, 10,000 or so years ago, and signs of their passage mark the Pine Forest Mountains to the east of Sheldon National Wildlife Refuge. At over 7,500 feet in the high alpine meadows of the range lie several glacial moraine lakes flanked by cathedral peaks.

As you leave Route 140 about 14 miles south of Denio Junction, there is little evidence of what is to come in the higher elevations. At first glance, the surrounding land is flat, sagebrush-covered desert with little to beckon one onward. With a second and third glance, however, you will see California quail and jackrabbits flitting about beneath the low-lying sagebrush, and sage thrashers feeding higher up in the brush.

Another glance upward will likely bring into view an American kestrel or golden eagle sitting on wires and utility poles along the road.

These are just the appetizers, though. As you drive farther along the route, you may spot mule deer, sage grouse and pronghorn along the road, or a California bighorn sheep on the mountain slopes to the north.

While you can cross the mountains on a day drive, I prefer to take several days in the 25,000 acres of BLM land. The road climbs the spine of the Pine Forest Mountains from flat sagebrush country to high-country meadows where you have great views that reach into Oregon to the north and California to the west.

Low-growing sagebrush covers most of the slopes, but aspen, along with mountain mahogany, grow along streams that cut through the steep canyons below. In spring, these provide a sparkling of light green as the new buds break into leaves. In early fall, the groves turn a vibrant yellow as the canyons add spots of color to the dusky green of sagebrush.

Wildflowers cover the flats and slopes in late June or early July. By that time, the snowpack has melted at the higher elevations and camping is excellent at Onion Valley Reservoir, where the BLM maintains a primitive campground with portable toilets.

A well-marked trail leads about a mile from the campground to the Blue Lakes, which include several lakes formed by glacial moraines. The largest of these are Blue Lake and nearby Leonard Creek Lake. This hike takes you from sagebrush country into one of the scattered stands of white-bark and limber pines that grow around the lakes and Duffer Peak to the south. In spring, you'll see lupine, globemallow and Indian paintbrush add splotches of color along the way as they begin their quick growing season.

The forest around the lake is home to several songbirds which are rare in this area of Nevada. These include the pine grosbeak and red crossbill. Chukar and sage grouse do their drumming dances as they mate and nest in the sagebrush near the lake.

I have never camped here without awakening to the gentle movement of herds of mule deer who have come to the lakeshore for water. If I stay still in my sleeping bag, I can often watch the herds for maybe half an hour before they move on.

If I am lucky, I'll catch a panful of trout for breakfast from one of the two major lakes and eat it as the early morning sun sparkles on the surface of the blue water.

Directions: Drive south from Denio Junction for 14 miles on Route 140. At the Blue Lake turnoff, head west on Alder Creek Road and continue for about 15 miles to Onion Valley Reservoir.

Fee or Free: This is a free area.

Camping: There is a semi-developed campground at Onion Valley Reservoir, and primitive camping is allowed anywhere in the area. Remember that Nevada law prohibits camping within 300 feet of livestock watering holes.

Lodging: The best bet for lodging is in Winnemucca, 100 miles south.

Contact: BLM Winnemucca District Office, 705 East Fourth Street, Winnemucca, NV 89445; (702) 623-3676.

3

McGill Canyon

In northwestern Nevada

The sounds of violent clashes echoed off the walls of the narrow canyon, and I knew I had come to the right place—a place where muscular bighorn rams run free and challenge each other for territory and harems without the interference of humans.

McGill Canyon cuts through jagged limestone ridges and rock outcroppings that rise high above the canyon floor. It is a remote desert sanctuary where golden eagles ride the thermals, scanning the sagebrush with sharp eyes for hidden jackrabbits, cottontails and ground squirrels. I enjoy and appreciate the raptors and their prey that struggle to survive in this dry and desolate land, but it is the bighorn sheep that draw me back to this hard-to-reach site.

This is the best place I have ever found to view these majestic animals, and you can't miss glimpsing them here year-round. An especially good time to visit, however, is between March and April, when the ewes are lambing on the upper slopes of the canyon, and in the fall, during rutting time, when the rams collect their harems.

If you head into the canyon during either of those times, though, remember that you should take care not to intrude upon the sheep's immediate surroundings to

---

avoid disturbing them during crucial times. This is when you want to set up your viewing scopes and long camera lenses and watch from afar.

McGill Canyon, which covers about 3,500 acres, is very remote, and has no maintained roads or hiking trails. Venture into it at your own risk and take plenty of food, water and fuel. If you get stuck here, it is a long way out.

This is a place where you can truly watch wildlife—and there is excellent viewing of raptors, predators such as coyote and kit fox, bighorn sheep and reptiles year-round—in peace and solitude.

Directions: Take US 95 north from Winnemucca 31 miles to Route 140. Turn west onto Route 140 and continue another 35 miles northwest to Leonard Creek Road. Turn west on Leonard Creek Road and drive 7.5 miles to the end of the pavement. The mouth of the canyon is another 19 miles over unmaintained dirt road.

Fee or Free: This is a free area.

Camping: Primitive camping is allowed anywhere in area. There may be water in streams, but you should bring a good supply anyway.

Lodging: The only nearby lodging is in Winnemucca.

Contact: BLM Winnemucca District Office, 705 East Fourth Street, Winnemucca, NV 89445; (702) 623-1500.

Pyramid Lake

Near Reno

———————— ————————

State Road 445, an arrow-straight road, heads north from Sparks and bisects a narrow valley between ridges of the Virginia Mountains. No trees grow here, nor does much else that is green. Only the dusky gray-green of the low-lying sagebrush keeps the land from being totally devoid of plantlife.

The route is dry, hot in summer and cold in winter. But after you pass the Pyramid Lake Store about 25 miles from Sparks, you round a sharp turn in the road. Suddenly you are faced with a wide expanse of blue. It is a deeper blue than the endless Southwest sky—the blue of Pyramid Lake.

Pyramid Lake is the largest remnant of prehistoric Lake Lahontan, which once covered most of the Great Basin region in Nevada. Roughly 200 miles long by 175 miles wide, it once reached from what is now Winnemucca to Susanville, California.

Today the much smaller, 110,000-acre Pyramid Lake is a blue sea surrounded by gray desert hills, which are tinged with pink as the setting sun drops behind the Sierra Nevadas to the west.

The beauty of the lake is stark rather than lush. Long stretches of sheer tufa cliffs, piles of tufa rock and tufa domes occasionally break the gently sloping sand that leads to the waters of the lake. In fact, the large pyramid-shaped island that gives the lake its name is one huge block of tufa.

Tufa forms as mineral deposits grow around underwater springs, and the fantastical shapes—like whitish-gray drip castles—have long held the imagination of those who come to Pyramid Lake, much like at Mono Lake in California.

Even the islands in the lake, such as the Needle Rocks, are formed of tufa. When the water level of the lake dropped precipitously in the 1960s, Pyramid Island and the Needle Rocks became part of the mainland. Many visitors defaced them, and the leaders of the Pyramid Lake Indian Reservation declared both off-limits to visitors. Once again, you can visit these islands, but you should be careful not to harm them in any way.

Most visitors are not drawn to the lake for its natural beauty, however, but for its outstanding trout fishing. It is considered to be among the top five lakes in the country for trophy trout.

Also found in Pyramid Lake is the cui-ui, an endangered sucker fish that is found nowhere else. It lives in the depths of the lake at about 300 feet, and comes to the surface only to spawn from April to June. The species does this only once every 15 to 20 years, however, so consider yourself among the very lucky if you view a cui-ui run up the Truckee River toward Verdi.

Others come to view the colony of white pelicans that breed and nest on Anaho Island, a national wildlife refuge in the middle of the lake, with one of the largest white pelican nesting colonies in North America. Double-crested cormorants, Caspian terns and California gulls also nest here.

Although Anaho Island is closed to the public, as are the waters around it for a distance of 500 feet, you can get great views of the colonies from several sites around the lake and from boats. You may get permits and rent boats at Paiute Tribal Headquarters in Sutcliff. The best launching facilities are at Pelican Point.

A word of warning: Boating can be dangerous here in

high winds. I was once slowly moving around the lake in a small motor boat, not paying much attention to the weather, when a storm approached. My boat began to jump about in the increasingly choppy waves before I noticed anything amiss. By the time I reached shore, I was having to bail out water to keep from capsizing.

Summer can be hot here, and winter winds cut to the bone. The best times to visit are during spring nesting season and during the fall bird migration.

Directions: From Interstate 80 in Sparks, take State Road 445 north for about 25 miles to Sutcliff. Ask for directions to various sites at the ranger station.

Fee or Free: Day use costs $5 per vehicle; camping is $5 per night, first come, first served.

Camping: There are some developed campgrounds around the lake, all of which are owned and operated by the Paiute Tribe.

Lodging: There are some motels on the Indian reservations, but the best bets are in Sparks, where motel rooms are abundant, and in Fernly.

Contact: Anaho National Wildlife Refuge, c/o Stillwater National Wildlife Refuge, P.O. Box 1236, Fallon, NV 89406-1236; (702) 423-5128. Pyramid Lake Paiute Tribe, P.O. Box 256, Nixon, NV 89424; (702) 476-1155.

❺

Santa Rosa Mountains

In north-central Nevada

Several years ago, I was hiking along the Summit Trail in the Santa Rosa/Paradise Peak Wilderness Area when I saw the unmistakable imprint of a mountain lion on the trail ahead. I quickly looked around, not out of fear but out of a desire to see one of those elusive predators. While I had seen several mountain lions in California mountains, I'd never seen one in Nevada. But whatever had left that imprint was nowhere in sight.

The Santa Rosa Mountains, where the Summit Trail is located, is the area where I have seen the most mountain lion signs over the years. One reason is the large herd of California bighorn sheep that can frequently be spotted jumping from ledge to ledge on the granite cliff faces of the higher peaks.

The 12-mile Summit Trail crosses the top of the Santa Rosa Mountains above 8,000 feet, and is an excellent place to see the bighorns. It leads through pockets of aspen along streams where downy woodpeckers, mountain bluebirds and many species of warblers feed. In early summer, bluebells, lupines and other bright spring wildflowers add color to the trailsides.

Those who aren't up to making a 12-mile hike (across country where you must carry your own water) can drive Forest Service Road 084 to Hinkey Summit at 7,867 feet. Here, herds of mule deer browse, yellow-bellied marmots loaf in the heat of the midday sun, and golden eagles roost in the spectacular rock outcroppings to the east. The higher you get, the more forested it is, but down low, this is dry sagebrush country.

I often see pronghorn browsing on the plateaus in this range and find that it is relatively easy to track a herd for several miles while snapping photographs of them.

I like to visit the range during a new moon in mid-summer, when I can sleep out under the Milky Way, watching satellites on their orbit around the Earth and meteorites that leave streaks of trailing light as they flash across the dark sky.

Directions: Take US 95 north from Winnemucca to both the Summit Trail and the rest of the Santa Rosa Mountains. For the Summit Trail, take State Road 290 east off US 95, 21 miles north of Winnemucca. Drive 17 miles to Singas Road (Forest Service Road 092), then turn west and drive six miles on a gravel and dirt road to the trailhead.

To reach Hinkey Summit, follow the directions above, but stay on State Road 290 for 18 miles to Paradise Valley. Take State Road 792 (which becomes Forest Service Road 084) along Indian Creek out of Paradise Valley as it climbs toward the summit.

Fee or Free: This is a free area.

Camping: Primitive and backcountry camping are allowed anywhere in the national forest.

Lodging: The best bet for lodging is in Winnemucca.

Contact: Agriculture Service Center, Santa Rosa Ranger District, 1200 Winnemucca Boulevard East, Winnemucca, NV 89445; (702) 623-5025.

Jarbridge Wilderness

Along the Idaho border in northeastern Nevada

As you hike along the crest of the Jarbridge Range in northern Nevada, which stays at over 9,800 feet for about seven miles, you get a great feel for what isolated means. Even the Shoshone Indians steered away from this rugged wilderness. So do most Nevada residents.

The small community of Jarbridge is the most remote town in a state noted for remote towns. It is 47 miles over a gravel road to this community near the boundaries of the 100,000-acre Jarbridge Wilderness in Humboldt National Forest. The town's several hundred residents are all that remain from a much larger population that settled here in the 1910s and '20s when the area was the largest gold-producing region in Nevada. Today, there is no gold left, and most of the residents make their living as ranchers.

Although the region abounds with excellent outdoor getaways, few people take advantage of the offerings. One of these is a five-mile hike along the spine of 8,000-foot Biroth Ridge, in the northern portion of the region near the Idaho border. As you wander through the ridge's conifer forests, you are sure to see plenty of Rocky Mountain elk and mule deer, which often rest beneath the tall firs during the day. At Bruneau Meadows farther south, you can hike and picnic among the many songbirds and pronghorns that frequent this lush meadow. And these are only a sample of the getaways in the range.

During my first trip to the area, I stopped at the Wild Horse Crossing Campground before heading farther into the wilderness and had a delightful time. The campground is located along a quiet stretch of the Owyhee River among steep volcanic cliffs where swifts and swallows nest. As I walked among the groves of aspen and willows along the river I spotted lots of fallen trees and beaver dams.

As the sky darkened, I waited quietly near a grove of young willow, hoping a beaver would venture out of the water for a bite of food. Despite plenty of rustling movement, I couldn't see a single beaver. Soon one crawled slowly up the bank and began nibbling on the bark of a sapling. As I moved to position my camera, I snapped a twig. Oops—that was my last chance for a photograph. With a slap of his tail and a sharp whistle, the large rodent disappeared into the water. I heard numerous others follow the warning.

I was sorely disappointed until a great horned owl swooped low over the path as I was walking back to camp, and that kept my adrenaline flowing until bedtime.

The next day, I backtracked to Bruneau Meadows and drove toward Bear Creek Summit. I wouldn't recommend this drive to anyone who is anxious about mountain roads. The steep, one-lane gravel road often exceeds a 15-percent grade, and the many birds that flit alongside the road are a real danger to a serious birdwatcher. I frequently pulled over and stopped when the birding became too good to pass up.

Finally I made it to the end of the road and came to the community of Jarbridge. The town sits in Jarbridge Canyon, a half-mile-deep river gorge surrounded by high mountains, plateaus and rugged lava flows. North of town, a road climbs to the boundary of the wilderness area, and a moderate trail leads to Jarbridge Lake.

This remote, rugged area has yet to be discovered. A few visitors search it out each year for the solitude and beauty it offers, but nowhere does it get what could be called crowded, or anywhere close to it. While the Shoshone may have been smart in avoiding the region, the Jarbridge Wilderness Area and surrounding national forest lands are perfect for those of us who like to enjoy our outdoor getaways where few others dare to tread.

Directions: Head north form Elko on State Road 225 for 55 miles to County Road 746. Bruneau Meadows and Bear Creek Summit are located along the next 47 miles. To reach Biroth Ridge, cross over the Idaho state line at Rogerson. From Rogerson, head west for 38 miles on Three Creek Road to the small town of Three Creek. Take the Pole Creek Guard Station turnoff and head south for nine miles to the Humboldt National Forest Boundary. At that point, the road becomes Forest Service Road 074. Continue for five miles to another sign for the Pole Creek Guard Station. Turn south and continue one mile past the station. Turn west and continue another mile, then turn south and continue a half mile to the trailhead.

To reach Wild Horse Crossing Campground, continue on State Road 225 past County Road 747 for another 16 miles to the campground. It is located eight miles north of Wild Horse Reservoir.

Fee or Free: This is a free area.

Camping: A developed campground is available at Wild Horse Crossing, and primitive camping is allowed anywhere on national forest land.

Lodging: Lodging is available in Elko to the south.

Contact: Humboldt National Forest, 2035 Last Chance Road, NV 89801; (702) 738-5171.

7

Angel Lake

South of Wells in the Ruby Mountains

I lay in my sleeping bag and watched the colors of the morning sun change as they reflected off the waterfalls cascading down the sheer cliffs across Angel Lake. A chill was holding in the air and I was reluctant to move from my cocoon until I spotted movement on a ledge above the waterfalls.

Even with my binoculars, I couldn't tell if I was watching a mountain goat or a bighorn sheep, but it was deftly jumping from ledge to ledge in its search for food on the rocky cliff. It was only when I could see its large curved horns as it crested the ridge that I knew it was a bighorn ram.

It's not everyday that you can spot bighorn sheep without getting out of your sleeping bag, but it does happen at the forest service campground at Angel Lake, southwest of Wells. You can also see them during late evening and early morning hours as they exhibit their nimble forms on the cliffs around this cirque basin lake.

Although the lake is only 12 miles from Interstate 80, it is seldom crowded. Most of the people who visit here are interested in keeping the area quiet as they look for the sheep and goats. The paved road to the lake leads through rugged country with pine- and juniper-covered slopes.

The blue, 400-acre lake sits among tall cliffs in a glacier-carved cirque. I head here when I want a scenic outing with little effort, and I am never disappointed. Late spring is my favorite time to visit, when the cascading falls, located near the campground, are at their fullest and the wildflowers around the lake are at their peak.

Painted lady butterflies flit among the wildflowers as they feed on the nectar, and mule deer browse in the open areas near the cover of scattered pine and aspen. Here, the noises of Clark's nutcrackers reverberate as they feed in the trees.

In the low brush around Angel Lake, I frequently spot blue grouse as they fly near the ground and hermit thrushes as they pick seeds from the brush. In the skies above, golden eagles and red-tailed hawks are common as they soar on the lookout for careless rabbits and rodents that have unwisely left the pine's protective cover.

Directions: From the town of Wells, take the West Wells exit south off Interstate 80 to State Road 582 and continue south for 12 miles to the campground. Warning: The last four miles are steep and winding. Don't attempt them with a trailer or large RV.

Fee or Free: Camping costs $6 per night, $3 for each additional vehicle.

Camping: There is an excellent campground at the lake.

Lodging: There are adequate motels in Wells.

Contact: Humboldt National Forest, Ruby Mountain Ranger District, P.O. Box 246, Wells, NV 89835; (702) 752-3357.

Ruby Mountains

In northeast Nevada

Angel Lake is located at the northern end of the Ruby Mountains, and for years I would say that I was going to the Rubies when I headed for Angel Lake. Then I explored deeper into the range and realized that the lake is just the beginning of this wondrous alpine range, high above the deserts of central Nevada.

Once, on my way across Nevada, I stopped in Elko and decided to take a detour into the Ruby Mountain Scenic Area along Lamoille Canyon. The detour took so long that I never reached my destination. I just stayed in the canyon and explored the region's alpine valleys.

Glaciers really worked their wonders here. They formed rugged cliffs, which rise above cirque lakes full of tasty trout, leaving U-shaped valleys and moraines in their wake as they slowly advanced and receded.

I made my decision to stay and explore the region long before I reached the end of the 12-mile-long canyon. The paved road curved around 11,429-foot Ruby Dome, the highest peak in the range, as it led up the canyon where huge, erratic boulders stood as geological signs of past glacial activity.

The sheer cliffs, hanging valleys and broad valley floor were reminiscent of Yosemite Valley, but on a smaller scale. Not only is the canyon smaller, but so are the crowds. Nowhere did I have to fight for a parking space or campsite, even though I was here in the middle of summer.

This was midweek, though, and by the weekend the campground was full of visitors from nearby Elko. Even so, I was able to get away from the crowds by taking short hikes on the trails that lead out from the campground.

The 40-mile Ruby Crest National Recreational Trail leads out from the rear of the parking lot at the end of the road. There are 10, count 'em, 10 lakes that the trail skirts on its way to the crest of the Ruby Mountains.

I struggled up a particularly steep section of the trail on my first visit, and was wondering whether the effort was worth it when the trail suddenly leveled out. Any doubts of why I was working so hard vanished. In front of me was a cirque basin, complete with an azure lake and sheer cliffs. On those cliffs was a herd of mountain goats, and along the ridge I spotted a solitary bighorn ram just as he darted from sight.

I didn't hike far along the trail on my first visit, but I have returned since to complete the entire 42-mile trek from Lamoille Canyon to Harrison Pass to the south. Along the way the trail skirts glacier-formed canyons, lakes and streams as it winds through thick conifer forest where lazuli buntings, blue grouse and mule deer feed.

From beaver to golden eagles, this remarkable subalpine range seems more like Colorado or California than Nevada, and you can enjoy all that it has to offer without having to rub shoulders with hundreds or thousands of others.

Directions: From Elko on Interstate 80, take State Road 227 southeast for about 20 miles. About a mile before the small community of Lamoille, a sign directs you south on Lamoille Canyon Road to Lamoille Canyon and the Ruby Mountain Scenic Area. Continue on this road for 12 miles to its end.

Fee or Free: There is a $5 fee to stay at Thomas Campground, but the rest of the area is free.

Camping: There is a developed forest service campground here; primitive and backcountry camping is allowed on national forest land.

Lodging: There is plenty of lodging in Elko.

Contact: Humboldt National Forest, 2035 Last Chance Road, Elko, NV 89801; (702) 738-5171.

Ruby Lake National Wildlife Refuge

Along the eastern slope of the Ruby Mountains

The rugged eastern slope of the Ruby Mountains rises to the west and sagebrush adds a wispy tinge of gray-green to the uplands that flank the freshwater bulrush marsh that comprises most of the Ruby Lake National Wildlife Refuge.

The marsh is a remnant of prehistoric Franklin Lake, which once covered over 470 square miles. Its water comes from over 200 hot and cold springs which originate high up the slopes and peaks of the southern Ruby Mountains. These slopes are primarily porous limestone, and the accumulated runoff from winter rains and snow filters down the slopes in underground aquifers before finally rising to the surface at Ruby Lake.

The springs feed over 37,000 acres of wetlands that have been diked to maintain a constant water level within the refuge. Over 200 species of birds stop over on their annual migrations or stay to nest in the protected waters.

My favorite time to visit is in late spring and early summer when about 130 species of birds and waterfowl nest in the rushes. Patches of spring wildflowers add color to the sagebrush lands that radiate out from the marshlands.

If you miss the spring nesting season, you may want to head for the refuge in late fall when trumpeter swans and bald eagles take over as the primary attractions.

At either time, you can catch coyote stalking unsuspecting prey in early morning and late evening. As night falls, the yips of the coyote join the deeper sounds of great horned owls, which come out at night to feed.

Although not often seen, mountain lions frequently roam the edges of the refuge in search of easy prey among the large herds of mule deer that come to the marsh for water. The Ruby Mountains above the refuge are thought to harbor the largest concentration of mountain lions in the West, and you have a better chance of seeing this reclusive hunter here than almost anywhere else.

I often bring a kayak with me when I head for the refuge, and use it to stealthily explore the shore of Ruby Lake. On these jaunts, I have come upon numerous coyote as they hunted on shore. While I have yet to see a mountain lion here, I plan to keep looking.

Directions: From Wells, take US 93 south for 28 miles to State Road 229. Turn west and continue for about 15 miles to the signs for the refuge. Head south on the gravel Ruby Valley Road for about 30 miles past the Ruby Valley Indian Reservation and the community of Ruby Valley to the refuge headquarters.

Fee or Free: This is a free area.

Camping: There are several developed forest service campgrounds nearby.

Lodging: There are motels in Elko, Wells and Ely to the south.

Contact: Ruby Lake National Wildlife Refuge, HC 60, Box 860, Ruby Valley, NV 89833; (702) 779-2237.

Goshute Mountains

Along the Utah border

A Cooper's hawk swooped by, a sharp-shinned hawk followed, and then so many raptors came that I couldn't tell you what species were included. Soon a rare peregrine falcon darted by as a golden eagle soared overhead.

No, I wasn't dreaming. I was just in raptor-lover's heaven. Over 20,000 birds of prey follow the ridgeline of the Goshute Mountains in eastern Nevada each fall on their way south along one of the largest raptor flyways in the western U.S. It is seldom that you see fewer than 200 birds of prey per day along the ridge during migration season, and it is not unheard of to see over 1,000.

At the ridge's 9,000-foot elevation, Cooper's and sharp-shinned hawks are abundant between mid-August and mid-October each year, and over a dozen other raptors are common. These include golden and bald eagles, prairie and peregrine falcons, osprey, northern goshawks and American kestrels, as well as red-tailed, Swainson's, ferruginous, red-shouldered and rough-legged hawks.

In fact, 18 different species of birds of prey have been spotted along the ridge during migration season.

The area provides such excellent raptor watching that Hawkwatch International uses it as a monitoring site for their program, and welcomes those who want to participate in its counting and banding studies.

Raptor watching is not the only reason to head for the Goshute Mountains. Goshute Canyon Natural Area offers some of the best, and least crowded, backpacking in Nevada. Limestone crags reach far above pristine meadows where cool springs provide water for large aspen groves. Hiking is excellent along the canyon floor as it heads into the large natural amphitheater of Goshute Basin at the headwaters of Goshute Creek.

Among the tall mountains that ring the basin are 1,500 feet of underground passages that have been eroded out of the limestone formations to form Goshute Cave. Spelunkers head for the cave to explore the passages and look at the rare limestone formations there.

Although this is a prime year-round destination, few people visit it. Summers are delightful, with moderate days and cool nights. Fall is beautiful as the trees turn. Wildlife is extremely active in the spring. Winters can be cold and snowy, but if the roads are clear, hiking can still be good along the creek.

Directions: Head south on US Alternate Route 93 for 24 miles from Wendover to the old Ferguson Highway Maintenance Station. Turn west on a dirt road at the station and continue for two miles to a T-junction. Take a right at the junction and go another mile, then bear left at the top of a hill. Follow the jeep road to its end in Christmas Tree Canyon. Take the marked trail from the parking area to the raptor-viewing site. The trail climbs about 1,600 feet in two miles.

To reach Goshute Canyon, take US 93 north from Ely for 45 miles to State Road 489. Turn west on State Road 489 and continue for nine miles to a local road (signed for Goshute Canyon) that heads northeast. Stay on this road for 11 miles to Goshute Creek. Hike into the canyon from the parking area.

Fee or Free: This is a free area.

Camping: Primitive camping is allowed on BLM lands.

Lodging: You'll find motels in Wendover and Ely.

Contact: For Goshute Canyon Natural Area: BLM Ely District Office, 702 North Industrial Way, Box 33500, Ely, NV 89301; (702) 289-4865. For Goshute Raptor Migration Area: BLM Elko District Office, P.O. Box 831, 3900 East Idaho Street, Elko, NV 89803; (702) 753-0200. For Hawkwatch International: P.O. Box 35706, Albuquerque, NM 87176; (505) 255-7622.

Chapter 7

Central Nevada

Maps 19, 20, 21

Map 19

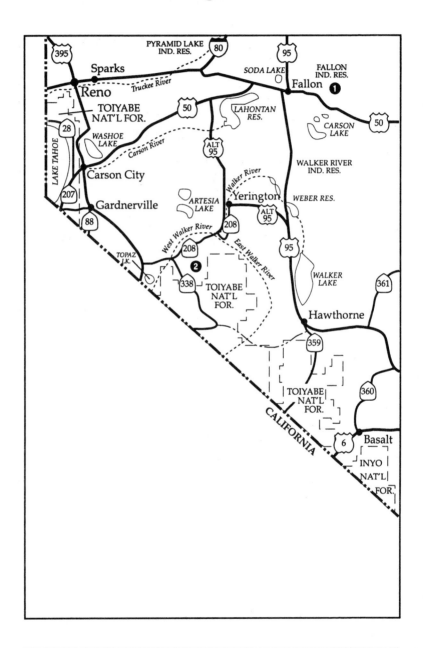

Map 20

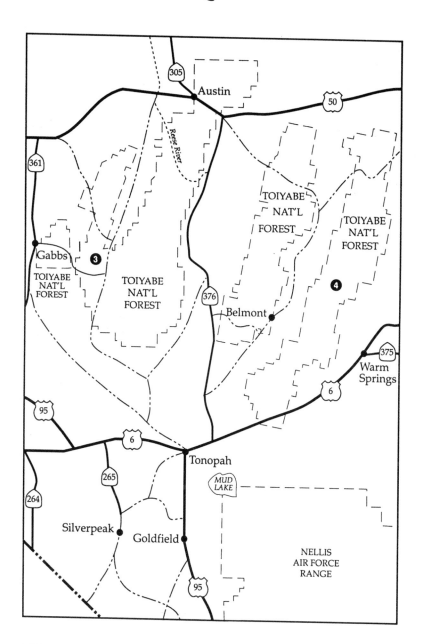

Map 21

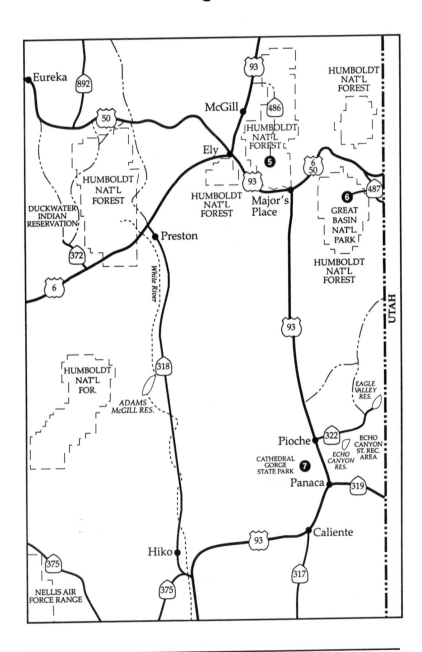

Stillwater National Wildlife Refuge

Off US 50 near Fallon

I hit a good year to visit the Stillwater National Wildlife Refuge. The spring runoff had been excellent, and the water levels of the 78,000-acre refuge had remained high throughout the year. Canvasback ducks floated by the thousands among the much larger and more stately white pelicans, tundra swans and Canada geese.

As I walked along the levees and dikes, however, I thought of the last time I had visited the refuge. Nevada had just gone through several years of drought, and there simply had not been enough water to supply the needs of the Reno-Sparks Water District, the Lahontan Valley Irrigation District and the wildlife refuges of the region. Stillwater was a refuge with little water to fill the many holding ponds where hundreds of thousands of waterfowl and wading birds come to spend the winter and mate during spring. Nevada had already lost two national wildlife refuges due to lack of water, and it appeared that

---

a third was on the road to extinction.

Recent wet years and the work of conservationists have given new life to this refuge, however, and there is hope for the whistling swans, white pelicans and almost 175 other bird species that use the refuge.

I head for the flat desert lands in the fall, when there is still enough water to provide a sanctuary for 250,000 waterfowl. During the winter, the refuge has the largest concentration of bald eagles anywhere in Nevada.

The refuge is only a part of the much larger Stillwater Wildlife Management Area. Stillwater's 162,000 acres are operated by a wide-ranging group of government and private conservation organizations working together as the Lahontan Wetlands Coalition. This group spear-headed the effort to have the region designated as an essential site in the Western Hemisphere Shorebird Reserve Network, and continues to monitor water sources and contaminants.

You can get good views of the flocks by driving along the roads in and around the management area, but the best views are from hikes along the dikes and levees inside the refuge. There you can see the colorful flocks and hear the wild sounds as the Paiute Indians did for thousands of years, before the Europeans came and diverted the waters to the marsh to "reclaim" the surrounding desert for farmland.

Directions: From Fallon, take US 50 east four miles to Stillwater Road and follow signs to the refuge.

Fee or Free: This is a free area.

Camping: There is a primitive campground on the refuge.

Lodging: Motels are available in Fallon.

Contact: Stillwater National Wildlife Refuge, P.O. Box 1236, Fallon, NV 89407-1236; (702) 423-5128.

2

State Road 208 through Wilson Canyon

Along the Walker River

Roaring waters wind through a narrow canyon with sheer walls of volcanic cliffs where swifts, swallows and rock wrens nest on crevices and ledges. As you drive on State Road 208 along the rocky gorge, looking down over the rushing West Walker River and up to the craggy cliffs where raptors make their homes, the stark beauty of Wilson Canyon is undeniable.

Hiking here is limited to walks along the river near the many pullouts along the road. From these, you have good views of the cliffs that rise above the river. Scan them for signs of the bulky stick nests of golden eagles and red-tailed hawks. Whitewashed rocks signal the pothole nests of prairie falcons in the cliffs. Since traffic is generally light, you can hike along the road in many places.

The American dipper, otherwise known as the water ouzel, nests in holes in rocks and ledges above the water, and this wren-on-steroids can be seen as it searches for

---

food among the river shallows. Its characteristic bobbing motion is unmistakable. You may even get lucky and see it walk along the bottom of a deep pool as it digs up larvae on the rocky bottom.

Although the bird population is smaller during the winter, I like to head for this area to see the large herd of mule deer that congregate in the Pine Nut Mountains. Snow covers the canyon walls above the rushing Walker River along State Road 208 between Yerington and Wellington, and the riparian growth is barren of greenery. At this time of year, the river canyon is at its most striking.

As you leave the canyon, you enter the Smith Valley. For outstanding views of winter mule deer herds, turn north on Upper Colony Road off State Road 208, about two miles past Wellington.

Along the west side of the road, you can scan the low-lying sagebrush, bitterbrush and juniper that cover the steep slopes in search of the large herds of deer that come here to browse during midwinter.

Directions: Take State Road 208 south from Yerington and continue on it for about 15 miles to the head of Wilson Canyon. Follow the road through the canyon for 12 miles to Wellington. For the deer herds, continue through Wellington to Upper Colony Road and turn north.

Fee or Free: This is a free area.

Camping: The deer herds congregate on private property, and there is little flatland to camp on in Wilson Canyon. Camping is available in Toiyabe National Forest off State Road 338 to the south of Wellington.

Lodging: There are motels in Yerington and Wellington.

Contact: BLM Carson City District Office, 1535 Hot Springs Road, Suite 300, Carson City, NV 89706-0638; (702) 885-6000. Toiyabe National Forest, Carson Ranger District, 1536 South Carson Street, Carson City, NV 89701-5291; (702) 882-2766.

Berlin-Ichthyosaur State Park

In Toiyabe National Forest

Ichthyosaurs in Nevada? Well, not recently, but they were there about 185 million years ago, and at least 40 of the 60-foot fossils of these marine dinosaurs were unearthed in excavations during the 1950s. Today, three of these are exposed for viewing in this isolated state park that was once a company-owned mining town.

It isn't easy reaching Berlin, but the ride from Gabbs along State Road 844 to the park takes you on a scenic route across the heavily forested Paradise Range before it drops onto the sage flats of Lone Valley. The route then climbs back up the slopes of the Shoshone Range before it ends in the park.

The 1,200-acre park is open year-round, but late spring is the best time to take the trek out here. Then Indian paintbrush, prickly poppy and small-leaf globemallow, among more than 80 flowering plants that grow along the route to the park, burst into bloom after the snow melts.

The 14 sites in the campground are seldom filled, and the slopes above the old structures that remain from the park's boom days as an old mining town offer excellent hiking.

The partially exposed dinosaur fossils lie in the ground where they were buried millions of years ago along the banks of an ancient sea. The 60-foot, 35-ton animals were the prehistoric ancestors to today's large whales and their remains are impressive. A trail with interpretive signs leads among the fossils.

Directions: Take State Road 844 east from Gabbs for 18 miles to a fork in the road. Take the right fork another seven miles on a well-maintained gravel road to the park.

Fee or Free: Entry to the park is free. Camping costs $3-$6 per night.

Camping: There is a developed campground in the park.

Lodging: The best bets are in Fallon, about 100 miles to the north, and Hawthorne, about 80 miles to the south.

Contact: Berlin-Ichthyosaur State Park, Route 1, Box 32, Austin, NV 89310; (702) 964-2440.

Table Mountain Wilderness

In Toiyabe National Forest

Monitor Peak rises to 10,856 feet as it towers over the plateau of the Table Mountain Wilderness Area. A spring trip here offers the chance to hike through wildflower-covered meadows where beaver are busily repairing dams and lodges from damage inflicted by the snowmelt runoff.

Over 100 miles of trails lead through pinyon-juniper forests where jackrabbits and desert cottontails thrive, and into spectacular green aspen groves where you can hear dozens of small songbirds singing as they establish their territories and prepare for nesting.

Golden eagles and northern goshawks soar overhead as they search for food, and Rocky Mountain elk browse in open meadows during summer. I have never seen an area with so many forest-dwelling hawks, many of which leave the shelter of the forest to scour the open sagebrush lands beyond for rodents and small rabbits.

Flooded areas of some mountain streams have aspen along the water's edge, which have the distinctive shew marks of our largest rodent, the beaver. If you watch carefully at dawn and dusk, you may see these busy animals as they come ashore in search of new trees for food. At night, keep alert for the sound of a coyote yipping and the fleeting sight of a cougar on its night prowl.

The trail to Monitor Peak (elevation 10,856 feet) offers wildflower-filled meadows, pine forests and spectacular views of deep canyons.

And you can enjoy all of this with no one else around. This wilderness area is truly remote. Few people venture into it, and there are no facilities. Be prepared to experience Nevada wilderness at its best.

Directions: Take US 6 east from Tonopah for six miles to State Road 376 and head north. Take the Belmont turnoff after 13 miles and drive another 26 miles to the town. Continue two miles, then head northeast for four miles to the Barley Creek turnoff. Turn east and continue for 12 miles, past a guard station, to the trailhead leading into the wilderness area.

Fee or Free: This is a free area.

Camping: Wilderness and primitive camping are allowed on forest service lands.

Lodging: If you want lodging, don't head for this wilderness area. The nearest motels are in Tonopah, 60 miles away.

Contact: Toiyabe National Forest, Tonopah Ranger District, P.O. Box 3940, Tonopah, NV 89049; (702) 482-6286.

5

Cave Lake State Park

In the Schell Creek Range

I came upon Cave Lake State Park by chance. Its beautiful emerald lake reflected the sheer granite cliff that rises behind it high in eastern Nevada's Schell Creek Range. I had come to the region for the scenic auto tour along County Road 486 as it follows up Duck Creek Basin toward Success Summit between US 93 and Water Canyon.

I certainly wasn't disappointed with the trip as I drove through beautiful eastern Nevada ranch country before heading down into Boneyard Canyon and up a rocky road to Success Summit. As I passed over the 8,950-foot summit, I stopped to see what the view offered, and was surprised to see a small herd of Rocky Mountain elk feeding on an open sagebrush-covered hillside across the road. Later I discovered that the scattered herds that feed on the higher slopes of the range congregate at winter feeding grounds along US 93 south of Ely—in fact, you can see as many as 200 to 300 elk within sight of the highway from fall to spring.

As I descended down Steptoe Creek, in the canyon where the road runs, through a leafy canopy of riparian growth that reached out over the road, I stopped and looked high overhead as the canopy opened up to give me a view of limestone cliffs and rock outcroppings. Above, I spotted an eagle's nest, as well as signs of prairie falcons' roosting spots where droppings made the rocks below look whitewashed.

After what seemed like a dozen switchbacks, I spotted a sign for 1,820-acre Cave Lake State Park, and was glad to find a good place to rest from the tortuous drive over rocky, winding roads. What began as a rest stop turned into an overnight. I just couldn't resist the promise of a hike through the pinyon-pine and juniper forest that covered the slopes above the lake. The five-mile interpretive trail had outstanding views to the west. Wildlife watching was excellent as I sighted a ferruginous hawk and blue grouse, as well as more elk.

That evening, I fed on rainbow trout from the recently stocked lake and enjoyed the sunset as it colored the granite cliffs above the lake. As the sun sank lower and lower, the lake took on the color of the cliffs until both slowly turned blue and then black as evening fell.

Although I have never visited this region in the fall, I'm convinced it has to be outstanding. The aspen and cottonwood in the canyons should add touches of gold and yellow, and the elk viewing along US 93 south of Ely is supposedly some of the best in the country.

Directions: From Ely, take US 93 north six miles past McGill. Turn east on unpaved County Road 486 and follow it south.

Fee or Free: Day use of the park costs $1 to $3 per vehicle; camping is $3 to $7 per vehicle.

Camping: There is developed campground in park, plus several forest service campgrounds along the drive before the summit.

Lodging: Lodging is available in Ely.

Contact: Humboldt National Forest, Ely Ranger District, 350 8th Street, P.O. Box 539, Ely, NV 89801; (702) 289-3031. Nevada State Parks, District 5 Office, P.O. Box 176, Panaca, NV 89042; (702) 728-4467.

6

Great Basin National Park

Along the Utah border in central Nevada

Wheeler Peak captures the imagination long before you reach the turnoff to Great Basin National Park along the Nevada-Utah border. At 13,063 feet, the second highest peak in Nevada stands all alone above the flat valleys of the Basin and Range Province. From a distance, the peak and slopes all blend into one large gray formation. It is only as you get closer that you realize that the top 3,000 feet of the peak reach above treeline.

As the peak rises 8,000 feet above the surrounding desert, the dark-green forests of the lower slopes gradually separate from the lighter gray of the treeless upper slopes. Here, the southernmost ice field in the country is found.

US 50, which passes to the north of the park, is called the "Loneliest Highway in America," and it is easy to see why. Even crossroad communities are hard to find along the route. The tiny town of Baker (population 50) is the nearest one to the park. Unlike most large national parks in this country, there is no gateway community with dozens of motels and glitzy entertainment centers to distract you as you head into the foothills of Wheeler Peak, the centerpiece of the park.

This is truly a wilderness park, offering acres and acres of backcountry where you can hike among bristlecone pine that are over 4,000 years old and look out over hundreds of miles of desert ranges and valleys where the deer and antelope still roam and the people are few.

In 1961, a scenic road was constructed that leads to the 10,000-foot level on the peak. Along the road you'll find the Wheeler Peak Campground, which you can use as a base for your excursions into the park's miles of backcountry trails. Many lead to exceptional alpine lakes and scenic overlooks. The five-mile Wheeler Peak Trail is one of the best, climbing over 3,000 feet in the last four miles on a steep and exhilarating climb to the summit.

Lower in the park, you can join other visitors on tours through the colorful rooms of Lehman Cave, a limestone cave with dramatic sculptures and fanciful formations.

This is just about my favorite national park. It has caves, wilderness areas, forests of the oldest-living trees in the world, fantastic views, high alpine lakes, good campgrounds and very few people. Fewer people come to this park in a year than can be found in the larger and more popular national parks in a day.

A visit here in the fall is great. The aspen and other deciduous trees on the lower slopes turn gold and yellow and the nights are nippy. Even less people are in the park in fall than in summer, and hikes along the trails at the higher elevations in the cooler weather are truly invigorating.

Directions: From Ely, head east on US 50 for about 60 miles (just past the small community of Baker) to State Road 488. Turn west on State Road 488 and continue to the visitor center.

Fee or Free: Entrance to the caves costs $3 for adults and $3 for kids. Camping costs $5 a night (you must bring your own water in winter).

Camping: There are several developed campgrounds within the park, and primitive camping is allowed in national forest to the south.

Lodging: Lodging is available in Ely. There is one small motel in Baker, as well as one about 15 miles farther east on US 50.

Contact: Great Basin National Park, Baker, NV 89311-9701; (702) 234-7331.

❼

Cathedral Gorge State Park

Near Panaca

As you leave US 93 about a mile north of the small town of Panaca, you enter a gorge whose walls have been carved into cathedral-like formations over millions of years. The formations were carved out of 1,500 feet of sedimentary layers of silt and clay left from an ancient lake.

Even few native Nevadans seem to know about small, scenic Cathedral Gorge State Park, but they should. Here, you can hike into deep and narrow slot-like canyons and below cliffs so dramatic that they have been the backdrop for passion plays and local pageants. As the sun drops below the mountains in the west, the slanting rays turn the cliffs into fire-washed rocks with overtones of red and orange that slowly become darker and darker until only the silhouettes of the spires and ledges stand out in the dark night sky.

This is when I set up my cameras and wait. Sometimes I just watch and never bother tripping the shutter, because the hues are so subtle that I know that I will never be able to capture them on film. At other times, they are so vibrant that I know that I can't miss with any shot.

Trails lead through canyons, to overlooks, and into the desert from the tree-shaded campground. Some of these canyons are so narrow that they have come to be known as caves. Moon Cave and Canyon Cave are two of the most popular ones, and they narrow down to passages so thin that only small children can pass through them.

The first time I walked through these winding passageways, I felt out of place and time. The vertical walls rose so high that I had no sense of where I was headed.

The campground in the park sits in a valley surrounded by strange eroded rock formations that look like organ pipes, and a good interpretive nature trail leads out from it through 100-foot-high cliffs. It passes through a rich variety of desert plants, including bitterbrush, rabbitbrush, desert barberry, greasewood and Mormon tea.

Directions: Head north on US 93 from Panaca for two miles and turn left at the signs to the park.

Fee or Free: Day use costs $1 to $3 per vehicle; camping runs $3 to $7 per night.

Camping: There is a developed campground in the park.

Lodging: There are motels in Panaca and Pioche to the north.

Contact: Nevada State Parks, Division 5 Office, P.O. Box 176, Panaca, NV 89042; (702) 728-4467.

Chapter 8

Southern Nevada

Maps 22, 23

Map 22

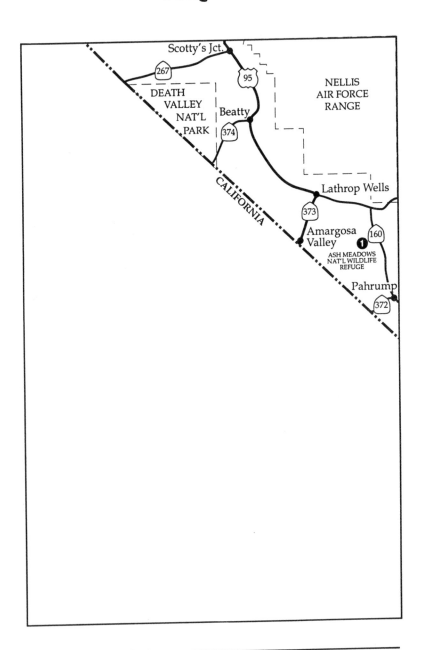

Map 23

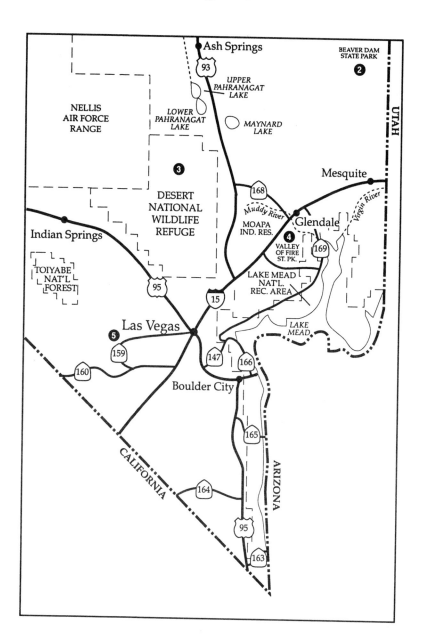

Ash Meadows National Wildlife Refuge

In southwestern Nevada

North from Pahrump along the eastern edge of Death Valley National Park, you'll find some of the bleakest parts of the Mojave Desert. Even the names, such as Devil's Hole, are bleak.

But all is not what it seems. As you drive north, you do pass through a bleak and desolate landscape, but after about 25 miles you find yourself in an oasis. This particular oasis has been considered so important that it has been designated as a wetland of world significance.

Twenty-six plants and animals found nowhere else in the world live here. Four of these are small fish that find hospitality in an inhospitable world in the wetlands at Ash Meadows. With 30 seeps, springs and streams that feed water to these desert wetlands, the 12,736 acres of Ash Meadows National Wildlife Refuge are a veritable paradise in the desert, not only for its native plants and animals, but for visitors as well.

One spring, I decided to find out what the raving was about and headed for Ash Meadows after a visit to Death Valley. I really didn't expect to find anything much different from what I had seen at dozens of other desert water holes over the years—a grove of mesquite and some sedge growing around a seep with a few pupfish swimming in the shallow waters.

Was I in for a surprise... Brilliant blue pupfish (their spring coloration, I later discovered) dashed about 10 to 12 feet down in the crystal-clear water of large cavern pools as they fought each other for territory. One such pool, Devil's Hole, has its own special species.

Hot springs bubbled to the surface and fed warm water ponds where other pupfish flourished. Great blue herons and white-faced ibis fed in the marshy areas around two reservoirs. Meanwhile, American avocets, Wilson's phalaropes and dowitchers moved among the shallows in search of food.

There are no set hiking trails in the refuge, but the open country makes them unnecessary.

All in all, Ash Meadows far exceeded any expectations that I had. Even the lushness of the vegetation is so great that many small pools are almost hidden by the greenery, and the open ground is dotted with splotches of color from the spring blooms of wildflowers, many of which are endemic to the area.

Directions: From Pahrump, head north on State Road 160 for 8.5 miles to Bell Vista Road. Turn west and continue 17.5 miles to a fork in the gravel road. Take the right fork and continue to the refuge.

Fee or Free: This is a free area.

Camping: Primitive camping is allowed on BLM and park lands. This may change with the change of status of Death Valley from a national monument to national park, so check before camping.

Lodging: There are motels in Pahrump.

Contact: Death Valley National Park, Highway 190, P.O. Box 579, Death Valley, CA 92328; (619) 786-2331. Ash Meadows National Wildlife

Refuge, c/o Desert National Wildlife Refuge, 1500 North Decatur Boulevard, Las Vegas, NV 89108; (702) 372-5435.

Beaver Dam State Park

In the southeast corner of Nevada

Six miles of paved road from the nearest community, then 19 miles of gravel road, and then a final 13 miles of dirt road—by the time I reached Beaver Dam State Park, I certainly understood why it has been called Nevada's most remote state park.

It also lives up to its description as one of the loveliest parks in the state. I had left the barren, desert country near Caliente behind as I climbed to over 5,000 feet into green mountains with plenty of water. Pine forests covered the slopes and streams cut through the small canyons.

I soon discovered the pleasures of hiking through the 2,300-acre park. Although there were few marked trails, it was easy enough to wander wherever I wanted along the pinyon-pine-covered slopes.

Everywhere along Beaver Dam Wash there were signs of the industrious animals who gave the area its name. Fallen trees lay along the banks of ponds impounded behind log dams, and lodges rose from the deeper waters in the middle of the ponds. Great blue herons took advantage of the beavers' engineering skills and fished along the shallow edges.

For wildlife watchers who crave rare sightings, the park offers the chance to spot the smallest of all ground squirrels, the white-tailed antelope ground squirrel.

In the evening, I fished for planted rainbow trout in Beaver Dam Reservoir alongside families whose children swam along the shore. As I cast, I got to know my neighboring campers. They had ventured to the park from Las Vegas, trying to beat the midsummer heat.

We watched the bats flit and jerk in the darkening light of dusk, enjoying the warm evening as the cloudy Milky Way stretched across the night sky. As I joined the others who had gathered at this isolated spot, stories were traded around a campfire. It was a relaxing end to the day as we settled in for the night in a corner of Nevada that few know about.

Directions: From Caliente, head six miles north on US 93 to the signs for the park that mark a gravel road. Continue on this road for 32 miles to the park.

Fee or Free: Day use costs $1 to $3; camping is $3 to $6.

Camping: There is a developed campground in the park.

Lodging: Motels are available in Caliente and Panaca.

Contact: Nevada State Parks, Division 5 Office, P.O. Box 176, Panaca, NV 89042; (702) 728-4467.

3

Desert National Wildlife Refuge

North of Las Vegas

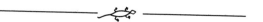

From the top of a desert peak, over 3,000 feet above where we had camped, we quietly searched the distant slopes for signs of desert bighorn sheep. We had been told that there was about an 80-percent chance of seeing them if we climbed higher than they usually ranged. This meant a long, hard hike to over 6,000 feet in elevation—there were no established trails through the sagebrush country.

We had been ready for the climb, though, after a night of desert camping when the sparkle of the stars seemed near enough to touch and the yip-yipping of the coyotes was close enough to easily distinguish the individual coyotes as they called to one another. We even saw the outline of several owls against the night sky as they silently flew over the campground.

After over an hour of concentrated effort in the early morning, we were rewarded with a sighting of a small herd of about a half dozen sheep grazing about a mile away. We watched them for a while, and then were distracted by a badger digging for rodents in the hillside below the sheep.

After the badger and sheep departed, we stayed on

the peak scanning the surrounding countryside for other wildlife. Above us, we spotted a pair of golden eagles riding the thermals, and on our way down we literally ran into a slow-moving desert tortoise, which was half the size of a basketball, as it was moving from shade to shade in search of green plants.

This was a normal day of wildlife watching at this large (2,400-square-mile) national wildlife refuge, which was established to protect bighorn sheep. Today, the largest population of bighorn sheep outside Alaska roams the mountain crags of this beautiful and raw region.

Mountain lions may be found near the sheep as they hunt in search of easy prey, and kit foxes can be seen in late evening as they move around beneath the low-lying desert scrub, searching for unsuspecting rodents.

Even the birds in the refuge are worth a trip here, as the oasis near the refuge headquarters at Corn Creek attracts large numbers of songbirds. During April and May of just one year, the sightings of 21 species of vireos and warblers were recorded at the headquarters.

One Las Vegas birder told me that it isn't unusual to spot over 50 species of birds in a morning on the refuge, and that he has made such extraordinary sightings as a wood stork and Mississippi kite.

From Corn Creek, Mormon Well Road goes through several life zones as it heads into the high country, where the sheep are most abundant, and back down to the low desert along US 93 near the Pahranagat National Wildlife Refuge, where ponds are diked and flooded for thousands of waterfowl that stay over in the winter.

Directions: Take US 95 north from Las Vegas for 22 miles to the refuge sign. The Corn Creek Headquarters is four miles from the sign.

Fee or Free: This is a free area.

Camping: Primitive camping is allowed on the refuge. Please avoid camping too near springs, which the wildlife depend on for their survival. Developed campgrounds are available at Lake Mead, about 40 miles south.

Lodging: There is excellent lodging in Las Vegas.

Contact: Desert National Wildlife Refuge, 1500 North Decatur Boulevard, Las Vegas, NV 89108; (702) 646-3401.

❹

Valley of Fire State Park

Near Lake Mead

The brick-red is what catches your eye first. Then the many shades of yellow, lavender, brown, pink and gray. It is only later that you begin to pick out the wondrous shapes that time, rain and wind have carved out of the limestone and sandstone, which was deposited in the Valley of Fire at the bottom of ancient seas and lakes over 200 million years ago.

The first time I drove into the valley, I came from the north along State Road 169, braving the dips and rises between Interstate 15 and Lake Mead. Suddenly, my windshield was filled with a mass of red rocks, which extended to the horizon and took on odd and whimsical shapes. This was the Valley of Fire, which got its name from its color, not its origin.

Red rocks dominate the landscape, and the many fantastical, sculptured formations have just as fantastical names—Duck Rock, Elephant Rock, Cobra Rock, Poodle Rock, Arch Rock and Balancing Rock are among the more popular ones. Dome-shaped mounds encircled with horizontal lines are known as the Beehives. The Rock of Gibraltar needs no explanation, and the Grand Piano is only one of many platforms with multiple legs in the park.

Most people who come to the 46,000-acre park do so for a day trip, and it is well-laid out for those. Everything is within a half-hour drive of everything else, and the park is only an hour's drive from downtown Las Vegas. During fall and spring weekends, the park is crowded, although only moderately so by most populated areas' standards. During midweek year-round, the park is almost always empty.

I prefer to spend several nights in one of the two campgrounds in the park, though, because it is only at sunrise and sunset that you can truly appreciate the colors of the rocks. At those times of indirect light, the colors come alive, and are constantly changing as the sun rises higher and drops lower.

During midday, I like to hike among the wonderland of canyons, caves and arches that have been carved from the sandstone by wind and water over centuries. There are no marked trails in the park, but you can explore among the washes and canyons as you please. Many of the canyons are so narrow at spots that only children can crawl through the passages. Unlike many parks where you view scenic attractions from afar, this park offers everyone an opportunity to experience the whorls and hollows up close.

You can spend hours exploring the many wind-carved features, and in many of the shelves and caves there are signs of wildlife. Droppings and the remains of the previous day's meals challenge your senses of sight and smell as you come upon the home of bats and owls.

Sometimes you might even encounter the animals themselves in your adventures. Back up and enjoy these encounters, but leave the creatures be. It is their home, after all. You are only a guest in their fascinating, colorful home.

The park is bordered on the south by the Lake Mead National Recreation Area, and the drive along State Route 167 to the lake is one of the most scenic in Nevada as it crosses tablelands above Lake Mead. The 45-mile drive back to Las Vegas and its glitzy casinos gives you time to decompress. It takes a little while to realign your thinking. Vegas' neon lights can seem quite strange after observing the truly spectacular lights of nature that you find in the Valley of Fire.

Directions: From Las Vegas, take Interstate 15 east 36 miles to State Road 169 at Glendale. Turn south and continue 12 miles to the park entrance.

Fee or Free: Day use is $3 per vehicle; camping costs $7 per night, first come, first served.

Camping: There are two developed campgrounds in park. No backcountry camping is allowed.

Lodging: There is plenty of lodging in Las Vegas.

Contact: Valley of Fire State Park, P.O. Box 515, Overton, NV 89040; (702) 397-2088.

5

Red Rock Canyon National Conservation Area

West of Las Vegas

The 3,000-foot high escarpment that extends the length of Red Rock Canyon stands high as you head west from Las Vegas on State Road 159. It is easy to see the fascination the area has for rock climbers from around the world.

The canyon isn't just for rock climbers, however, for it is only a half-hour drive from downtown. This makes the area an ideal outdoor getaway for visitors to Las Vegas who don't have the time to explore areas such as the Valley of Fire.

You know you have something special when you reach an area where the BLM has set up a visitor center and interpretive trails. And that is what greets you as you begin the 13-mile loop drive through Red Rock Canyon. Stop at the center, one of less than a half dozen operated by the BLM across the West, and study the exhibits on the geological and natural history of the canyon before you continue along the loop drive.

A number of vista points and pullouts provide parking at trailheads, allowing you to hike into the canyon where wildlife congregates around water sources and riparian growth. The abundant water makes the flat canyon floor a mecca for deer, rabbit, coyote, songbirds and small rodents. These in turn bring animal hunters, such as bobcat and cougar, which make the rounds at night when humans are banned from the canyon floor.

One unusual plant for this region is the Joshua tree. A good forest of these large members of the lily family grows along the bottom of the canyon.

This is strictly a day-use area, and its proximity to Las Vegas makes it crowded on weekends, but the chance to see the multicolored cliffs up close makes this a "don't miss" trip if you are in town.

Directions: Head west on State Road 159 (Charleston Boulevard) for 15 miles to the entrance to the canyon.

Fee or Free: This is currently a free area, but a $5 fee was being proposed at press time.

Camping: There is no camping in the canyon, but head to BLM and national forest lands outside the canyon for primitive camping.

Lodging: There is plenty of lodging in Las Vegas.

Contact: BLM Las Vegas District Office, 4765 West Vegas Drive, Las Vegas, NV 89108; (702) 647-5000.

Utah

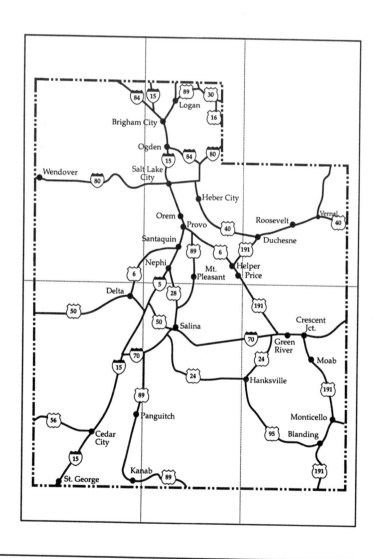

Introduction to Utah

Several things stand out about Utah. It is the only Western state that was settled and developed by a single religious group. It has the largest inland saltwater lake in the country. Some of the most popular ski resorts in the country are located in the Wasatch Range near Salt Lake City. And its southern third contains the most fantastic group of natural sites to be found anywhere in the nation. Once you get past these items, however, people seem to know little about this diverse state.

Yet there is plenty more to Utah than its religious majority, the Great Salt Lake, its great skiing and the dozen national park units that are located in its canyonlands. Of all the states in this guidebook, only California has higher mountains. The western half of Utah is desert studded with small mountain ranges. These rise high enough to catch winter rains that help at least minimal vegetation grow on the slopes of the peaks. Some of the best caving in the West is also found in the Wasatch Range.

Although Utah does not have the low deserts with prickly plants that are found in Arizona and New Mexico, it is still desert country. Most of the state is so dry that evaporation exceeds precipitation. Only Nevada, out of all

50 states, is drier overall than Utah. While parts of the Wasatch Range receive over 50 inches of precipitation annually, other sections of the state receive less than 10 inches.

The Basin and Range Province, which extends between the Rocky Mountains and the Sierra Nevadas, begins in Utah, and most of the western portion of the state lies within the province. This region is part of the Great Basin Desert, and shares both topography and climate with Nevada.

The canyonlands of southern Utah are located along the Colorado Plateau, and are one of the prime natural attractions of the Southwest. These areas include a number of national parks and monuments, as well as several popular state parks.

Nearly 80 percent of Utah is controlled by one government agency or another. The Bureau of Land Management administers 43 percent of the land itself. The six national forests in the state cover more than nine million acres.

There are great outdoor getaways for just about every taste in Utah, from mountain biking—which has become even more popular than hiking in some areas—to whitewater rafting in the Virgin, Green and Colorado rivers. And only a few of the most popular areas draw large enough crowds to be called heavily used. You'll also find excellent high-country backpacking, spelunking and slot-canyon hiking in southeastern Utah's national parks, and in the Wasatch and Uinta mountain ranges. If you want solitude, you can easily find it in Utah.

Chapter 9

Northern Utah

Maps 24, 25, 26

Map 24

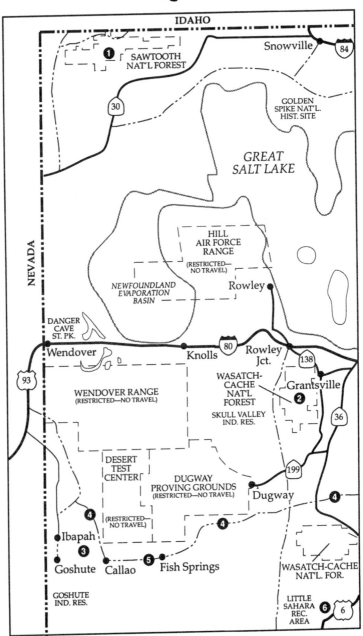

Map 25

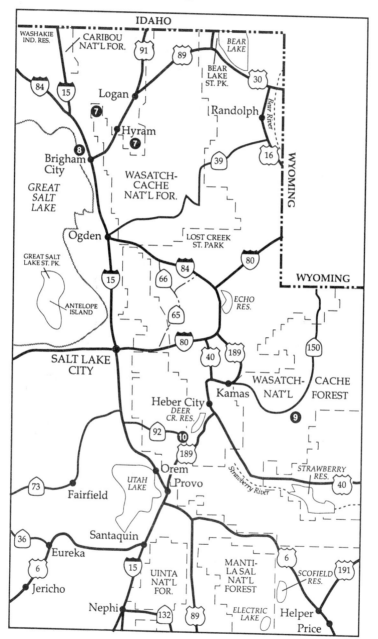

Map 26

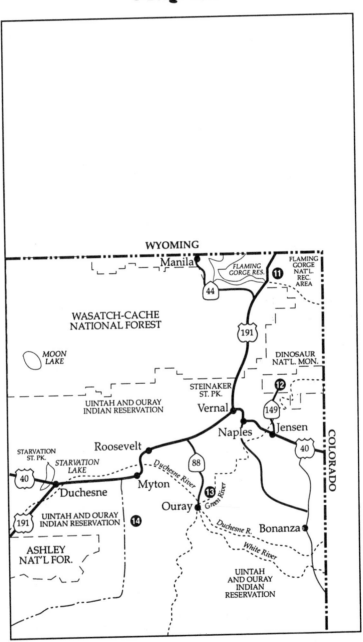

Northern Utah (maps on pages 322-324)

Raft River Mountains

In Sawtooth National Forest

If you'd like to hike along a rolling crest where you look down upon aspen and fir forests on the lower slopes and out across wide expanses of desert and the Great Salt Lake, head for the 50 square miles of the Raft River Mountains in the northwest corner of Utah. Few people seem to know about this lively range—including natives.

There are so few hikers in this alpine wonderland that the few existing trails are actually only expanded animal trails. The lack of trails is no problem, though, because the crest of the range is open grassland; from here you can see where you want to go with no chance of getting lost. Because the hills only rise up a few hundred feet from the already high ridge, even the highest peak, 9,931-foot Bull Mountain, is almost indistinguishable from other nearby knolls.

Campers and hikers must stay to the north of the crest. Ranchers who own the land to the south bar hikers for fear that they will spook their cattle. That's fine with the few people who come to this isolated area, because the alpine forests and cirque lakes of the most scenic areas are along the north slope. Jeep trails crisscross this area of the range, and access to the best hiking and camping is from here.

Most visitors head for Clear Creek Campground at 6,400 feet on the north side of the range. This improved forest service campground sits among aspen and alders where deer come to browse, even when campers are present. The campground is a good base from which to explore the region.

The best hiking starts at a trailhead in Lake Fork Canyon about four miles past the campground. From the trailhead, you can hike three miles to Bull Basin Lake, which lies in a rugged glacial cirque just to the north of Bull Mountain. From the lake, you can scramble up to the peak to see the excellent views of mountain ranges in Utah, Idaho and Nevada, plus vast areas of desert and the Great Salt Lake.

Although there are pumps and springs at the campground and creeks and lakes on the hikes, you should bring your own water for emergencies.

Winters are harsh here and the snowpack is heavy. After it melts in the spring, wildflowers begin their quick growth in alpine meadows and along mountain streams. During midsummer, the temperatures are moderate both night and day, and hiking is easy. By fall, the trees along the canyon floors begin to turn and their leaves add spots of color to the range.

Directions: Take exit 5 off Interstate 84 just north of Snowville, and head west on State Road 42 for 25 miles to Strevell, Idaho. Take a left on the gravel road marked "Yost" in Strevell, and then another left after 3.5 miles at the forest service road signed for the campground. The campground is six miles from the last intersection. The best hiking is about four miles past the campground in Lake Fork Canyon. You should always have topographic and forest service maps when you travel in this region.

Fee or Free: This is a free area, including the campground.

Camping: There is good camping at Clear Creek Campground, and primitive camping in the forest.

Lodging: The nearest lodging is about 75 miles west in Tremonton and Logan.

Contact: Burley Ranger District, Sawtooth National Forest, Route 3, 3650 South Overland Avenue, Burley, ID 83318; (208) 678-0430.

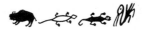

❷

Deseret Peak

In the Stansbury Mountains

The Stansbury Mountains rise from arid, desolate, desert land to 11,031-foot Deseret Peak. A trip to the Stansbury Range takes you from hot, parched land with no vegetation to stands of Douglas fir, aspen and pine on the mountains' higher slopes and in their canyons.

This area is within easy driving distance of Salt Lake City and surrounding population centers, and is fairly popular. On summer weekends, the campgrounds in the Stansbury Range section of Wasatch-Cache National Forest can be crowded, and you will meet a number of other hikers as you trudge along the trails of the Deseret Peak Wilderness Area.

During midweek and in the off-seasons of spring and fall, you will have the range almost to yourself, though. These are the most scenic times to visit the area. Wildflowers dot the mountain meadows in the late spring, and the aspen add gold to the slopes as fall approaches.

The eastern slope of the range is the most accessible, and that is where you will find forest service campgrounds. I like to camp at the Loop Campground, where a moderate 7.5-mile loop trail leads to the top of Deseret Peak, as well as to four lower peaks nearby. The views along the trail and from the peak are especially inspiring in the early fall when the air is crisp from night frosts and the gold and yellow aspen line the canyons below.

On a clear day, you can see forever from the peaks. Or almost, for the Wasatch Range is visible to the east, the Great Salt Lake to the north, Pilot Peak in Nevada to the west, and a number of desert ranges to the south.

On summer days, the lower elevations that spread out in all directions from the range are hot and dry, but the 10,000-foot-plus peaks offer a cool relief from the enervating heat.

The trails that traverse the Deseret Peak Wilderness Area begin in campgrounds in the adjoining South Willow Canyon Recreation Area. Two other popular trails in the recreation area originate about five miles northwest in the town of Grantsville—the Black Canyon-Big Hollow Trail, which goes to Box Elder Pass, and the trail from South Willow Lake through the Mining Fork of the South Willow Canyon.

Directions: Take Interstate 80 west from Salt Lake City for about 25 miles to State Road 36 at exit 99. Turn south on State Road 36 and go four miles to State Road 138. Head west and go 10 miles to Grantsville. At Grantsville, head south for five miles on South Willow Road. At the signs, turn southwest and continue for another five miles to the Loop Campground in the South Willow Canyon Recreation Area. The campground is at the edge of the Deseret Peak Wilderness Area.

Fee or Free: This is a free area.

Camping: There are developed campgrounds without water along the South Fork of Willow Creek. Primitive and hike-in camping are allowed on national forest land.

Lodging: There is plenty of lodging in Salt Lake City.

Contact: Salt Lake Ranger District, Wasatch-Cache National Forest, 6944 South 3000 East, Salt Lake City, UT 84121; (801) 943-1794.

❸

Deep Creek Mountains

In west-central Utah

As you head along Interstate 80 near the Nevada-Utah border, you are in hot, dry country where you can travel for miles without seeing any sign of water. About 50 miles south of Interstate 80, you can see high peaks rising above the horizon. These are part of the Deep Creek Mountain Range, where you will find water—enough to supply eight year-round streams complete with rainbow and cutthroat trout. They flow down the eastern slopes of the range, and nourish adequate, if not lush, vegetation that feeds antelope, mule deer and desert bighorn sheep.

The peaks reach over 12,000 feet high into the sky, and a rich wildlife population lives on the slopes and in the canyons. If it weren't for the many informal roads created by the off-road travel of miners, ranchers and hunters, which reach into every nook and cranny of the range, this would be an excellent wilderness area.

As it is, you can have a wilderness experience in solitude without having to trek long distances. You can drive to almost any part of the range with a high-clearance vehicle on old mining roads and camp in privacy.

Backcountry camping is great at glacial cirque lakes carved from the nearly white granite cliffs that make up most of the summit ridge. You won't find hiking trails in this area, but you will find some pine forests, high desert scrub and sub-alpine tundra near the summit.

Directions: You can reach the range from the east via the 140-mile Pony Express Route that begins in Fairfield. This improved gravel road leads through desolate country where you are as alone as you would have been a century ago. Another, faster route to the range is to take US 93 south from Wendover, Nevada for about 10 miles. Turn east at the marked gravel road to Ibapah and Goshute. Continue for about 25 miles to a four-way junction. There you can turn left and head 22 miles to Callao on the eastern side of the range or go straight ahead for about 20 miles to Ibapah on the western side. From either, you can head up into the range to explore hidden canyons and creeks. The best water is on the eastern slope.

Fee or Free: This is a free area.

Camping: There is primitive camping on BLM land and at a developed campground (an old CCC site) about four miles south of Callao.

Lodging: Some lodging is available in Wendover.

Contact: BLM Richfield District Office, 150 East 900 North, Richfield, UT 84701; (801) 896-8221.

4

Pony Express Route

From Fairfield to Ibapah, across central Utah

Pony Express riders risked life and limb to take mail across the great American deserts from St. Joseph, Missouri to Sacramento, California. Although they only rode the 1,838-mile trail for about 18 months from 1860 to late 1861, their exploits are a vital part of our Western heritage. Many sections of their route have been covered by asphalt or pavement, while others have been almost lost as wilderness has reclaimed its own.

The 140-mile stretch of the trail between Fairfield, just to the west of Utah Lake, and the Nevada border is preserved by an improved gravel road that takes you through some of the most desolate country in Utah. During the days of the Pony Express, riders stopped at stations spaced approximately 12 miles apart all along their route.

Today you can start in Fairfield (you just follow the sign from downtown to the beginning of the route) and drive slowly along the road across Utah, stopping as often as you like to explore the country. If you do stop, you should stay on the roadway, for the sand and mud flats can be deceptive. The last thing you want is to be stuck off the road here.

The route is scenic as it winds over open plains and among small mountain ranges. Several springs are located along the route. The BLM maintains a campground at Simpson Springs (about 40 miles west of Fairfield), where there is water year-round, and one south of Callao, at the end of the route. There are no other facilities of any kind along the way, except for two gas station/grocery stores in Ibapah near the Nevada state line.

A reconstructed stone cabin that was once a Pony Express station stands at Simpson Springs, and the campground sits on high ground with good views of the surrounding country. The cabin offers an interesting glimpse into the minimal, bare-bones existence of the riders who used it as an overnight stop along the route.

Between Simpson Springs and Callao is the 10,000-acre Fish Springs National Wildlife Refuge, which is certainly worth a visit (see the following story).

This trip can take one day or it can take several weeks. Either way you will relive a part of our history as you skirt the worst of the Great Salt Desert and leave behind the speeding traffic of Interstate 80. Few people take the time to drive this route, and those that don't really don't know what they are missing.

Directions: From Fairfield, head west for 140 miles over the Pony Express Route to Ibapah.

Fee or Free: This is a free area.

Camping: There is developed camping at the two BLM campgrounds or primitive camping on BLM lands.

Lodging: There is no lodging after Fairfield. Some is available in Wendover, Nevada to the north of Ibapah.

Contact: BLM Salt Lake District Office, 2370 South 2300 West, Salt Lake City, UT 84119; (801) 977-4300.

5

Fish Springs National Wildlife Refuge

At the southern edge of the Great Salt Desert

Desert oases always attract birds and plenty of other wildlife, and the oasis near Fish Springs on the southern fringe of the Great Salt Desert is no exception. Every second, these springs bring 43 cubic feet of water (at a constant 70 degrees) from deep beneath the earth to feed the desert lake and marsh, where up to 100,000 waterfowl and wading birds congregate during the spring and fall. Lush green growth rises from the water of the springs and surrounding marsh in stark contrast to the barren brown desert.

Archaeological evidence indicates that humans have inhabited this area for over 6,000 years, but today it is more than 100 miles to the nearest motel and 45 miles to the nearest gas station. This is obviously one of the most inhospitable places in Utah, but that is what makes it such a special site.

Trumpeter swans, Caspian terns, long-billed dowitchers, Canada geese, pie-billed grebes and nine kinds of ducks are just a few of the birds you can see in large numbers at this oasis. Although many of these are here only during migration periods, others, such as the white-faced ibis, snowy egret, and black-crowned and great blue heron, choose to nest in colonies at the refuge.

Coyotes come for the water, too, as do mule deer. Muskrats by the thousands are found in the bulrushes, and kit foxes occasionally may be seen nearby.

The best way to explore the marsh and open water is by canoe (you must bring your own). When the water is high, the canoeing is excellent as you weave in and out among the bulrushes in search of birds and muskrats. Some areas are off-limits during nesting season, however, to avoid disturbing the birds.

Several warnings: The roads can be muddy and slippery after just a small amount of rain, and flash floods often come without warning after as little as a half inch of rain. These frequently leave boulders and mud deposits in road dips where you cannot see them until the last minute. Drive carefully at all times.

For many, the address of the refuge will dredge up memories of the Cold War and biological weapons. Dugway Proving Grounds were used by the U.S. Army to test a wide variety of biological weapons between the 1950s and 1980s. The testing grounds received plenty of press coverage for a number of years, but they have since disappeared from public scrutiny.

The testing grounds lie to the northeast of the 17,692-acre refuge and apparently there are no programs underway that are in any way dangerous to those who venture into the southern end of the Great Salt Desert.

Mountains rise to over 8,000 feet near the refuge. On a clear day, a climb to the top of any of the nearby peaks offers views that stretch out for over 60 miles. While there are no formal trails from the refuge to the peaks, hiking is easy through the desert scrub.

Directions: Take State Road 36 south from Interstate 80 at exit 99 (near the Lake Point road stop) and follow it for about 50 miles to the Pony Express

Route. Turn west and continue for another 65 miles over gravel road to the refuge.

Fee or Free: This is a free area.

Camping: Primitive camping is available on BLM land outside the refuge and at an improved BLM campground at Simpson Springs 42 miles to the east.

Lodging: There is no significant lodging available outside Salt Lake City and Wendover, Nevada, which are 75 and 70 miles away, respectively.

Contact: Fish Springs National Wildlife Refuge, P.O. Box 568, Dugway, UT 84022; (801) 831-5353.

6

Little Sahara Recreation Area

In south-central Utah

Sand dunes are central to many people's image of deserts, but only limited sections of the great Southwest have sand dunes of significant size. One area in Utah that deserves note is the giant sandbox between Eureka and Delta. There, the Little Sahara Recreation Area includes over 60,000 acres of free-moving sand dunes set among sagebrush-covered flats and juniper forests along the higher ridges.

This is a popular area for dune buggies, motorcycles and off-road vehicles, which can roam at will over most of the region. Some play areas for children have been set aside near campgrounds, and here you can hike without fear of mechanical creatures roaring over dunes and crushing you. (Although these areas are supposed to be for children to play in, there is nothing that says that adults can't enjoy a casual hike in the quiet dunes.)

Another place where you can hike in solitude and quiet in the shifting sands is the Rockwell Natural Area in the western part of the dunes. The area includes 9,150 acres that have been set aside for nature study. While most people may think that nothing lives in these shifting mounds of sand, several sturdy plants have set root and

---

formed small plant communities. Frequently I spot footprints of small rodents who scurry across the sand at night here. Sometimes I even come upon the remains of a rodent that became careless and lost its life in a struggle with a sidewinder, coyote or owl.

The dunes originated 150 miles away along the southern shore of Lake Bonneville over 10,000 years ago. Prevailing winds moved sand from the lake shore at a rate of about 18 inches per year until Sand Mountain deflected the winds and the large dunes were deposited downwind.

Directions: From the town of Jericho Junction on US 6, take County Road 148 four miles west. Take a left (south) there and follow the signs to the recreation area.

Fee or Free: There is a $5 per vehicle day-use fee.

Camping: There are three developed campgrounds with water and one primitive camp without.

Lodging: There is some lodging in Nelphi, but the closest abundant lodging is in Provo to the north.

Contact: BLM Fillmore District Office, P.O. Box 778, Fillmore, UT 84631; (801) 743-6811.

7

Hardware Ranch & Wellsville Mountains Wilderness

In northwestern Utah

Near the town of Logan in Cache Valley, there are several day outings and a popular state park where you can camp while exploring the surrounding sites. Hyrum State Park is located along the shores of a 450-acre reservoir on the Little Bear River, and most people who head for the park like to waterski and sun on the sandy beaches.

I prefer to make my base nearer to Hardware Ranch, an operation of the Utah Division of Wildlife Resources. During the winter, you will see herds of elk there because the ranch provides them with winter feed; you'll frequently see elk during the rest of the year as well. The road from Hyrum leads through the scenic Blacksmith Fork Canyon, where sheer cliffs rise above the canyon

---

floor and tall cottonwood trees line the creek. There are several campgrounds located along the road. Pioneer Campground is developed and has water; Friendship and Spring campgrounds are without water. All are open from mid-May through late October, and I like to visit in the fall after the aspen that grow in the canyons and on the mountain slopes have turned bright yellow and gold.

For summer outings, I like to head for the Wellsville Mountain Wilderness, about 20 miles west of the ranch, across Cache Valley. This steep range rises 5,000 feet almost straight up on the west side of the valley. From the tops of its peaks, you have a great view of the Great Salt Lake to the west.

Overnight backpacking trips aren't recommended in this terrain; the slopes are too steep to camp on and the exposed ridges are constantly buffeted by high winds.

An excellent day-hike is the trail to the top of Mendon Peak (elevation 8,766 feet) where you have outstanding views of the Wasatch Mountains to the east and canyons leading from the Wellsville Mountains down to Cache Valley. Birding, particularly for raptors, is also good along the trail and on the ridge. Hawks come through the area in large numbers during the fall migration, and almost year-round you can spot several species riding on the thermals below the ridges.

You climb 2,700 feet in three miles from the trailhead in Deep Canyon to the ridge. There, the trail intersects with the Ridgeline Trail. If you are making the climb to look for hawks, the best viewing is from a point to the north of Mendon Peak. Take a right at the intersection and continue another mile to a mountain that is simply called "Peak 8585." For Mendon Peak, turn left and continue for about one-half mile to the top.

Directions: To reach Hyrum State Park, go south on Hyrum Road for seven miles from Logan. The park is along the shore of the lake. To reach Hardware Ranch, take the Blacksmith Fork Canyon Road east from Hyrum for 16 miles to the ranch. For the Wellsville Mountains Wilderness, take Mendon Road 11 miles west from Logan. In Mendon, go west on Third

North for two miles to a parking area on the right. The trailhead in Deep Canyon is another half mile along an unimproved dirt road that is unsuitable for most vehicles.

Fee or Free: Day-use is $3 per day in Hyrum State Park, and camping costs $9-$10 per night.

Camping: Campsites are available in Hyrum State Park and in Blacksmith Fork Canyon.

Lodging: There is plenty of lodging in Logan.

Contact: Hyrum State Park, 405 West 300 South, Hyrum, UT 84319; (801) 245-6866. Hardware Ranch, Utah Division of Wildlife Resources, 1596 West North Temple Street, Salt Lake City, UT 84116; (801) 538-4700. Wellsville Mountains Wilderness, Wasatch-Cache National Forest, Logan Ranger District, 860 North 1200 East, Logan, UT 84321; (801) 755-3620.

8

Bear River Migratory Bird Refuge

Along the shore of the Great Salt Lake

In the mid-19th century, an explorer, having wandered into large flocks of waterfowl along the Bear River in northern Utah, said, "I have seen large flocks of birds before...but never did I behold anything like the immense numbers here congregated together."

At the mouth of the Bear River as it flows into the Great Salt Lake, flocks of birds have congregated for hundreds, maybe even thousands, of years. Today, the largest number of tundra swans found anywhere in the country, up to 12,000 at a time, come through each fall. Five hundred thousand ducks of various kinds join with over a million other birds on the fall migration.

In the spring, thousands of golden-tufted-eared grebes float on the Bear River and a half-million swallows form clouds as they pick insects from the sky above. Canada geese goslings bob like dustballs in batches of up to 20 as they follow their diligent parents across the shallow waters along the shore in search for food. Graceful avocets feed along the dikes and white pelicans with nine-foot wingspans fly low over the lake.

Spring and fall are the best times to visit this beautiful 65,000-acre wildlife refuge, but you can't miss any time of the year. I like to come in the fall when the waterfowl are most numerous and almost shut out the sun as they move in large formations from one feeding pond to another.

My favorite time is late in the afternoon, before the sun sinks behind the Promontory Mountains to the west and while the snow-capped Wasatch Range is still in full light to the east. As the sun sinks, the western sky turns pink and reflects off the feeding ponds where the waterfowl are just settling in for the night. As I listen to the cackling and gurgling of birds squabbling for a favorite location in the flock, I turn to the east as the white snow on the peaks of the Wasatch transforms into a pink wash that matches the sky. You just can't ask for a better way to end a day.

In the mid-1980s, the refuge was flooded by record snowfall and runoff that covered the dikes and ponds and made it impossible to drive in to see the flocks. This was followed by five years of drought, however, and the refuge was restored. Now you can once again drive along the 12-mile auto-tour route that leads through the interior of the refuge.

Directions: From Brigham City, take Forrest Street, which turns into Bird Refuge Road, 15 miles west to the refuge.

Fee or Free: This is a free area.

Camping: There are several forest service campgrounds in the Cache National Forest about five miles east of Brigham City. Willard Bay State Park, which lies just south of the refuge, also has developed campgrounds.

Lodging: There is plenty of lodging in Brigham City.

Contact: Bear River Migratory Bird Refuge, 866 South Main Street, Brigham City, UT 84302; (801) 723-5887.

High Uintas

In northeast Utah

Towering peaks, lush meadows, large stands of coniferous forests, cold, clear streams, and thousands of tiny alpine lakes all combine to make the High Uintas one of the premier backpacking regions in the nation. Glacier-carved sheer cliffs and sharp ridges rise above broad basins and great moraines, creating a remarkable setting for outdoor adventures.

You can backpack into country where you will encounter few others, or you can set up a base camp at one of the many campgrounds in Wasatch National Forest, from which you can explore the peaks and canyons.

The Uintas have gentler terrain than the Wasatch Range and this makes cross-country hiking easier. On both day and overnight hikes, you can enjoy a true wilderness experience in the Uintas as you look for elk, moose, mule deer and Rocky Mountain goat. Fishing is great in the streams, and even the most remote lakes are stocked regularly.

The best introduction to this region is to take the Mirror Lake Highway (State Road 150) that connects the small communities of Kamas, Utah and Evanston, Wyoming. The highway climbs from 6,500 feet at Kamas to 10,678 feet as it crosses Bald Mountain Pass. Because of its high elevations and the heavy snowfall in the region, the highway is closed from October to mid-June most years.

As the road crosses the range, it passes by numerous meadows where wildflowers provide a dash of color in the green grass. At turnouts along the road, you can enjoy great views of distant peaks and canyons.

Snow stays on the ground in the high country until well into June in most years. In mid-July and early August, campers and hikers overflow the campgrounds, particularly those around lakes, during weekends and holidays. At most other times, however, you can find yourself all alone in the campgrounds, from which you can explore the gentle backcountry.

The Uintas is a unique range that runs east and west rather than the more usual north and south of other ranges in the region. Most of the range to the east of State Road 150 is a designated wilderness area, and it is this region that draws the majority of the backcountry hikers that come here. If you are seeking more seclusion, visit the lands to the west of the highway. Although they are not designated wilderness areas, they have many of the same attractions and are much less crowded.

Dozens of national forest campgrounds are located along the highway, and many are lightly used. On your first trip, you may want to just car camp and explore the region from a base camp. If you like it, you can come back later for longer backcountry hikes.

One popular trail into the wilderness begins at the Henrys Fork Trailhead on the north side of Kings Peak. (Access is from the community of Lone Tree.) From there, you can take the 16-mile hike to the top of 13,528-foot Kings Peak, the highest point in Utah. The 32-mile round-trip hike climbs 4,100 feet from the trailhead, and most people take at least three days to complete it.

Directions: From Salt Lake City, take Interstate 80 east for about 30 miles to US 189. Head southeast on US 189 for about nine miles to the community of Kamas. Take State Road 150 (Mirror Lake Highway) east from Kamas as it heads into the High Uintas.

Fee or Free: This is a free area, although there is a fee at some of the campgrounds.

Camping: There are plenty of forest service campgrounds along the highway.

Lodging: There is plenty of lodging in Salt Lake City.

Contact: Several national forests have jurisdiction in the Uintas, and about a dozen ranger districts are involved. Your best bet is to contact the Wasatch National Forest, 8230 Federal Building, 125 South State Street, Salt Lake City, UT 84138; (801) 524-5030.

Timpanogos Cave National Monument

In the Wasatch Range

Caves hold a special fascination for many people. Maybe that explains the popularity of Tolkien's *Lord of the Rings* trilogy. It could be that we have an attraction for Middle Earth and think that we can reach some sort of magical world by heading deep beneath the planet's surface.

Whatever the reason, caves such as those at the Timpanogos Cave National Monument continue to draw visitors from around the world. What makes Timpanogos different is that you don't just drive up to the caves; you have to hike 1.5 miles, climbing 1,065 feet from the visitor center, before you can even come to a cave.

This hike takes you along a spectacular trail with views of the American Fork Canyon below and the Utah Valley to the west. You then take a half-mile tour through the caves before returning to the visitor center.

The hour-long tour inside the cave leads through limestone formations such as branching helictites and

---

graceful flowstone formations, which range in color from pure white to delicate hues of green, yellow and red.

Rangers also lead nature tours outside the caves, and the surrounding Wasatch Mountains have many sites that you can explore. Little Cottonwood Canyon, about 15 miles to the north, is one of the more popular destinations for its many trails. The cliffs of 11,750-foot Mount Timpanogos rise 7,000 feet above Utah Valley to the west. The strenuous climb to the top is a great day-hike.

One trail to the peak, the Timpooneke Trail, begins at Timpooneke Campground off State Road 92, and another, the Aspen Grove Trail, begins at the Theatre in the Pines Picnic Area. If you want to experience both, you can even combine the two with a car shuttle, taking one route to the peak and the other back.

Directions: Head south on Interstate 15 from Salt Lake City and take the Alpine exit (exit 287). Follow State Road 92 (Alpine Scenic Loop) two miles east up American Fork Canyon to the visitor center.

Fee or Free: Entrance to the monument is free, but the cave tour costs $5.

Camping: A number of forest service campgrounds are near the caves.

Lodging: There is plenty of lodging in Provo and Salt Lake City.

Contact: Timpanogos Cave National Monument, Route 3, Box 200, American Fork, UT 84003; (801) 756-5239. Pleasant Grove Ranger District, Uinta National Forest, P.O. Box 228, Pleasant Grove, UT 84062; (801) 785-3563.

Flaming Gorge National Recreation Area

Near the Wyoming border

I have to admit this up front: This is not one of my favorite outdoor getaways in Utah. But it is a favorite of millions who come to this vast region for its deep gorges and its reservoir, which extends for over 90 miles along the Green River near the Utah-Wyoming border. This large expanse of water attracts boaters, anglers, rafters and swimmers in noisy numbers that just turn me off.

There is no denying, though, that there are attractions here. The view of the gorge from the Red Canyon Visitor Center is outstanding. As you gaze upriver, the reservoir sneaks through a gorge with sheer cliffs that rise from the water for over 1,500 feet, and the views of the 502-foot-high dam that contains nearly a million cubic feet of concrete are awe-inspiring.

As you drive through Sheep Creek Canyon Geological Area, you witness an almost mind-numbing amount of geological history—layer upon layer of sediment that the creek has cut through over millions of years. To help you understand it all, the recreation area has developed a guidebook for a self-guided tour through a series of numbered stops and overlooks. There are also three picnic areas along the route where you can stop for a break from the drive. No camping has been allowed in the canyon since 1965, when seven members of a single family lost their lives during a flash flood.

Along the east side of the reservoir, Antelope Flat has a nice campground where you can fish or observe wildlife. Deer and pronghorn casually approach the water's edge, even when humans are present and active.

I like to visit during the off-season when few people are at the campgrounds and no one is darting around the lake in loud motorboats. Some dedicated anglers still come to the area with their boats even when sections of the lake have iced over, but they are neither numerous nor irritating to the ears.

The river below the dam is a favorite rafting area, and is quite busy during the summer. The rapids are calm enough for beginners to enjoy short trips, and there are several designated pull-outs downstream.

There are some hiking trails in the recreation area, although they are not highly advertised. Rather than ask about these at the visitor centers, you should contact the rangers at the Flaming Gorge District Office in Manila for backcountry information.

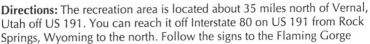

Directions: The recreation area is located about 35 miles north of Vernal, Utah off US 191. You can reach it off Interstate 80 on US 191 from Rock Springs, Wyoming to the north. Follow the signs to the Flaming Gorge Dam and Visitor Center. The center has maps of the area with campgrounds and trails.

Fee or Free: Day-use is free; camping costs $5-$15 per night. Some campgrounds may be reserved ahead; call (800) 283-2267.

Camping: A number of developed campgrounds are located in the recreation area around the reservoir.

Lodging: There is some lodging in Rock Springs and Vernal.

Contact: Flaming Gorge Ranger District Office, P.O. Box 279, Manila, UT 84046; (801) 784-3445.

Dinosaur National Monument

Along the Green River

As much as I shy away from Flaming Gorge National Recreation Area (see previous entry), I gravitate to Dinosaur National Monument. Part of my attraction to the monument is my longtime interest in dinosaurs and the excavation of their bones. The other part is the 200,000 acres of desolate backcountry where few people venture. This includes a long stretch of the Green River where you see plenty of people floating along, but almost no one on the shore.

In the summer months, when whole families make their pilgrimage to the best exhibit of exposed dinosaur bones in the world, the monument is a busy place indeed. Between 1909 and 1924, over 350 tons of bones, including 22 complete skeletons, were removed from the site and transported to museums back east. After that, quarry work was shifted to exposing bones in relief in their natural positions in the large blocks of sandstone.

Most of the visitors to the monument head to the modern, air-conditioned building that covers the wall where the current excavation is taking place. Inside the building, you can see the exposed bones of aptosaurus, stegosaurus, diplodocus and camptosaurus that roamed here over 140 million years ago. Not only can you watch scientists at work in the quarry, you can discuss their findings with them as well.

Only relatively few visitors stay to explore the rest of the monument, and those who do discover rock art, old ranch buildings, miles of river and a good campground where you can camp beneath tall cottonwoods and watch the summer night sky. If you are here in mid-August, this is a great place to watch the Perseid meteor showers.

For a decent hike, follow the trail that leads uphill to an old cattle ranch, which was run by a single woman, Josie Morris, until she was well into her 80s. Her primitive home still stands as it was when she died earlier in this century. You can look inside for a glimpse of how simply she lived on this secluded ranch. Along the way, you can examine Fremont rock art that was left here on exposed boulders by prehistoric tribes thousands of years ago.

Directions: Take US 40 east from Vernal for 13 miles to Jensen. Turn north on State Road 149 and continue for seven miles to the monument entrance.

Fee or Free: Day-use costs $5 per vehicle ($40 per van). Camping costs $8 per night.

Camping: There is a good campground on the tributary of the Green River.

Lodging: The best bet for lodging is in Vernal.

Contact: Dinosaur National Monument, P.O. Box 128, Jensen, UT 84035; (801) 789-2115.

Ouray National Wildlife Refuge & Pelican Lake

On the Green River

South of Vernal, the land is dry and desolate. An average of seven—that's right, *seven*—inches of rain falls each year there. Yet, in the midst of this, one may find Ouray National Wildlife Refuge, a green oasis where dinosaurs still reign supreme, or rather their modern descendants—the waterfowl and wading birds that come by the hundreds of thousands during fall and winter. Many even stay on, nesting in the refuge during the spring and raising their young during early summer.

The water for this 11,061-acre refuge and oasis comes from the 12-mile stretch of the Green River that meanders through it. The river attracts just about every large mammal for miles around at one time or another, and the diked feeding ponds are home to a wide variety of birds and waterfowl.

A number of raptor species, including golden eagles, nest in the tall trees of the refuge, and others come through in large numbers during spring and fall migrations. The primary attraction for serious birders, though, are the Lewis' woodpeckers, which forage and nest here in the stately cottonwoods.

You can view the birds from an observation tower, by hiking along the dikes through the midst of the noisy flocks, or by taking the auto tour of the refuge. My favorite way to explore the area, however, is by canoeing or kayaking along the Green River, where I can watch for busy beavers along the shore, and enjoy a peaceful float as I keep an eye out for the many ducks that dive for food in the shallows along the shore.

As for the large mammals that frequent the refuge, the coyotes don't seem to fear human intruders in this wild place, nor do the large mule-deer bucks with five-point racks. They are frequently seen each fall, standing in regal poses for photographers.

Just to the west of the refuge is Pelican Lake, where large flocks of birds also congregate. You can canoe or hike around this large lake to look for birds. No swimming is allowed because of the schistosomes in the water. These parasitic flatworms are a danger to humans.

The BLM maintains a primitive campground beside the lake for those who don't like to camp out in the flats without any facilities.

Directions: Take US 40 west from Vernal for 14 miles to the first refuge signs. Head south on State Road 88 for another 15 miles to the refuge entrance. Pelican Lake adjoins the refuge to the west.

Fee or Free: This is a free area.

Camping: There is a BLM campground and boat launch at Pelican Lake, and good campgrounds at Dinosaur National Monument, about 25 miles from the refuge. Primitive camping is allowed on BLM land outside the refuge.

Lodging: There are motels in Vernal and Roosevelt to the north.

Contact: Ouray National Wildlife Refuge, 266 West 100 North, Vernal, UT 84078; (801) 789-0351.

Nine Mile Canyon

In east-central Utah

Along Nine Mile Canyon Road south from Myton on US 40, you can stop by petroglyphs and pictographs, ruins, historic cabins and great wildlife observation areas. As the road leads through a scenic sandstone canyon and across high plateaus for 78 miles to Price on US 6, it follows the historic Price-to-Myton Road, which was built by the U.S. Army's 9th Calvary in 1886.

Even farther back, early Native Americans lived and flourished in this region and left one of the richest areas of rock art in the country. Contact the Utah Travel Council for a brochure with details of the archaeology of the route.

I like to take several days to drive this route, stopping on BLM land off the road for overnights and exploring the ridges and canyons nearby after I set up camp. Daytime temperatures rise to nearly 100 degrees during midsummer, so I hike in the early morning before packing up and driving slowly along the gravel road for several hours during midday.

I take my time setting up camp, allowing the temperature to drop enough for me to hike in the cool of late afternoon and early evening. On these walks, I attempt to find rock art, look for birds in the pinyon pine and juniper forests, and wait for the rays of the sinking sun to highlight the red in the sandstone cliffs.

Although the road is open year-round, sometimes snow and rain make it impassable for periods of time.

Before taking the trip, obtain a BLM map of the region. This will let you know where BLM land stops and private land begins, and also give you an up-to-date map of the road and the less-used side roads that branch off from it along the way. Marked pull-outs are scattered along the route where you can see historic or archaeological exhibits and sites.

Directions: From US 40 at the town of Myton, take Nine Mile Canyon Road south to Price.

Fee or Free: This is a free area.

Camping: Primitive camping is available on BLM land.

Lodging: There is lodging in Price and Myton.

Contact: BLM Price River Resource Area, 900 North 700 East, Price, UT 84501; (801) 637-4584. For a brochure on the archaeology of Nine Mile Canyon: Utah Travel Council, Council Hall/Capital Hill, Salt Lake City, UT 84114; (801) 533-5681.

Chapter 10

Southern Utah

Maps 27, 28, 29

Map 27

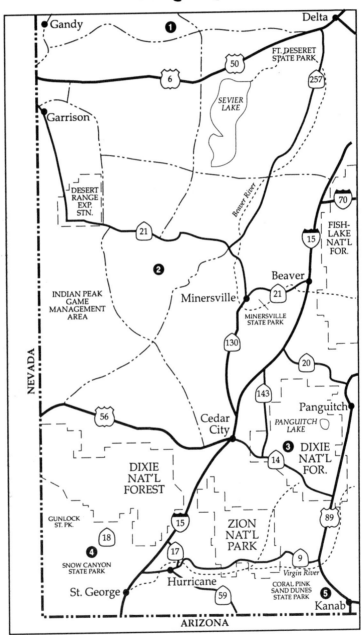

Map 28

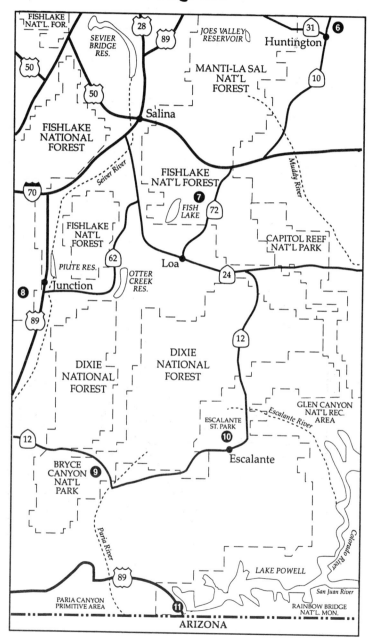

Map 29

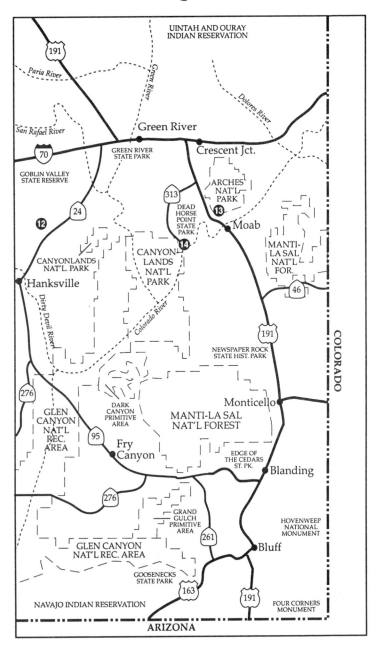

The House Range

West of Delta in central Utah

The House Range of mountains has trilobites (extinct marine arthropods) in fossil form, caves, great vistas, scenic drives and outstanding wilderness hiking. It doesn't reach great heights (9,669-foot Swasey Peak is its highest point), but it has spectacular, massive sandstone cliffs with faces of up to 2,500 feet and rugged canyons.

The steep west side of the range is an escarpment that rises rapidly from the surrounding desert and indicates the fault line that runs along the side of the range. The eastern slopes are much gentler than the western ones and are easier to hike on. They do not offer the spectacular vistas and massive cliff faces of the western side, however.

Juniper, pinyon pine, mountain mahogany and sagebrush cover the dry lower slopes, although some of the higher slopes are covered by several types of pine, Douglas fir and aspen. The most interesting trees in the range are the ancient bristlecone pine. These are the longest-living trees in the world, and you may find them along the high ridges of Swasey and Notch peaks in the House Range.

In the evening, near Sawmill Basin in the northeastern portion of the range, wild horses seek water at creeks and pools, and you can hear their sounds of battle during mating season as stallions challenge one another for the

---

Great Outdoor Getaways to the Southwest

control of herds of mares.

Golden eagles and peregrine falcons nest in nooks and crannies along the sheer cliffs and are frequently seen in the sky overhead as you hike along the ridges.

The roads throughout the range are quite good, and you can reach far into most areas on them. There are a few marked trails to the higher peaks, but most hikers simply head across country here. If you plan on doing so, be sure you have a good topographic map of the region, know how to read your compass and have plenty of water. There are a few springs in the backcountry, but they are not dependable. Most hikers simply car camp and make day-hikes into areas away from the dirt roads. You can reach even to the top of Swasey Peak on the Swasey Peak Loop Trail in a long half-day hike, and other scenic areas are even closer. The trail begins in Sawmill Basin.

The most impressive peak in the range is Notch Peak, whose 2,700-foot sheer rock face is only 300 feet shorter than Yosemite's El Capitan. A relatively easy nine-mile hike from behind it takes you to the top of this impressive rock face where you have great views over desert ranges to the west.

Many visitors to the range go down instead of up, however. Two caves popular with spelunkers are Antelope Spring Cave near Dome Canyon and Council Cave on Antelope Peak between Notch and Swasey peaks. The limestone formations inside the winding tunnels of the caves attract spelunkers from near and far. Some have been explored very little, and advanced cavers head for those as they reach the range. The opening of Council Cave is so large that it can be seen from 50 miles away.

As with any caves, you should be experienced before attempting to investigate them. The BLM provides information about the caves' dangers. Check with them before heading out. The Utah Caving Society also provides caving information for those who are interested; contact David Langston at (801) 584-4422 between 8 a.m. and 5 p.m.

Directions: Take US 50 about 45 miles west from Delta and turn north on a gravel road to the House Range. The road is between Sevier Lake and Shell Rock Pass. If you reach the pass, you have gone about five miles too far. The road curves gently to the west after about 15 miles when you can see the spectacular face of Notch Peak. Use a BLM or forest service map to help you navigate the interior of the range.

Fee or Free: This is a free area.

Camping: Primitive camping is allowed in the national forest and on BLM land.

Lodging: There are motels in Delta.

Contact: Fishlake National Forest, Fillmore Ranger District, 390 South Main, P.O. Box 265, Fillmore, UT 84631; (801) 743-5721.

❷

The Wah Wahs

In west-central Utah

About 50 miles due south of the House Range are the Wah Wah Mountains, which are in one of the most remote and untouched areas in all of Utah. This is the place to go if you really want to be in the outback of America. The name Wah Wah comes from a Paiute term for salty or alkaline seeps.

The snow-white slopes of Crystal Peak rise to 7,106 feet, and are visible from over 50 miles away. My eldest son Matt and I once drove cross-country on US 50. Even from that distance, we could see the peak beckoning to us, and I was sorely tempted to drive to it for an overnight stay. Our schedule didn't allow the extra time it would have taken, but I have made the trip several times since and have found the peak even more impressive up close.

Crystal Peak is the primary attraction for the few visitors who travel to the range and most like to climb to the top. The climb is fairly easy, but you have to be careful in the soft, white tuff (soft volcanic rock) that gives the peak its distinctive coloration.

There are other peaks in the central portion of the range, but none have a dependable supply of water, and neither does Crystal Peak. This is one of the driest sections of Utah and any trips here must include sufficient water for day-to-day living and emergencies—don't count on anyone stumbling upon you in your time of need.

While little else survives in this wild and arid range, it is a critical year-round habitat for golden eagles. They nest on the sharp ledges that jut out from steep mountain faces and forage for game from there.

The lower reaches of the range have a sparse covering of sagebrush, juniper and pinyon pine where the eagles hunt for prey, but some of the higher slopes have aspen, fir and pine. This pristine high country should be a draw to anyone who wishes to explore far reaches of the wilderness, but the lack of water keeps most people away from the range.

A BLM report from the mid-1980s indicated that the Wah Wah Mountains Wilderness Study Area, which covers about two-thirds of the range, had only 155 visitor days per year. That is only about one person every two days. Talk about solitude. You can surely get it in the Wah Wahs.

Directions: Take State Road 21 west from Interstate 15 in Beaver for 24 miles. As the road passes through the San Francisco Mountains at milepost 54, turn left on an unmarked gravel road and head into the range. Crystal Peak is unmistakable near the north end of the range. Use a BLM map to decide how to reach other sections of the range.

Fee or Free: This is a free area.

Camping: Primitive camping is permitted on BLM land.

Lodging: There are motels in Beaver.

Contact: BLM Richfield District Office, 150 East 900 North, Richfield, UT 84701; (801) 896-8221.

❸

The Markagunt Plateau

In red rock country

To the west of Cedar City is open grasslands and flat desert broken by an occasional small mountain range. To the east, you quickly rise onto the top of the Markagunt Plateau, with its gently rolling terrain, forests and lakes.

State Road 14 runs across the southern portion of the plateau, and along this scenic stretch is a variety of outdoor getaways where you can enjoy both the geological beauty for which the region is noted and great hiking. Throw in some lakes with good fishing, a hike to an unexpected waterfall and a cave where you can explore the inside of a lava flow and you have a great place to visit.

The vast expanses of flat desert to the west of Cedar City appear to be brought closer during summer storms as low clouds and bursts of lightning settle over the small mountain ranges. I had never seen such storms from on high, however, until my first visit to the plateau. On that day, I encountered one of the most powerful storms that I have ever experienced as I drove up the winding highway to the top of the plateau. I pulled over and looked back to the west just as the storm broke.

The late-afternoon sun peaked through the dark

clouds moving west. The first rays hit one of the small peaks rising from the desert in the west, while the surrounding grasslands remained under the dark shadow of the clouds. I turned to the east and saw the sunlight and shadows covering the pink cliffs and dark green forests with amazingly contrasting colors. From that moment, I have always gotten a special feeling when I travel along this high plateau.

A number of spectacular views of both Zion National Park and Cedar Breaks National Monument are along this route, and my favorite is off State Road 143 just north of State Road 14 in Cedar Breaks. The road skirts the lip of a 2,500-foot-deep natural amphitheater where you can stop to look over the pastel-colored badlands below.

The best stops in the monument are at the Cedar Breaks Visitor Center and at the Chessman Ridge Overlook. From the visitor center, take the four-mile round-trip Wasatch Rampart Trail, which leads past Spectra Point to the rim of the amphitheater. At Chessman Ridge Overlook, a short hike leads to a small grove of bristlecone pine, the oldest living things on the planet, on the Bristlecone Pine Trail. You can also hike on the trail alongside the highway for about 1.5 miles to Alpine Pond and back.

Farther along the route is the turnoff to Navajo Lake. This recreation area centers around a 3.5-mile-long lake that has no surface outlet. All water from the lake drains through sinkholes in the limestone beneath it and emerges at Cascade Falls and Duck Creek. The lake is held by a natural dam, which was formed by lava flows thousands of years ago.

Green groves of aspen, fir and spruce dot the lakeshores, and several forest service campgrounds are located among them.

Nearby Cascade Falls drop over the colorful Pink Cliffs on the south rim of the plateau as the water gushes from a cave in the face of the cliffs on its way to the Virgin River below. The flow is at its peak in late spring, and splotches of white snow frequently remain on the crevices and ledges of the cliffs to add a touch of winter to the scenic falls.

With truly spectacular scenery, a lava-dammed lake, one of the largest waterfalls in southern Utah and plenty of campgrounds, the 30 miles of State Road 14 between Cedar City and Duck Creek Village are a great place to spend a week exploring and camping.

For even more scenery, continue on State Road 14 for another 2.5 miles past Duck Creek Village, where the red-rock formations have been used as a backdrop for Westerns since the 1940s, to the gravel road that heads south for nine miles to Strawberry Point. Zion National Park, countless ridges and canyons and the Arizona Strip are all visible from there.

Directions: From Cedar City, head east on State Road 14 for about 18 miles to State Road 143, then head north to Cedar Breaks National Monument. The Navajo Lake turnoff is 25.5 miles east of Cedar City. Cascade Falls is less than a half mile from State Road 14 on the road to Navajo Lake. Turn left on a gravel road and continue three miles to the half-mile trail to the falls.

Fee or Free: Day-use is free. Camping costs $7 a night; to reserve, call (800) 280-2267.

Camping: There are plenty of campgrounds at Cedar Canyon, Cedar Breaks, Navajo Lake and Duck Creek.

Lodging: There is adequate lodging in Cedar City.

Contact: Dixie National Forest, 82 North 100 East, P.O. Box 0580, Cedar City, UT 84721-0580; (801) 865-3700. Cedar Breaks National Monument, P.O. Box 749, Cedar City, UT 84720; (801) 586-0787.

St. George & Zion National Park

In southern Utah

St. George gets hot—very hot—during midsummer, and its temperate winter climate earned the region the nickname "Little Dixie." Brigham Young retreated to the area during the cold winters in Salt Lake City, and the land around the city is rich agricultural country.

There are several other attractions nearby, though, which bring thousands of visitors each year. The town is the jumping-off point for Zion National Park to the east, and two less-visited areas to the west, Snow Canyon State Park and the Pine Mountains.

When I'm in the area, I never miss at least a short trip into Zion to see its awe-inspiring, towering cliffs, but I generally head west for longer trips. Snow Canyon State Park has it all—red-rock canyons with steep cliffs whose colors metamorphose as the sun rises and sets each day, huge pink sand dunes, volcanic cinder cones, and lava tubes where you can find artifacts left by Native Americans who lived in the region thousands of years ago.

I hike along the miles of trails in the park during late spring when delicate wildflowers dot the slopes beside the trail or after the second bloom in early fall. These blooms are set against the red sandstone cliffs that rise 500 to 750 feet to enclose the three-mile-long canyon.

To the northeast of State Road 18, massive blocks of magma have been exposed by years of erosion. Signal Peak tops the range at over 10,000 feet, and it is the centerpiece of the Pine Mountain Recreation Area. Even in the midst of a summer heat wave, the trails of the wilderness area lead through cool mountain forests and make this an excellent backpacking destination. Trails lead by streams fed by the winter snowmelt. A plentiful supply of water is available in late spring and early summer, and the wildflowers are at their peak bloom then.

While it is possible to take day-trips into the Pine Mountains, most of the trail loops are too long for just a day-hike. It is best to plan for at least one overnight, if not several, so you can explore among the range's jumble of volcanic rubble.

I don't mean to shortchange Zion, but it has been so written about, and is so heavily visited (at least along the primary drive through the park and around park headquarters), that I just don't spend much time there. That isn't to say it isn't worth a visit.

At Zion, sculpted cliffs whose pastel colors change before your very eyes as the sun moves across the sky tower thousands of feet above narrow canyons. First-time visitors should stop at the visitor center where you can join a number of ranger-led hikes into such areas as The Narrows of Orderville Canyon, Angels Landing, the Watchman Trail, the Canyon Overlook Trail and the Emerald Pools Trail to Middle Pool. These are excellent introductions to the over 100 miles of developed trails that crisscross the park.

Fewer than 10,000 backpackers head into the backcountry of Zion out of the more than two million visitors who come to the park each year, but they enjoy some of the premier backpacking in the Southwest. Zion is one of the few parks in the region where water is plentiful in the backcountry. Few trails are without a good supply, and that gives hikers great flexibility in planning cross-country treks.

The most popular backcountry area in the park is the Kolob Canyons Wilderness in the Timber Creek drainage, where hikers follow the path of narrow slot canyons. Other areas such as Hop Valley and Wildcat Canyon are less crowded but just as spectacular as you hike through canyons cut through red rock.

You must obtain free permits from either the Zion Canyon Visitor Center or the Kolob Canyons Visitor Center before heading into the backcountry on overnight trips. You don't need a permit for day-hikes, unless you plan to hike into The Narrows (which few people do on day trips).

Directions: For Snow Canyon State Park, take State Road 18 northwest from St. George for about 12 miles to State Road 300, which leads into the park. To reach the interior of the Pine Mountains, take State Road 18 northwest from St. George for about 25 miles to the small crossroads community of Central. Take the paved road from Central east for about five miles to Pine Valley. From there, use forest service maps to trailheads within the wilderness area. Zion National Park is northeast of St. George about 40 miles on State Road 9.

Fee or Free: Day-use at Zion costs $5 per vehicle. Camping costs $7, first come, first served. Pine Mountain Recreation Area is free.

Camping: A number of developed campgrounds are located in both parks and in the Pine Mountain Recreation Area near the wilderness area. Primitive and backcountry camping are allowed on national forest land.

Lodging: There is plenty of lodging in St. George.

Contact: Snow Canyon State Park, P.O. Box 140, Santa Clara, UT 84765; (801) 628-2255. Dixie National Forest, Pine Valley Ranger District, 345 East Riverside Drive, St. George, UT 84770; (801) 652-3100. Zion National Park, Springdale, UT 84767-1099; (801) 772-3256.

5

Coral Pink Sand Dunes State Park

In south-central Utah near Kanab

Camping under a full moon among the white sand dunes of White Sands National Monument is one of my favorite getaways (see page 231 in the southern New Mexico chapter), but when I finally spent a night with a full moon at Coral Pink Sand Dunes State Park near Kanab, I was even more entranced.

At White Sands, the pale moonlight seems to gain strength as it bounces from one dune to another, making the whole area appear brighter. At Coral Pink Sand Dunes, you don't get the amplification of light you do at White Sands. Rather you get a soft light—with a pink tinge.

As the full moon rises above the distant horizon, the pink slopes of the dunes take on a luminescence from the cool light of the moon, and the dunes seem to become a source of light themselves, one where the light is warm pink instead of cool white.

Now I know that the light doesn't really warm up in the cold desert night, but it certainly appears to. You can't read a newspaper the way you might at White Sands, but everything in view is touched by the tint of pink, giving the whole scene an otherworldly feeling.

The large, ever-moving dunes in this valley to the west of Kanab cover over 2,000 acres in the 3,700-acre state park. They form as churning desert air currents are funneled by surrounding mountains to the valley. There, sand carried by the strong wind is regularly deposited in dunes that rise to heights of several hundred feet.

The color comes not from ground-up pink coral, but from the tiny particles of rose quartz that make up the sand.

While the area appears devoid of animal life, you can find tracks that lead from bush to bush, and coyotes' yips are often heard at night. The coyotes feed upon the small rodents that scurry across the dunes during the cool of the night, and leave only footprints for you to spot the next day.

The dunes are extremely popular with off-road-vehicle afficionados, and the park is very crowded, especially on weekends between Memorial Day and Labor Day. If you do visit during the busy season, head for the areas that have been set aside for hikers, where you won't have to worry about onrushing machines. I like to visit in the off-season anyway—the daytime temperatures are more moderate, and there are fewer people among the dunes.

Directions: Take US 89 west for 13.5 miles from Kanab. Turn south on the paved road that is signed for the park.

Fee or Free: There is a $3 entry fee per vehicle. Camping is $9 to $10; for reservations, call (800) 322-3770.

Camping: There are two developed campgrounds in the area, one in the park and one on BLM lands just to the north of the dunes. Primitive camping is available on BLM lands outside the park.

Lodging: There is lodging in Kanab, Zion National Park and towns to the west of Zion.

Contact: Coral Pink Sand Dunes State Park, P.O. Box 95, Kanab, UT 84741; (801) 874-2408.

6

Huntington Canyon

Near Huntington in central Utah

Mormons didn't settle the eastern side of the Wasatch Plateau until the late 1870s, long after they had transformed the deserts to the west into productive farmland. It was only after adequate water and good land to the west began to run short that the first settlers began to colonize the eastern side of the plateau.

Now vacationers follow in the footsteps of the Mormons, moving toward the east of the plateau after having filled most of the parklands on the west side. Huntington Canyon is one of the places where they are heading.

This destination features fortress-like cliffs that rise above the canyons and alpine backcountry with cool forests and meadows, where you can hike and camp in comfort away from sweltering midsummer heat and with few other people.

Cold streams with cutthroat trout, groves of spruce, fir and aspen where deer browse in the open meadows, and scenic drives along the top of the plateau are all popular with the few visitors who come to this section of Manti-La Sal National Forest.

Although there are a dozen or more campgrounds in the area, I head for the Forks of Huntington Campground off State Road 31, about 18 miles from State Road 10. This campground sits among fir and spruce trees in an intimate side canyon at 7,600 feet. The Left Fork of Huntington Creek National Recreation Trail begins at the rear of the campground and follows the creek up a wooded canyon. The easy trail continues for five miles to an open alpine valley where you can take a rest before heading back to camp.

Nearby, Huntington Lake State Park features water sports and fishing for those who are more aquatically inclined.

Directions: The small town of Huntington sits at the mouth of Huntington Canyon near the junction of State Roads 10 and 31. Huntington Lake State Park is off State Road 10 just to the north of the town. State Road 31 leads up Huntington Canyon from the town.

Fee or Free: Day-use in the state park costs $3 per vehicle, $1 for hikers and bikers. Camping costs $9-$10; for reservations call (800) 322-3770. Designated camping in the national forest costs $5-$6. Day-use in the national forest is free.

Camping: There are plenty of excellent developed campgrounds in the state park and national forest. Primitive camping is allowed on national forest lands.

Lodging: The best chances for lodging are in Price about 20 miles north of the canyon on State Road 10.

Contact: Huntington Lake State Park, P.O. Box 1343, Huntington, UT 84528; (801) 687-2491. Manti-La Sal National Forest, 599 West Price River Drive, Price, UT 84501; (801) 637-2817.

❼

Thousand Lake Mountain

In Fishlake National Forest

Thousand Lake Mountain is not a mountain, nor does it have a thousand lakes. It is really a large plateau with only a few lakes. But it does have scenic overlooks, hiking and camping options, and a little-used campground.

From the highest peak in the area, 11,306-foot Flat Top, and other spots atop the plateau, you get excellent views of Cathedral Valley in Capitol Reef National Park to the east and the wooded valleys around Fish Lake to the west.

A well-maintained forest service road from the west follows a winding route for eight miles to the top of the plateau and a small forest service campground. Just before the campground, the road passes by the Desert View Overlook, which offers great views of Capitol Reef to the east, as well as vast expanses of desert.

I like to make my base camp here at the Elkhorn Campground, which is set at 9,300 feet. The campsites are surrounded by forests of fir, spruce and aspen. Deer frequently browse in the open alpine meadows that are hidden among the stands of trees. From this peaceful campground, you can take day-hikes to nearby lakes and Flat Top.

Directions: From the small community of Loa on State Road 24, head north and east on State Road 72 for 12 miles to Forest Service Road 206. Turn left and continue for eight miles to the Elkhorn Campground.

Fee or Free: This is a free area.

Camping: There is a good developed forest service campground. Primitive camping is allowed on forest service land.

Lodging: Some lodging is available in Bicknell and Torrey along State Road 24 to the east of Loa.

Contact: Loa Ranger District, Fishlake National Forest, 138 South Main Street, Loa, UT 84637; (801) 836-2811.

The Tushar Mountains

In Fishlake National Forest

The Tushars. Sounds like mountains that would be found in Afghanistan, not in Utah, and they might as well be, as far as most people are concerned. Although they are higher than the Wasatch Range, these delightful mountains, located in Fishlake National Forest, are relatively unknown even to Utah natives.

I like to drive across the mountains along State Road 153 even if I am not planning on camping or hiking. Both the campgrounds and hiking trails here are so inviting and uncrowded, though, that I can seldom just drive through. I usually stop at one of the half-dozen excellent forest service campgrounds along the route for at least a night, if not longer.

From these, day-hikes lead into the high alpine country where mountain meadows are surrounded by groves of aspen, fir and spruce. Longer hikes lead to the tops of the Tushars' three peaks, all of which rise above 12,000 feet. These are 12,082-foot Mount Baldy, 12,139-foot Mount Belknap and 12,169-foot Delano Peak.

The trails to each of these involve ascents of only about 2,000 feet and are easy day-hikes. In my youth, I

---

once climbed all three in a single day with a friend, but that was then. Today, I am satisfied with taking a leisurely stroll to the top of just one, and spending time there taking in the outstanding views of desert and mountains.

Trailheads to all three peaks are located along Big John Flat Road, which leads north from State Road 153. Although all three hikes are excellent, I prefer to head for Mount Baldy from Blue Lake, about three miles away. Then I have a delightful small mountain lake to sit beside as I rest after the hike.

For more sedentary types, there is plenty of good fishing in the lakes and streams of the range, and several of the campgrounds are located near reservoirs where fishing is good.

Directions: Take State Road 153 east from Interstate 15 at Beaver. The first 19 miles are paved, and the next 21 miles are dirt. You reach the town of Junction along US 89 at the end of the dirt road. Forest service roads lead off State Road 153 at intervals; many lead to campgrounds. Use a forest service map to locate the campgrounds.

Fee or Free: This is a free area, except for campground fees which run $4-$6.

Camping: There are plenty of developed forest service campgrounds in the national forest. Primitive camping is allowed on forest service land.

Lodging: The best bet for lodging is in Beaver.

Contact: Beaver Ranger District, Fishlake National Forest, P.O. Box E, Beaver, UT 84713; (801) 438-2436.

9

Bryce Canyon National Park & Vicinity

In the canyonlands of southern Utah

Red Canyon, Powell Point, Kodachrome Basin, Cottonwood Canyon, Upper Paria River Canyon-Vermillion Cliffs Wilderness Area—each of these is worth a long visit in itself, and all are located within miles of each other near Bryce Canyon National Park, one of the most colorful of all the canyonland parks that dot the southern Utah landscape.

With such a range of things to see and places to explore, it is difficult to decide where to head when you have only a short time in the Bryce Canyon area, so I always plan to spend at least two weeks in the region. I just couldn't make up my mind where to go and what to do if I spent any less time there.

The first time I drove into Bryce I didn't even make it to the turnoff to the park. Red Canyon was just too captivating as I passed through it on State Road 12. I couldn't imagine that I wasn't already inside the park as I gaped at the red-rock cliffs that rose above the highway on both sides. The rocks in the canyon are part of the same Wasatch Formation that is exposed at Bryce, and they are just as colorful as any located inside the park.

On that first trip, I was content to spend a night in the Red Canyon Campground and hike along the three trails that lead to outstanding views of the brilliantly colored cliffs. I could have stayed even longer, but when I pressed on to Bryce later the next day, I was glad I had.

If you've never been to Bryce Canyon, don't miss a chance to visit. When you reach the park, head for the visitor center, which has great exhibits about the geological events that shaped the canyonlands here.

After watching a slide show, looking over the exhibits and talking to the rangers, you will be more than ready to explore the park's trails. All of the trails lead down below the rim into the breaks (eroded formations), and that means you're in for a stiff climb back to the parking areas.

The effort is worth it, though, because the hiking here gives you views that change with every bend in the trail. What look like seemingly repetitious formations from above become endlessly varied eroded forms as you hike among them.

My favorite hikes are the Navajo Loop and Queen's Garden trails, but less-used trails to the north of Bryce Point include the Peekaboo Loop and Fairland trails, which are longer and steeper. To the south of the point, you can try the Under-the-Rim and Riggs Spring Loop trails.

While Bryce is not a disappointment by any stretch of the imagination, I must admit that I spend less time here than in other getaways where I see fewer people and can explore more out-of-the-way areas.

Among those places is what I consider the most superb vista in Utah, Powell Point. This lookout is located at the southern end of the Table Cliff Plateau, which is about 15 miles northeast of Sunset Point in Bryce Canyon. An added attraction to this vista point is that you are likely to have it all to yourself. Surprisingly few people know about the site, or care to make the effort to reach it.

Regular passenger vehicles with good clearance can only get to within about four miles of the point, but high-clearance vehicles can get to within a half mile. From either spot, the hike to the point is well worth the effort. For those with mountain bikes, the four-mile ride from where you park low-clearance vehicles is an outstanding ride in some of the most scenic country in Utah. Hikers can make the round trip to the point and back in an easy day's hike.

The drive in to the point, while interesting in itself, is only the prelude to this getaway. From the end of the unimproved road (where there is a good campsite for those who wish to make this an overnight), you take a half-mile trail to the tip of Powell Point. This footpath leads you through a weather-beaten grove of bristlecone pine, and the scars left on many of the trees from previous lightning storms give you fair warning that this is not where you want to be in a severe summer thunderstorm.

The views begin long before you reach the point, but once there you have a panoramic view of large chunks of southern Utah and northern Arizona as the red-rock country stretches out to the far horizons in waves of canyons and plateaus that gradually turn from bright red to pink to dark gray.

Directly beneath the point, the bright reds of the Wasatch Formation drop off into steep cliffs that the wind and rain have eroded into fantastic formations.

Another destination outside the national park is Kodachrome Basin State Park. Here, set among colorful cliffs, you can see "sand pipes," which are unusual rock pillars found nowhere else in the world. Over 60 of these pillars, ranging in height from six to nearly 170 feet, are located within the park, and I like to hike the trails through them at dusk as the sun sinks over the western horizon and the low rays highlight the reds and pinks in the rocks and cliffs.

Farther south and east are the true wildlands of the Cottonwood Canyon area. This was where I first hiked in the slot canyons that are scattered throughout the canyonlands of southern Utah. These narrow canyons have become popular in recent years among those searching for the sense of excitement that comes from hiking canyon floors where you are battling through water as often as you are on dry land. In these narrow slots, you must be constantly on the alert for flash floods that will drive you to higher levels within the steep canyon walls.

Even farther south, after the dirt road has joined US 89, you come to the Paria Canyon-Vermillion Cliffs Wilderness Area. In my opinion, this is the premier canyon-hiking area in Utah. You can hike from here all the way to the Glen Canyon Recreation Area in northern Arizona, along up to 45 miles of trails that lead through canyons with 1,600-foot-high walls.

Aside from the very real dangers of flash floods, hiking along the Paria River or Cottonwood Creek is an awe-inspiring adventure. You wander among vermillion cliffs that rise high enough to snuff out the sun. Windows carved out of the sandstone cliffs by high water offer the only place to dry your feet as you take a break. The arches and tunnels along the way lead you into a fairyland that brings out the shutterbug in even the least-experienced photographer, and the geologist in the least-informed science student. The layers of sandstone (Navajo, Kayenta, Moenave and Chinle) attest to the lively geological history of the region, and present a scenic diorama of events that long preceded human intrusion into this wild corner of the state.

This three- to four-day hike has become so popular, however, that you may want to pass it by. If you do, you can head back up Cottonwood Canyon Road to Hackberry Canyon along the Paria River. Canyon hikers have yet to descend upon this area as they have the areas farther downstream.

If you'd like to try one of the many other hiking options in the region, you can check in with the BLM Kanab Resource Area office to map out a trip that will take you where few others go.

Directions: Take State Road 12 east from US 89 south of Panguitch as it winds through Red Canyon. The Red Canyon Campground is four miles from US 89. The turnoff to Bryce Canyon National Park is another 10 miles past the campground.

To reach Powell Point, take State Road 63 (gravel) north from the junction where you turn south to Bryce Canyon. Continue 11 miles to Forest Service Road 132 and the sign to Pine Lake. Continue on Forest Service Road 132 another six miles past the lake. As you reach the top of the plateau, watch for a narrow dirt road on the right. If you don't have a high-clearance vehicle, you can park here and hike or bike to the point. With a high-clearance vehicle, you can drive the dirt road for just under four miles to the Powell Point Trailhead.

To reach Kodachrome Basin State Park, follow the signs from the small community of Cannonville, which is 12 miles southeast of the Bryce Canyon National Park turnoff on State Road 12. The park is nine miles from Cannonville, and only the first three miles are paved. You have to ford the normally dry Paria River along the way.

To reach Cottonwood Canyon, continue south on the road from Cannonville past Kodachrome Basin State Park for another 35 miles to US 89.

To reach Paria Canyon-Vermillion Cliffs Wilderness Area, take US 89 to the junction with Cottonwood Canyon Road and head about four miles west.

Fee or Free: At Bryce Canyon, day-use costs $5 per vehicle; camping is $7 per night, first come, first served.

Camping: There are plenty of developed campgrounds in the national forest and state and national parks. Primitive camping is allowed on national forest and BLM lands.

Lodging: There are motels in Panguitch, Bryce Canyon National Park and Escalante.

Contact: Powell Ranger District, Dixie National Forest, 225 East Center Street, P.O. Box 80, Panguitch, UT 84759; (801) 676-8815. Bryce Canyon National Park, Bryce Canyon, UT 84717; (801) 834-5322. BLM Kanab Resource Area, 318 North First East, Kanab, UT 84741; (801) 644-2672. Kodachrome Basin State Park, P.O. Box 238, Cannonville, UT 84718; (801) 679-8562.

Escalante Area

In the canyonlands of southern Utah

When I want strenuous outdoor activity along with scenic beauty, I head for the area around the small town of Escalante. Just outside town, you can mountain bike, hike in slot canyons, drive into scenic forests, take the historic route along the Hole-in-the-Rock Road, search for outcroppings of petrified wood, or hike along the misty Calf Creek Falls Trail. All of these take you into wild and semi-wild places where you can enjoy some of the finest red-rock country getaways in Utah.

It's almost impossible for me to decide beforehand what I am going to do when I reach the Escalante area. I just wait until I get there and then follow my instincts. If the weather is extremely hot, as it gets in midsummer, I head for the cool highlands along Hell's Backbone Road. This scenic road leads through country that rises above 8,000 feet (it reaches 9,200 feet before descending to State Road 12 almost 40 miles from Escalante). Unimproved roads lead to backcountry lakes and streams on both sides of the road as you wind through aspen and ponderosa pine forests.

Steep canyons drop down from the road, and deer browse in the high meadows. Camping in the forest service campgrounds is excellent, with cool nights and warm days, as long as you don't mind being with other people. I like to head for level campsites in the national forest, away from the developed campgrounds, where I can find solitude and total quiet.

The open forests invite hiking, and you don't have to worry about developed trails since the understory is so open. There is a short, mile-long trail that leads from Posey Lake off Hell's Backbone Road to an old fire-lookout tower, however, which you might want to take. From the tower you get great views of the surrounding country.

If the weather is cooler and I don't feel like immediately heading into the backcountry, I head into the Escalante Petrified Forest State Park just outside of town and set up camp. From there, I explore the trails in the park that lead to outcroppings of petrified wood. The best of these includes a longer hike to the Baily Wash area. There, a nature trail leads through one of the largest displays of petrified wood that I have seen outside Petrified Forest National Park in Arizona.

For anyone who hasn't hiked the slot canyons and wants to get a taste of what canyon hiking is like, the Lower Calf Creek Falls Trail just east of Escalante off State Road 12 is a must. You walk up a flat canyon floor where steep cliffs of Navajo sandstone streaked with desert varnish shade Calf Creek. As you hike upstream, you will pass beaver ponds and cool swimming holes, you'll be able to explore Indian ruins, view pictographs, and finally reach the 126-foot-high falls after about three miles.

The canyon here is not as narrow as the slot canyons that have become so popular for serious backpackers, but the high cliffs offer shade nearly all day. The grotto at the bottom of the falls is a great place to stop, swim and relax for a while before heading back to the parking area.

Sheer sandstone cliffs block any further progress up the canyon past the falls, but adventurous sorts may want to check with locals about how to reach Upper Calf Creek Falls by another route.

The Hole-in-the-Rock Road is a legacy from the days when Mormons were colonizing the wild areas of southern Utah. Today, it remains the only major route into the scenic western canyons of the Escalante River tributaries.

The network of slickrock (smooth, red rock) canyons and meandering streams along both sides of the Escalante River are among the most popular backpacking areas in southern Utah, and you should expect any canyon you choose between late spring and early fall to be crowded, at least by Utah standards.

The drive along the Hole-in-the-Rock Road is well worth the trip all by itself, even if you don't head into the region to backpack. The 56 miles of road were built by Mormons as they attempted to colonize the wild lands around the San Juan River. Construction on the road began in 1878, and the first 50 miles were fairly easy. The last six were more difficult, however, as they had to construct the road over rugged slickrock country to the Hole-in-the-Rock. There they found a sheer, 45-foot drop to an extremely steep slope of rock that covered the remaining three-quarters of a mile to the Colorado River.

Today, you can drive the entire route, although I recommend a high-clearance vehicle if you venture past Dance Hall Rock to the Hole-in-the-Rock. Devil's Garden and Dance Hall Rock are both scenic sidetrips along the way, but I always head straight to the end of the road. There I hike out across the rock to the notch known as the Hole-in-the-Rock for a view of Lake Powell below. The Mormons gave the notch this name since, from afar, it appeared to be a hole completely encircled by rock.

The first time that I visited this area there was no lake, only the Colorado River far below, and it was an overnight hike down to the river and back. Today, the lake level is only about 600 feet below the notch, and it is only a strenuous half-mile round-trip hike. Much of the road excavation that the Mormons used to get wagons down to the river is still visible, although over two-thirds of the route from the notch to the former river now lies under water.

Directions: From downtown Escalante, take Hell's Backbone Road north to Posey Lake and continue on it as it turns east before ending at State Road 12 near Boulder. Escalante Petrified Forest State Park is off State

Road 12 about two miles northwest of town. The Lower Calf Creek Falls Trailhead begins at Calf Creek Recreation Area, just over 15 miles east of Escalante on State Road 12. The Hole-in-the-Wall Road turns south off State Road 12 about five miles east of Escalante.

Fee or Free: Day use at the state park costs $3 per vehicle. Camping is $9 to $10; for reservations, call (800) 322-3770. Most of the surrounding areas, however, are free.

Camping: There are developed campgrounds at the state park, along Hell's Backbone Road in the national forest, and at the Calf Creek Recreation Area. You may primitive camp outside the developed campgrounds on national forest and BLM lands.

Lodging: There is some lodging in Escalante and more to the north in Torrey and Bicknell.

Contact: Escalante Ranger District, Dixie National Forest, 2770 West Main, P.O. Box 246, Escalante, UT 84726; (801) 826-4221. Escalante Petrified Forest State Park, P.O. Box 350, Escalante, UT 84726; (801) 826-4466. BLM Escalante Resource Area, P.O. Box 225, Escalante, UT 84726; (801) 826-4291.

Glen Canyon National Recreation Area

Along the shore of Lake Powell

I head for Lake Powell in the Glen Canyon Recreation Area when I feel nostalgic. As I boat over the cold water of the second-largest man-made lake in the world, I remember the deep slickrock canyons with sheer sides where eons of weathering had left dark desert varnish markings that could be seen for miles against the red sandstone.

On warm summer nights with a full moon, I am sure that I can still see the canyon walls as I float across the smooth waters in a modern houseboat. It is then that I realize how deeply attached I was to the region before the Glen Canyon Dam rose above the Colorado River in the early 1960s for hydroelectric and water supply purposes.

I don't often visit the lake during the peak summer season, though, because there are just too many people roaring about in their motor-powered water crafts. I prefer to come toward the end of the season after the crowds have thinned, if not disappeared altogether. Then I can charter a small houseboat, take along a canoe or kayak, and explore the many inlets formed in the tributary canyons of the Colorado in quiet solitude.

I still try to make my trips coincide with a full moon, however, when the nights are quiet except for the occasional yips of coyotes staking out their territories on the desert cliffs that rise above the lake. The moon lights the world twice—once from the sky and once from the water, where its ghostly white reflects the memories of what is forever drowned by the lake's cold waters.

On land, the moon highlights the spires and arches that rise above the surrounding desert and give life to these strange and wonderful shapes, long revered by the Native Americans of the region.

On my trips, I generally float around from one arm of the lake to another during midday, and hike among the red-rock country during early morning and late evening when the small animals and birds are most active near the water's edge. The land near the water is completely barren, because the fluctuating water levels prevent any plant growth; this makes hiking easy. It is only a short distance to desert scrub, though, where wildflowers sprout after the summer rains have ended.

Since there are so many places to explore around the lake, and there are a half-dozen marinas to rent boats, I always head for the Carl Hayden Visitor Center to check out what is going on in the natural world around the lake. I then decide which marina to head for.

A note: I mentioned the smooth waters of the lake above, but they are not always smooth and calm. Storms in the region bring gusts of winds of up to 60 miles per hour, and waves on open expanses of the lake can exceed six feet from crest to crest. These are steeper than ocean waves and can toss small craft around mightily.

Directions: The Carl Hayden Visitor Center and Glen Canyon Dam are located along US 89 about three miles north of Page, Arizona. The various marinas are located along the shoreline of the lake. Directions to each is included in information provided by the visitor center.

Fee or Free: Day use is free. Staying at Wahweop Campground costs $8.50 per night, first come, first served.

Camping: Several developed campgrounds are located near the marinas around the lake, and primitive camping is allowed in the backcountry with permits.

Lodging: Motels are available in Page and at the various marinas.

Contact: Glen Canyon National Recreation Area, P.O. Box 1507, Page, AZ 86040; (602) 645-2471.

The San Rafael Swell & Goblin Valley State Park

In east-central Utah

State Road 24 heads south from Interstate 70 about 12 miles west of the tiny community of Green River. (With a population of 1,000, Green River is considered a large town in this section of Utah.) For the next 50 miles, it parallels the eastern edge of the San Rafael Swell, a huge anticline that was formed as forces deep beneath the surface pushed the overlying strata of rock high above the surrounding area. The edge of the swell is known as the San Rafael Reef, and the brightly colored cliffs of the reef stand in striking contrast to the flat, featureless desert to the east of the highway.

About halfway down the reef, a dirt road turns off to the west toward Temple Mountain. As you take this, you begin to head into wondrous canyon country. It's an area you won't want to visit on Halloween, that is unless you like goblins galore. In the midst of these canyons and buttes stand a group of toadstool-shaped mudhills that are outlandish in shape and size, even by southern Utah standards.

The valley where these formations rise was named Mushroom Valley in the late 1920s when it was first discovered by Europeans, but it was later renamed Goblin Valley by folks who thought the mudhills were more reminiscent of goblins than mushrooms. Today, 3,654-acre Goblin Valley State Park includes the best examples of the goblins. Carved out of the cocoa-brown Entrada sandstone, many are capped with a greenish-white Curtis formation of layered clay that gives them a distinctly Halloweenish character.

I like to come to this isolated park when I can walk among the goblins, spires and balanced rocks in the moonlight. At those times, the otherworldly setting gains an added dimension of light and shadows that is truly unique.

To the northwest of the state park is the San Rafael Swell area where you can explore a region with deep canyons amidst landscapes of red rock and red sand that could easily fit on Mars.

For those who like to mountain bike, the Temple Mountain Bike Trail leads along old mining roads, crosses ridges, and follows along wash bottoms to the north of the state park. The bike trail follows old jeep trails that were first used by uranium miners who explored the region in the 1940s. Most of the ore used to produce uranium for the Manhattan Project in World War II was mined from Temple Mountain. The scars from that period still mar the mountain. Old cabins and junked cars also add to the blight from that period.

You can see these as you bike along over 10 miles of marked trails that begin off Temple Mountain Road about 12 miles to the north of the state park. You reach the trailhead by returning seven miles to the junction of Goblin Valley and Temple Mountain roads. Take a left and continue west along Temple Mountain Road for five miles to the trailhead.

Before heading out into the wild country of the swell where the Temple Mountain Bike Trail is located, you should check with the rangers at the state park or the BLM San Rafael Swell Resource Area Office for complete information about the region.

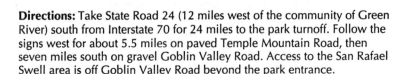

Directions: Take State Road 24 (12 miles west of the community of Green River) south from Interstate 70 for 24 miles to the park turnoff. Follow the signs west for about 5.5 miles on paved Temple Mountain Road, then seven miles south on gravel Goblin Valley Road. Access to the San Rafael Swell area is off Goblin Valley Road beyond the park entrance.

Fee or Free: Goblin Valley State Park has a $3 day-use fee. All other areas are free.

Camping: There is a developed campground in the state park. Primitive camping is allowed on BLM land outside the park.

Lodging: There is a motel or two in Green River and Hanksville, but the best bets are in Moab to the east and in Richfield to the west.

Contact: Goblin Valley State Park, P.O. Box 93, Green River, UT 84525; (801) 564-3633. BLM San Rafael Swell Resource Area, 900 North 700 East, Price, UT 84501; (801) 637-4584.

Arches National Park

North of Moab in southern Utah

The trail to Landscape Arch leads out from the Devil's Garden Campground in Arches National Park. Along it, you pass through slickrock country carved into a 300-foot-thick layer of red sandstone that was deposited over 150 million years ago during the time when dinosaurs roamed the countryside of what is now southern Utah.

Although you won't encounter any of the terrible "thunder lizards" along the trail, you will see seven huge arches that wind and water have carved out of the soft sandstone. In their own way, these arches are as spectacular as the dinosaurs were, and none is more spectacular than Landscape Arch. This thin strip of sandstone is never more than a few feet thick as it spans 291 feet. This is the longest natural arch in the world. As you come upon it, you are sure that the span cannot hold its own weight and will come tumbling down at any moment.

The trail to Landscape Arch is a six-mile loop that, while not strenuous, requires that you always carry extra water. Daytime temperatures regularly reach over 100 degrees during midsummer. As with any other hike into the desert, you must observe common-sense rules about survival.

More than 2,000 arches are located within the park, and you can reach most of them rather easily on short trails. The only trail that poses any problems is the one through the Fiery Furnace, a complicated maze of sandstone cliffs that are separated by dry streambeds. So many people have gotten lost in the maze over the years that you can now take the hike only if accompanied by a ranger.

Most visitors to the park just drive along its 17.5 miles of maintained road, past the trailheads that lead back into the formations. However, it is impossible to truly appreciate these natural wonders without walking among them. To do that, all you have to do is stop at any of the 11 marked trailheads along the road.

The trails vary from easy half-mile strolls to 15-mile treks. Get the park's detailed $2 hiking guide from the visitor center at the entrance and choose the hike that best meets your physical condition.

More adventurous sorts head for the infrequently maintained Salt Valley Road where they can get away from the crowds. Trailheads along this route lead farther away from the improved road into country where you will encounter few other hikers most of the year.

Summer gets extremely hot and winter is bitter cold at Arches, but spring and fall are both pleasant with mild temperatures.

Directions: The entrance to the park is off US 191, 27 miles south of Interstate 70 and five miles north of Moab.

Fee or Free: Day-use costs $4 per vehicle, $2 for hikers and bikers.

Camping: There is a scenic, full-service developed campground in the park.

Lodging: Several motels are in Moab.

Contact: Arches National Park, P.O. Box 907, Moab, UT 84532; (801) 259-8161.

Dead Horse Point State Park & Canyonlands National Park

Near Moab in southern Utah

The drive down US 191 from Interstate 70 passes by the strange landscapes of Arches National Park to the east and the rugged lands that are the eastern drainage of the Green River to the west. The drive through the canyon is bordered by tall cliffs of Wingate sandstone, and as you head up to Island in the Sky Mesa, the road passes by many interesting rock formations in a series of steep switchbacks. There is no doubt that you are in canyonlands here. The colors of the cliffs and formations range from red to pink to brown to white. Most of the lower slopes are dotted with bright green groves of juniper.

As you take State Road 313 west off US 191 about 20 miles south of Interstate 70, you head up Sevenmile Canyon toward Island in the Sky Mesa, where Dead Horse Point State Park provides outstanding vistas over these canyonlands of the Colorado River and its tributaries.

About seven miles from US 191 on State Road 313, steep brown bluffs rise to the right and large alcoves have been carved in their bases. Large, white, tooth-like stains from alkaline deposits create the illusion of white stalactites descending from the top of the alcoves against the dark back walls.

As you continue on the steady but gradual incline along the top of the mesa, you drive through a pygmy forest of juniper and pinyon pine. After a summer rain, the air is pungent with piney scents.

About 15 miles from US 191, the road forks. The right fork continues to Canyonlands National Park's Island in the Sky District and Grandview Point. Stay to the left and continue for another 6.5 miles and you reach Dead Horse Point State Park.

Island in the Sky Mesa rises some 2,000 feet above the Colorado River. The vistas from Dead Horse Point in the park rival those found at the Grand Canyon over 250 miles to the southwest. Far to the east, you see the peaks of the Manti-La Sal Mountains reaching almost 13,000 feet high as you drive out toward the point. Close to the point is a sign on a beautiful old pinyon pine that reads, "Stop, look, and listen. Listen to the sounds of the not-too-distant past. Listen for the thunder of horses' hooves running across the mesa top and the screaming cowboys behind them running in the blinding and choking dust. Look at the flaring nostrils and rippling muscles on the powerful mustangs' legs and sides as they run past you heading for the point."

The sign continues, "So it was during the late 1800s when the cowboys used to herd the wild horses that roamed throughout the area across the narrow neck of land that separates the point form the mainland. The point served as a natural corral. Once the mustangs were on the point, the cowboys fenced it off and captured the horses for their own use. The legend of Dead Horse Point states that a group of horses left stranded on the water-less point died within sight of the Colorado River, 2,000 feet below."

The first time that I visited the park, I watched the

sun descending in the west as I read the sign, and then drove on to the parking area at the point across the narrow neck, not more than 30 yards at its widest.

I didn't know what to expect as I walked up to the rim. What I did see was truly stunning. To the east were the Manti-La Sal Mountains that I had seen on the drive in. Over 50 miles to the south were the Abajo Mountains. All around were over 5,000 square miles of Utah canyonlands.

Towers, mesas and canyons were interrupted by monuments and monoliths of ever-changing hues of pink, red, purple and white as the slanting rays of the setting sun cast dark shadows on the multicolored layers of sandstone sediments from the last 250 million years.

Cutting its way through this jumble was the Colorado itself, 2,000 feet below. It was hard to tell its true color. At spots, the sun's rays reflected pink off the flowing water. In the shadows, it was a dark brown. Whatever the color, the legacy of the Colorado was spread out below me in the shear cliffs and deep canyons that had been carved by the river over millions of years as the area was constantly uplifted by geological movement far beneath the surface.

I had the point all to myself that evening, and I sat, still and focused on the vista below, until the dying sun was beneath the horizon and the chill of the desert night drove me back to camp. The only thing missing was a full moon rising in the east that would have shone its cold, white light on the cliffs that only moments before had been lit by the hot sun.

I am still planning to make the trip, to see the canyon when that moon rises full and completes the show of light and colors.

The next day, continuing my journey to Canyonlands National Park, I found that I could only explore the edges of this wild and wonderfully rugged park. No roads lead into the over 525 square miles of the park, where you'll find some of the most isolated land in southern Utah. To truly explore this region, you must backpack miles through the rugged gorges and canyons or raft through them on the rivers. The Green and Colorado rivers divide the Canyonlands National Park into four distinct "districts" that are geologically similar but isolated from one another by the tortured topography of the region.

One district is the Island in the Sky, and it is accessible from Dead Horse Point State Park. Much of the park can be seen from Grandview Point, and the strenuous White Rim Trail leads to remote arches and interesting side canyons. For the less hardy, there are short hikes to places such as Mesa Arch, Upheaval Dome and Whale Rock, a giant rock shaped like a whale.

Upheaval Dome is a real geological mystery. The three-mile-long, 1,200-foot-deep crater may have been caused by a meteorite, but no one knows for certain. An eight-mile trail leads all the way around the crater. Take it and see if you can form your own guess as to the crater's origin.

The cliff at Mesa Rock drops down, down and down to a canyon floor so far below that you almost feel as though you were standing on the edge of eternity.

To really know Canyonlands, you have to hike, and hike, and hike some more. The wild, tortuous canyons are accessible only by foot. As you hike through them, you gradually begin to identify with the sense of timelessness present all around you.

Directions: Take US 191 south from Interstate 70 for 20 miles and head west on State Road 313 to both the state and national parks.

Fee or Free: Day-use at Dead Horse Point State Park costs $3 per vehicle. Canyonlands charges $4 per vehicle for day-use.

Camping: Camping at Dead Horse Point State Park costs $7 per night; for reservations call (800) 322-3770. Needles Campground in Canyonlands costs $6 per night, first-come, first-served. Primitive camping is allowed outside on BLM lands that surround the park.

Lodging: The nearest lodging is in Moab.

Contact: Dead Horse Point State Park, P.O. Box 609, Moab, UT 84532; (801) 259-2614. Canyonlands National Park, 2282 "S" West Resource Boulevard, Moab, UT 84532-8000; (801) 259-7164.

Southern California Deserts

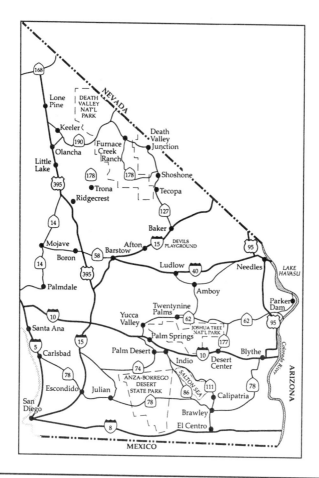

Introduction to Southern California Deserts

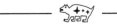

The California desert has become an increasingly publicized region in the past decade as conservationists and others squared off over the need for protective legislation. The conservationists have won. Large chunks of the Mojave Desert are now protected by federal legislation, and the national park system includes three new, large units, Death Valley National Park, East Mojave National Park and Joshua Tree National Park.

Joshua Tree and Death Valley were previously national monuments, and East Mojave was a national recreation area. Under the new legislation, all three have been enlarged as well as renamed.

Although the names and boundaries of these units have been changed, new regulations concerning land use in the expanded parks have yet to be published as of press time. Whether campers still will be allowed at undeveloped camping sites such as Darwin Falls and Eureka Dunes in the Death Valley region, as they were when the land was under the jurisdiction of the BLM, remains to be seen.

With that in mind, I have included the old contact agencies and numbers for all sites that were outside the previous monuments. Contact them for up-to-date information about new land-use rules. You can also contact the California Desert Information Center, 831 Barstow Road, Barstow, CA 92311; (619) 256-8313.

Chapter 11

Southern California Deserts

Map 30

Map 30

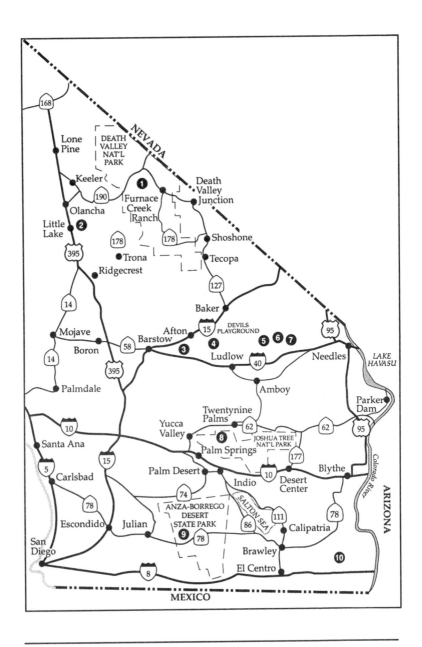

Southern California Deserts (map on page 404)

Darwin Falls & Death Valley National Park

East of Lone Pine along the Nevada border

Scotty's Castle, Furnace Creek, Stovepipe Wells, Zabriskie Point and Dante's View are all famous sites in Death Valley, but what about Darwin Falls, Wildrose Peak and Mahogany Flat? Never heard of them? If you haven't, you have missed some of the best sites in Death Valley. Not that the standard, popular sites aren't worth the visit, but there is more to the park than most people ever see.

Waterfalls and Death Valley aren't normally thought of together. I visited the monument numerous times over a quarter century and had never even heard of Darwin Falls until a geologist friend of mine mentioned it as a place to camp before my last visit.

"It's a great spot," he said. "You go down a dirt road about half a mile to this locked gate. Then you hike about another half mile to these great falls."

Well, he was right about the falls being great. He wasn't right about his directions. The half mile to the gate turned into almost three miles. The dirt road turned into a boulder-filled, marginally graded road that the Bureau of Land Management had deemed "For Four-Wheeled Vehicles Only." (Formerly, the falls were on land administered by the BLM, but they will be inside the new national park boundaries.) Considering that my twelve-year-old son Kevin and I were in our family mini-van pulling a tent trailer, the trek along the road to the locked gates seemed like an eternity.

Kevin was sure that we would never make it and would be stuck forever to suffer in Death Valley heat. It had reached the 100-degree mark that day, and the canyon walls seemed to close in on us as we went farther along the dry Darwin Creek that runs down the middle of the canyon.

He really had nothing to fear. Although it has its spots, you can pass over the road in most family cars. If you treasure your vehicle and keep it in pristine condition, however, you may want to avoid the trek. You would be missing a desert wonder, though.

When we finally reached the locked gates, there were several other vehicles in the level area where people appeared to camp, but there was no sign of water in the dry creek. I couldn't imagine that we were less than half a mile from falls of any sort, although my friend Terry had assured me they flowed year-round. There wasn't even any vegetation to speak of in the creek bed, which would at least have indicated an underground stream.

I put my trust in Terry's knowledge, though, and began a hike up the creekbed past the gates. We soon met several people who said, "Yes, there are falls, and they are great." They couldn't really give us an estimate of distance, but they did say we couldn't miss them, since this was a box canyon with the falls at the end.

Soon a wet strip of sand appeared in the creekbed, accompanied by vegetation. The vegetation got thicker and the sand got wetter. Before we were really aware of it, the wet sand became a small stream. Within a half mile, we were walking alongside a small but unmistakable creek. Within three-quarters of a mile, we reached a spot where the stream was flowing over an outcropping of rock, but this 18-inch waterfall couldn't be what we were looking for, could it?

No. There was a visitor booklet near the small falls, and the comments in it indicated the falls were still farther. Some people seemed not to have found them by their comments, while others extolled their beauty.

And beautiful they were. In the midst of the desert stood the falls, dropping over granite cliffs for about 30 feet to a pond covered with duckweed and surrounded by lush growth. The mile-long hike was worth it. And the hike back to the van seemed much shorter.

And the full moon, clear air and quiet evening walk along the road made the day a full and fruitful one. The moon was so bright that there was no need for a flashlight of any sort. The hills to the east of the canyon cast full shadows on the western slopes.

A more familiar outing for me is within the monument. When people think of Death Valley, few think of high mountains, yet Telescope Peak on the western side of the valley rises to 11,049 feet. The views from the peak take in Mount Whitney to the west, the highest point in the contiguous United States, and Badwater to the east, the lowest point. A seven-mile trail from Mahogany Flat passes through woods and brushy terrain to reach the summit, and is open only from April to October.

For those who aren't up to such a strenuous hike, a drive into Mahogany Flat may suffice. This is the highest point within the monument that can be reached by automobile at 8,133 feet. Two campgrounds at the end of the road are open from April to October, and a shorter trail near them leads to the top of Wildrose Peak at 9,064 feet.

One exciting feature of Mahogany Flat, as well as of Wildrose Campground nine miles farther west, is the braying of wild donkeys, which roam the mountainsides in small herds. These noisy animals are thought to be a nuisance by some, and when the herds get too large, some are captured and sold.

Personally, I enjoy their vocal antics when I camp at Mahogany or Wildrose, and feel that any animal that can survive in the harsh climate of Death Valley should be considered a part of the natural ecosystem.

Wildrose Campground is open year-round, but winter camping can be bracing at the high altitude.

Directions: Darwin Falls is about 47 miles east of Lone Pine on Highway 190 and one mile west of Panamint Springs. The dirt road leading to the falls is marked as you head west from Panamint Springs, but is unmarked as you head east from Lone Pine. Turn south on the dirt road and continue for just under three miles to the locked gates. You come to a fork in the road at about 2.5 miles. Take the less-maintained fork to the right and continue to the gates.

The road to Mahogany Flat is 18 miles east of Panamint Springs and six miles east of Stovepipe Wells. Turn south on Emigrant Canyon Road and continue for about 21 miles to the junction with Wildrose Canyon Road. Turn east and follow the signs for Wildrose Campground, which are on the left after about one-half mile. Continue nine miles to Mahogany Flat.

Fee or Free: Darwin Falls is a free area, but Death Valley National Park has a $5 entrance fee per car. Camping fees range from $6-$10.

Camping: Camping is allowed at present, but this may change—check with the park before heading out. There are several developed campgrounds in the park, and primitive camping is allowed on BLM land outside the park boundaries. All campsites are first come, first served, except for those at Furnace Creek Campground; for reservations, phone (800) 365-2267.

Lodging: There are several lodges in the park, including the expensive and luxurious Furnace Creek Inn. You must have reservations during the peak winter and spring seasons.

Contact: Death Valley National Park, Death Valley, CA 92328; (619) 786-2331. BLM Ridgecrest Resource Area, 300 South Richmond Road, Ridgecrest, CA 93555; (619) 375-7125.

❷

Fossil Falls

East of Death Valley, along US 395

US 395 cuts through a large volcanic field as it slices a straight path through the upper end of the Mojave Desert between Lone Pine and the junction with State Road 14, about 65 miles to the south. This route leads through one of the most desolate sections of California, and I am always on the lookout for interesting sidetrips as I reach the stretch of US 395 below Mount Whitney.

I had driven the route dozens of times when I noticed a sign to "Fossil Falls," which I had never seen before. On a whim, I took the turnoff, figuring that even if the falls were a bust, I could explore around in the volcanic field. If nothing else, I could climb the red cinder cone that stood beside the highway at the turnoff.

Fields of wildflowers on the slopes to the west of the highway filled my rearview mirror with blue, white and gold. Black-lava boulders rose from the patches of color, and added a harsh, rugged note to let me know that, although the slopes might nurture the wildflowers that softened the vistas in the distance, they were still inhospitable to any who might enter unprepared.

A look out the front windshield left no doubt about that. Cliffs of columnar basalt, cinder cones and stove-black lava flows dominated the region. I followed the signs through several turns as I crept along the road, con-

---

stantly looking for signs of water that would feed the falls, but not finding any.

As I pulled into the parking area, I did see the opening of a large gorge, but I neither heard sounds of the falls nor saw any water. It was only when I reached the end of the short, quarter-mile trail to the falls that I realized what their name truly meant. They were "fossil" falls—falls 60 to 80 feet high that had not flowed for thousands of years, but whose smooth path through the rugged lava flow had been fossilized as the river dried up.

As I walked along the lip of the gorge, I came upon a second set of falls, which dropped 20 to 30 feet on a smooth course. While I had the urge to slide down, I knew that even with water it would have been somewhat risky, and without water it would have been extremely so.

From the falls, I hiked around the lava field before deciding to set up camp farther along the dirt road on BLM land. The Easter full moon rose over the field to the east as I set up camp, and the coyotes were in full song that night as I closed my eyes to the otherwise quiet desert.

Directions: Approximately three miles north of the ruins of a hotel and gas station at Little Lake, turn east on Cinder Cone Road at Red Mountain. After about a half mile, turn south on a dirt powerline road and go just over a quarter mile to another road heading east. Take this road about a half mile to the parking area. The trail, poorly marked with splotches of paint, leaves from the rear of the parking area.

Fee or Free: This is a free area.

Camping: Primitive camping is allowed on BLM land. There are developed forest service campgrounds to the west of US 395 to the north.

Lodging: There are motels in Lone Pine to the north and Ridgecrest to the south.

Contact: BLM Ridgecrest Resource Area, 300 South Richmond Road, Ridgecrest, CA 93555; (619) 375-7125.

3

Afton Canyon

In the East Mojave Natural Area

Flowing water is unusual in the Mojave Desert except after the occasional summer thunderstorm when flash floods roar through canyons. In fact, one of the few places in the region where you can see flowing water year-round is in Afton Canyon. Here, the Mojave River runs above ground for about a dozen miles.

The Mojave River begins in the San Bernardino Mountains near Lake Arrowhead and flows east toward Soda Dry Lake near Baker. Most of its route is underground, but where it surfaces, there are trees, grasses, abundant wildlife and plenty of people. This is certainly true of Afton Canyon.

The canyon is one of the most accessible oases in the eastern Mojave Desert, and its harsh beauty attracts city dwellers on weekends when the campground is wall-to-wall campers. In the past, most visitors came with off-road vehicles with which they tore up the surrounding desert—the scarred hills nearby attest to this practice. The BLM banned this activity several years ago, however, when the region was first considered for national park status.

As you drive south from Interstate 15, you cross a basin that was once part of a 200-square-mile freshwater lake. If you look carefully, you can see the old shoreline of the lake.

The narrow, corridor-like canyon was no stranger to pioneers, as many historic figures, including Jedediah Smith, Kit Carson and John C. Fremont, traveled through it on their way west. William Adams Vale wrote in his journal, "I walked down the canyon looking at caves and deep gorges in the mountains...Oh! What a country—there is some grand scenery in Cave Canyon."

While its name has changed from Cave Canyon to Afton Canyon, its scenery has remained unchanged. Sheer cliffs rise as much as 600 feet above the river floor, and greenery that is out of place in this arid desert grows along the riverside. The steady water supply and abundance of green plants also attract migratory birds, which stop over on their way south in the fall. You can also see herons, egrets and ibises along the stream, where they hunt for frogs and minnows year-round.

If you make your trip during midweek in the spring, you can hike in solitude among fields of wildflowers and explore side canyons. Pyramid Canyon is the largest of these, and you reach it by crossing the river under the first set of railroad trestles just south of the campground. The water-carved cliffs of the two-mile-long canyon are home to golden eagles and red-tailed hawks, which can be seen soaring overhead.

Afton Canyon itself is eight miles long, and hiking along its floor is easy, although there are no real trails in either it or the side canyons. Although I have never explored it, I have been told that at a culvert marked 194.65 there is a cave-canyon that has many fascinating twists and turns as it winds its way up a very narrow side canyon. You need a flashlight to navigate the cave, and few people make it to the end because of its many turns.

In addition to the large crowds on weekends and prime camping periods, there is one other major intrusion into the desert quiet and solitude—trains. A much-used railroad track runs down the center of the canyon and it is busy day and night. If you're like me, however, you may get to like the intrusion. The first time a train came through it seemed distracting, but I soon looked forward to hearing the lonely, high tone of the whistle as the train signaled its approach.

Directions: Take Interstate 15 east from Barstow for 33 miles to the Afton exit. Follow a good dirt road southwest for three miles to the Afton Campground.

Fee or Free: This has been a free area, but this is subject to change.

Camping: There is a developed campground at the Mojave River. Primitive camping is allowed on BLM land away from the canyon.

Lodging: There is plenty of lodging in Barstow.

Contact: BLM Barstow Resource Area, 150 Coolwater Lane, Barstow, CA 92311; (619) 255-8700.

④

Cima Dome & Cinder Cone National Natural Landmark

In the East Mojave Natural Area

I pulled over to look for what I had been told was the world's largest, tallest and densest Joshua tree forest, but I couldn't find the dome that I was supposed to use as a reference point. It was only after taking another look at the topographic map that I realized what locals had long known—Cima Dome is something you drive on, not to.

This almost perfectly symmetrical dome is a geological rarity. Not only is it the most symmetrical dome formation in the U.S., it also covers 75 square miles and rises over 1,500 feet above the surrounding desert. It is only from afar, such as from the Mid-Hills Campground to the west, that you can get a good look at the gently sloping formation.

My reason for driving to the top of the dome was not just to see the Joshua trees. The dense forest and natural springs of the region attract a large number of bird species. These include two extremely rare birds that I hoped to find, Bendire's thrasher and the gilded common flicker. Bendire's thrasher is found in only a few other places in Southern California, while the gilded common flicker inhabits only one other spot, Clark Mountain, about 15 miles north of Cima Dome.

While I wasn't successful in my bird search, I had not wasted my time. Not only did I enjoy hiking among the Joshua trees, but also from the top of the dome I could see for miles across the surrounding desert. Almost due west were the 32 cinder cones of the 25,600-acre Cinder Cone National Natural Landmark. Remnants of the once-active volcanic field of the East Mojave, they are said to be denser than any other rocks on Earth. Geologists from the world over come to the field to study them.

I knew that Cow Cove, an outstanding petroglyph site, lay to the north of the cinder cones and Aiken Wash, my destination for the night, to the south. The view from Cima Dome gave me an opportunity to scout out my route to see what lay ahead.

Although I couldn't see the wash itself from the dome, my campsite turned out to be one of the most scenic areas in the East Mojave Desert. Willow trees, which thrive in the wash along with some Joshua trees and Mojave yucca, provided a little shaded relief from the 100-plus-degree temperature as I set up camp. You couldn't call it cool, however, as the solid black wall of basalt rock along the wash seemed to radiate extra heat.

Although the heat was enervating, it had the advantage of keeping others out of the desert. As night fell, I discovered that I had no neighbors beside the dry streambed.

The sinking sun washed the black and red cinder cones that were visible from the campsite with a red glow. With just a wee bit of imagination, I could see the cones glowing from volcanic activity, although even the youngest of the cones were over 1,000 years old. The oldest had not been active for over 10 million years.

As the night air began to cool, I knew that the heat

would not be bothering me the next day. I was headed into the cinder cone area where I would spend the day underground in a lava tube.

My last memory of the night was watching the dark silhouette of a giant Joshua tree above the wall of the wash as it stood like a sentinel against the milky stream of stars stretching across the night sky.

I wandered around the cinder cones the next day, searching for the great hole in the earth that was the entrance to the lava tube. Finding it was no easy task as the landmarks in this rugged area were quite confusing. (Be sure to check with the BLM ranger for specific instructions before heading out.)

The effort of locating the entrance was well worth it, though, for a day underground in the midst of midsummer in the Mojave Desert was a unique experience. Nothing was disappointing, from the climb down a rickety ladder to reach the floor of the tube, to having to flatten out on the floor of the tube and squeeze through a small opening to enter the large cave.

The lava tube is a fascinating place that was formed as fast-flowing lava cooled quicker on its surface than below. The tunnel formed as the lava continued to flow beneath the surface, leaving a cave-like formation with plenty of nooks and crannies to explore.

Inside the cave, beams of light broke the total darkness of the tube. These came from above, through openings in the lava ceiling, and flooded areas of the cave floor in bright light.

As I entered one recess, several bats awoke and flitted by. I don't know who was startled more—me or them. I also saw owl pellets scattered on the floor beneath several ledges, although I saw no owls.

I spent a good part of two hours exploring the nooks and crannies before returning to the heat of midsummer at the surface.

Note: If you plan to head into this area, it is strongly recommended that you talk to a ranger beforehand for up-to-date information on roads and directions.

Directions: Take Interstate 15 east from Barstow for 89 miles to the Cima Road exit at Valley Wells. Follow Cima Road for just under six miles, then turn due south on a dirt road leading to Valley View Ranch. The ranch is about 3.2 miles south, and as you near it, take the road to the left toward Deer Springs. If you find yourself at the main ranch house rather than passing by a windmill, you have gone too far. Continue past the windmill for about three miles to a cattle fence. Park there and hike around on the dome. Use a BLM road map to head for Aiken Wash and the Cinder Cone National Natural Landmark.

Fee or Free: This has been a free area, but it may have a fee with the new national park status.

Camping: Primitive camping has been allowed under BLM jurisdiction, but this area is to be included in the new national park, which may result in camping restrictions.

Lodging: There are plenty of motels in Barstow to the west and some in Baker to the east.

Contact: BLM Needles Resource Area, 101 West Spikes Road, Needles, CA 92363; (619) 326-3896. As the park is developed, it will fall under the jurisdiction of the Joshua Tree National Park. Contact them at 74485 National Monument Drive, Twentynine Palms, CA 92277-3597; (619) 367-7511.

5

Kelso Dunes

In the East Mojave Natural Area

As the sun disappeared in the west, the wind slowly exerted itself, blowing cool air over the warm sand. Then the sounds began.

They were low at first, not much more than a hint of a hum. Then, as the polished grains of rose quartz soaked up the low rays of the setting sun and glowed a dark pink that turned to a deep purple, the sounds grew louder. Not so loud that my son and I could really describe them, but loud enough that we knew they were not just our imagination. Finally, we knew that we were truly hearing the low vibrational sounds that make the Kelso Dunes famous as "booming dunes."

Everywhere these types of dunes are found in the world, whether in Egypt, Libya or Kelso, their sounds become part of the local folklore, and I can understand why. The sounds aren't something you hear every day in nature. In fact, they definitely have an unnatural quality to them that humans have long tried to define.

A part of the folklore at Kelso Dunes is that long ago a teamster started off across the dunes with a load of whiskey for the saloons in Kelso, but he had to abandon his wagon in the midst of a severe sandstorm. When he returned to recover his property, he could not locate it. It had been buried beneath the shifting dunes during the storm.

The story has it that he and his friends continued to search until their dying days, and the low, rumbling sounds you hear from the dunes on cold, clear nights are the celebration by their ghosts reveling in their discovery of the precious cargo.

I don't know about the ghosts, but low, rumbling sounds do emanate from the dunes as the polished grains of sand slide over the underlying surfaces, and they make for a soothing musical background against which to fall asleep. This is especially true on a night when the full moon rises high overhead to cast a cool light over some of the highest dunes in the United States.

Among the dunes in this 45-square-mile formation, some rise as much as 700 feet above the surrounding desert. The 1.5-mile trek from the designated parking area to the top of the dunes involves plenty of two-steps-forward, one-step-back hiking. With this in mind, we set out early the next morning as the rising sun brought a rose-colored glow to the dunes.

We headed north and watched for signs of animal activity that had occurred overnight. Beneath a bunch of tall grass, where the tips had scribed a circular pattern as they were blown by the winds that prevail in the area, we spotted the trail of a lizard and the tiny tracks of a kangaroo rat before we began our steady ascent into the dunes.

We had hoped to roust a sidewinder as we hiked along, but the best we could do was spot the sinuous route where one had crossed not long before.

By the time we reached the top, we found ourselves sinking to our knees into the soft sand. And we hadn't even attempted a frontal assault; we had hiked to a small saddle and then walked along the ridge to the highest dune. It had been obvious from the start that a frontal assault would have been near impossible.

As we ate lunch and prepared for a rapid descent, we had a 360-degree view of four different desert mountain ranges. Occasionally, one of us would shove a foot through the sand toward the lee side of the dunes, then watch the particles cascade down the steep slope and listen to the gathering rumble as the moving sand gained speed.

That rumble was nothing, however, compared to what we set off as we scampered down the steep slope after lunch. Every small avalanche was followed by one of the loud booms for which the dunes are famous.

Directions: Take Kelbaker Road south from the town of Baker on Interstate 15 for 34.5 miles to the community of Kelso. Continue past Kelso for another 7.2 miles to a signed dirt road leading west to the main part of the dunes. The parking area is three miles along this dirt road.

Fee or Free: This has been a free area, but it may have a fee with the new national park status.

Camping: Primitive camping has been allowed under BLM jurisdiction, but this area is to be included in the new national park, which may result in camping restrictions.

Lodging: The closest lodging is in Baker.

Contact: BLM Needles Resource Area, 101 West Spikes Road, Needles, CA 92363; (619) 326-3896. As the park is developed, it will fall under the jurisdiction of the Joshua Tree National Park. Contact them at 74485 National Monument Drive, Twentynine Palms, CA 92277-3597; (619) 367-7511.

Providence Mountains State Recreation Area

In the East Mojave Natural Area

In the Providence Mountains, volcanic formations are intermixed with limestone peaks, and it is among these mountains that I discovered Mitchell Caverns. Of course, the caverns themselves had been discovered many years before I found them (the Chemehuevis Indians used the caves for over 500 years before the first Europeans discovered them), but to me they were a wonderful surprise. I had been driving around the East Mojave Desert looking for new sights when I encountered the signs to the caverns and the surrounding Providence Mountains State Recreation Area.

The tour of the caverns themselves is really nothing spectacular, but it is certainly a relief from the stark landscape above ground. Rangers lead groups along paths with electric lights, railings and stairs to formations common to limestone caves. These include stalactites and stalagmites, flowstone, cave shields and cave ribbons in the two major chambers. It's not exactly what one expects to find in the midst of the Mojave Desert, but not all that unusual in limestone caverns. Nevertheless, finding a cool cavern to walk through during the midday heat in the East Mojave is a pleasure in itself.

If you want something a little more unique, you can arrange for some serious spelunking in Winding Stair Cave where the modern contrivances of electricity and paved paths have not taken away the excitement of underground exploration. Even without the modern conveniences, novices can still enjoy exploring this small cave without fear of becoming lost or trapped. Ask park rangers for useful instructions on how to enter and explore the cave.

The Providence Mountains State Recreation Area is small by desert standards at 6,000 acres, but there is a small campground near the caverns, as well as a self-guided nature trail and the mile-long Crystal Springs Canyon Trail, which takes you up into the pinyon pine and juniper groves of the higher elevations of the Providence Mountains. From there, you can see several 7,000-foot peaks, as well as sand dunes, buttes, mesas and wide-open desert valleys.

For those who want a solid introduction to desert camping, but don't want to get too primitive, this is a great getaway. And after you have stepped on a cactus or two and found yourself saying, "Yeah, I like desert travel," head just up the road to the next getaway, Wild Horse Canyon.

Directions: Head east on Interstate 40 from Barstow for 80 miles to the Essex Road exit. Continue northwest on Essex Road for 16 miles to the state recreation area.

Fee or Free: Cavern tours are $4 for adults, $2 for children. Most camping is free, except for the sites at the state recreation area, which are $12 per night.

Camping: There is a small campground at the recreation area. Primitive camping is allowed on BLM land outside the recreation area. There are two BLM campgrounds on Wild Horse Canyon Road to the north.

Lodging: There is plenty of lodging in Barstow.

Contact: Providence Mountains State Recreation Area, P.O. Box 1, Essex, CA 92332; there is no phone. BLM California Desert District Office, 6221 Box Springs Boulevard, Riverside, CA 92507; (909) 697-5217. California Desert Information Center, 831 Barstow Road, Barstow, CA 92311; (619) 256-8313.

7

Wild Horse Canyon Area

In the East Mojave Natural Area

I first visited the Providence Mountains in search of Mitchell Caverns, but my discovery of two outstanding campgrounds and a backcountry road in the Wild Horse Canyon Area, which happened to be the Department of Interior's first official Back Country Byway, proved to be the highlight of the trip.

Backtracking about five miles from Mitchell Caverns to the junction with Black Canyon Road, I headed north across wide-open country, past batches of fuzzy cholla cacti along the side of the road. The Providence Mountains rose to the west, and to the east was the distinctive and aptly named Table Mountain.

This is true Wild West country. One can easily conjure up visions of cattle searching for food in the barren desert as winds whip tumbleweed across the dry valleys. In the distance, the flat top of Wild Horse Mesa brings Zane Grey to mind—this was the setting for his book *Wild Horse Mesa*.

From a 1,700-foot elevation at Interstate 40, you make a steady climb to about 4,000 feet as you come to the turnoff for Wild Horse Canyon. The vegetation near the turnoff is still primarily cholla cactus, and the land-scape is wide open. It was a maze of volcanic rocks, however, that caught my eye as I entered the campground at Hole-in-the-Wall.

I soon discovered that this was just the beginning of a wondrous range of rocks which lead into Banshee and Wild Horse canyons. Wind and water have eroded the red volcanic rocks that descend from the campground to the canyons below into hundreds of holes and caves.

From the campground, I navigated through a series of passageways down a sloping trail. It was so steep that I had to depend upon iron rings, which were anchored in the rhyolite (a crystallized form of lava), to keep me from slipping and sliding to the bottom at a much faster rate than was healthy for my aging bones.

Once at the bottom, I was in Banshee Canyon. It was not named for the shrieking elves of Scotland, but for the calls of horned owls that intermesh with the sounds of wind whistling through the passageways at night. I hiked to the mouth of the canyon and picked a route northward along a wash. The indistinct trail led to the top of a small mesa. From there, I could see Wild Horse Mesa to the west and rock formations with desert varnish to the east. Farther up the canyon were magnificent stands of cholla, beavertail and barrel cacti interspersed with yucca, whose tall center stalks rose high above all else.

Night was coming as I returned by the same route to set up camp. As I climbed up the passageway, I could see several raptors soaring on the thermals overhead. One appeared to be a golden eagle as it rose higher than all the others to disappear in the evening sky.

Later, I learned that I could have continued up Banshee Canyon to Wild Horse Canyon. It was just as well that I didn't, however, because when I drove to Wild Horse Canyon's mile-high Mid-Hills Campground the next day, I discovered the upper end of a fine eight-mile trail that leads from the higher Mid-Hills Campground back to Hole-in-the-Wall. For a great desert hike, take this trail downhill to Hole-in-the-Wall Campground for a one-way trek.

The drive along Wild Horse Canyon Road, the first officially designated Back Country Byway, leads from the cactus-strewn country near Hole-in-the-Wall upward into sagebrush country, and finally into pinyon pine and juniper woodlands above 5,000 feet.

Scan the rocky, sagebrush-covered slopes as you drive along and you may see desert bighorn sheep or deer browsing in early morning or late evening.

Of all the campgrounds that I have visited in the East Mojave, none has views that can compare with Mid-Hills. North from the campground, the *café-au-lait*-colored Pinto Mountains rise from the desert floor. To the west, you see the rolling Kelso Dunes. Between the two, and visible from the north end of the campground, is the best view anywhere of Cima Dome, a 75-square-mile volcanic formation.

This getaway is one of the few in the East Mojave where you can feel comfortable during midday even in the summertime, for temperatures at the high elevation seldom reach above 90 degrees, and nights are pleasant. In winter, snow frequently blankets the hills, and cold winds drive all but the most hardy into sheltered hide-aways.

Directions: Head east on Interstate 40 from Barstow for 80 miles to the Essex Road exit. Continue northwest on Essex Road for 10 miles to the junction with Black Canyon Road. Take a right at the junction and continue another 10 miles to Hole-in-the-Wall and Wild Horse Canyon Road.

Fee or Free: This is a free area.

Camping: There are two BLM campgrounds on Wild Horse Canyon Road at Hole-in-the-Wall and Mid-Hills.

Lodging: There is plenty of lodging in Barstow.

Contact: BLM California Desert District Office, 6221 Box Springs Boulevard, Riverside, CA 92507; (909) 697-5217. California Desert Information Center, 831 Barstow Road, Barstow, CA 92311; (619) 256-8313.

8

Joshua Tree National Park

In the Mojave Desert

Joshua Tree National Park is a wild and undisciplined place where nature rules, as my family discovered on a recent visit. As a news report said later, "The very active San Andreas Fault runs near the southwest boundary of Joshua Tree, making the whole area somewhat unstable and creating numbers of smaller faults."

Reminding us of just how unstable some of those smaller faults could be, we awoke to a rumbling and shaking one morning during our spring vacation. While the quake tore buildings apart in nearby Yucca Valley, it did little damage in the campground where we were sleeping. Still, the fear of crashing rocks got us moving quickly as we skittered to open ground away from the jumble of boulders that rose above our campsite. What was scenic the previous evening as we set up camp was now threatening.

This temblor did little to change the landscape in the park, but the granite extrusions, steep peaks with exposed slopes of convoluted strata, and oases where water rises through the fault lines from underground aquifers all resulted from previous, more violent, geologic activity. This arid land is where the Colorado and Mojave deserts meet, resulting in the wonderfully varied desert vegetation that grows here. All of these features make Joshua Tree a special place to visit.

The region was long considered so inhospitable that only a small gold strike in 1873 brought any early settlers. These soon left, and the Chemehuevis Indians who lived and prospered in the desert must have thought that those were the last of the invaders. In the 1880s, another strike in the Dale District brought more prospectors, however, and by the end of the first decade of this century both the Native Americans and pronghorn that roamed the region were gone.

Today, what some have called "the ugliest trees ever" grow in profusion along the flat lands and slopes of the higher elevations of the park. These "ugly" plants are Joshua trees, the largest members of the lily family. They grow to 15 to 20 feet high, with arms that extend from the central trunk. All are covered with sharp leaves that give them a shaggy appearance. From a distance, the plants appear to be old men waving their arms. Early explorers named the tree "Joshua" because they imagined it resembled the biblical figure Joshua.

The trees are set among vast jumbles of rock which rise above them. Rock climbers come to the park in large numbers to scale the vertical faces of the larger boulders, and hikers head across open desert country along well-marked trails to explore the backcountry.

The Joshua trees slowly thin out as you head toward the lower elevations in the southern portion of the park. There, you enter the Colorado Desert with its large variety of cacti.

Most visitors head for the park between fall and spring, but the park is pleasant even in midsummer when the higher elevations moderate the intense summer heat.

Spring is the most crowded time to visit the region, because this is prime spring wildflower country. The many varieties of cacti burst into bloom throughout April and May, and some even into June. The Joshua trees turn white with blooms before forming large green seed pods. Patches of blue, red, gold and yellow rise from the dry ground after the spring rains, providing color which is absent from the region most of the year.

This park is so large, and there is such great variety in the landscapes, that a visit to one of the three visitor centers is almost a necessity if you want to get the most out of your visit.

While at the visitor centers, get information about the trails that lead into the rugged mountains away from the paved roads. If you don't have time to explore the backcountry, at least follow one or more of the nine self-guided interpretive trails that begin along the park roads and lead for up to a mile into cactus gardens and along washes.

Directions: From Los Angeles, follow Interstate 10 east to State Road 62. Head north on State Road 62 to Yucca Valley and Twentynine Palms. There are park entrances from both of these towns.

Fee or Free: There is a $5 per vehicle entrance fee. Most campgrounds are free, except Black Rock ($10 per night) and Cottonwood ($8 per night); for reservations (for Black Rock only), call (800) 365-2267.

Camping: There are nine developed campgrounds in the park. Only one has water.

Lodging: There is lodging in Yucca Valley, Twentynine Palms, Palm Springs and Indio.

Contact: Joshua Tree National Park, 74485 National Monument Drive, Twentynine Palms, CA 92277-3597; (619) 367-7511.

9

Anza-Borrego Desert State Park

In the Colorado Desert

California has an extensive state park system with dozens of parks, yet almost half of all the land in the system can be found in one large park in San Diego and Imperial counties. Anza-Borrego Desert State Park covers over a half-million acres of harshly eroded, barren, gullied badlands broken by tall, pine-covered mountains with shaded trails. Here, you'll find scattered springs and oozing cienegas where wildlife congregates among the lush vegetation.

The region is untamed and almost as wild as it was when the first Spaniards visited, but during April and May, the rugged desert land softens with the bloom of dozens of species of wildflowers.

Visitors do flock here in spring, but the park allows primitive camping anywhere in the vast park. That means you can set up camp far from the nearest person and enjoy in solitude the desert sunsets and fragrant smell of sage. No matter where you camp you'll discover that this desert isn't silent. Almost year-round, the dark of night is accompanied by the constant chatter of cicadas and other desert insects.

Dirt roads lead into backcountry canyons where you may get lucky and spot desert bighorn sheep or a golden eagle's nest.

This park is so large and undeveloped that I always stop at the park headquarters to pick up an updated map and talk with the rangers about where to go. The visitor center is located at Borrego Palm Canyon, along with the most developed campground in the park and many conveniences, including a grocery store, gas station and laundromat.

First-time visitors should make the three-mile round-trip hike on the Borrego Palm Canyon Trail. It heads from the campground to a spring-fed pool surrounded by tall stands of green palms. Those who want to stretch their legs a bit more can head for the campground at Bow Willow Creek. From there, you can take a six-mile round-trip hike up into a rugged canyon to the pygmy grove of palms on the Mountain Palm Springs Trail.

Directions: Heading east from Julian, take State Road 78 to the middle of the park. County roads S2, S3 and S22 all cross the park. State Road 78 and County Road S22 also enter the park from State Road 86 to the east.

Fee or Free: Park entry is free. Camping costs $9 to $14, except for primitive camping, which is free.

Camping: There are several semi-developed campgrounds and there is primitive camping throughout the park.

Lodging: Some lodging is available in Borrego Springs, but the best bets are to the west toward San Diego and Escondido.

Contact: Anza-Borrego Desert State Park, P.O. Box 428, Borrego Springs, CA 92004; (619) 767-5311.

Algondones Dunes

Near the Arizona border

The Algondones Dunes come in all shapes and sizes. Some are transverse, while some are longitudinal. Some are star dunes, while others are crescent-shaped dunes. Some are migrating dunes, while others are at least partially stabilized by vegetation. Some dunes are just small humps. Others rise 200 to 300 feet above the surrounding desert.

Given that Algondones is one of the largest dune systems in the country, this diversity isn't surprising, nor is the controversy that surrounds its future. Interstate 8 from Yuma to San Diego crosses the southern portion of the dunes, and the slopes there are constantly barraged with the sounds of off-road vehicles. This activity is anathema to conservationists who wish to see the dunes preserved in their natural state for all to enjoy without fear of being crushed by an airborne dune buggy.

The BLM has attempted to conciliate between the opposing parties, and has declared portions of the northern end of the 40-mile-long dunes above State Road 78 a wilderness area where motor vehicles are prohibited. This is where you should head for hikes across virgin dunes.

If you just want to spend some time climbing around dunes and sliding down their steep faces, the rest stop and campground off Interstate 8, about 15 miles west of Yuma, is a good spot.

I prefer to head north of State Road 78 and camp along the edges of the dunes on BLM land, heading in for day-hikes. On windy days, the sand blows off the ridges in wisps that soften the stark landscape. After a particularly strong storm, the rounded dunes extending for miles around look so pristine that you can imagine no one has ever set foot on them before.

Directions: Take State Road 78 east from Brawley for about 20 miles to the dunes.

Fee or Free: This is a free area.

Camping: Primitive camping is allowed on BLM land.

Lodging: The closest motels are in Brawley and El Centro.

Contact: BLM El Centro Resource Area, 1661 South Fourth Street, El Centro, CA 92243; (619) 337-4400.

INDEX

Index

Appendices

Hot Air Ballooning

The Southwest became a center for ballooning because of its predictable early morning wind patterns, excellent climate, and wide-open country. From Albuquerque to Farmington to Reno, balloon enthusiasts gather together at balloon festivals each year to celebrate this growing sport.

You can enjoy the sport yourself throughout the year, even when the festivals are not being held. Dozens of companies offer balloon rides to the public almost year-round, and these give you a chance to experience soundless flights above endless country where the views cover open expanses of desert, meandering green rivers, and majestic, snow-capped mountains.

Balloon Festivals

Albuquerque International
Balloon Fiesta
3300 Princeton Northeast
Albuquerque, NM 87107
(505) 821-1000

Coalville Balloon Festival
c/o Park City Chamber/Bureau
P.O. Box 1630
Park City, UT 84060
(801) 649-6100

Four Corners Hot-Air Balloon Rally
c/o Farmington Visitors Bureau
203 Main Street
Farmington, NM 87401
(505) 326-7602 or (800) 448-1240

Great Reno Balloon Race
c/o Reno/Sparks Visitors Authority
P.O. Box 837
Reno, NV 89504
(800) FOR-RENO

Balloon Trip Companies

Santa Fe Detours
100 E. San Francisco
Santa Fe, NM 87501
(800) 338-6877

World Balloon Corporation
4800 Eubank
Albuquerque, NM 87111
(505) 293-6800

Unicorn Balloon Company
15001 North 74th Street, Suite F
Scottsdale, AZ 85260
(800) 468-2478

Red Rock Balloon Adventures
P.O. Box 2759
Sedona, AZ 86339
(800) 258-3754

Balloon America Inc.
P.O. Box 31255
Tucson, AZ 85751-1255
(602) 299-7744

For a list of hot air balloon companies offering balloon rides near where you plan to vacation, call the nearest Chamber of Commerce or Convention and Visitors Bureau.

Houseboating on the Reservoirs of the Colorado River

You could spend several lifetimes exploring the many coves and inlets of Lakes Powell, Mead and Havasu. These humongous reservoirs lie behind large dams and provide great family outings for those who want to get away from the hustle and bustle of the crowds that come to the parks along the shores of the lakes, but who don't want to rough it too much.

Houseboats are little more than large, well-stocked motel rooms on pontoons. You can captain these across the wide expanses of water in comfort and safety, even if you have never handled a boat before in your life. They are easy to handle, and all the rental agencies offer complete instructions on navigating the lakes.

Summer is the busy season for houseboating in the Southwest, but I prefer the off-seasons when the air and water temperatures are lower, but the crowds are smaller.

At either time, it is relatively easy to move away from the most crowded areas of water to quiet coves where you can fish, swim and hike in solitude.

Houseboat Rentals

Lake Powell
Hall's Crossing Marina
P.O. Box 5101
Lake Powell, UT 84533
(801) 684-2261 or (800) 528-6154

Lake Powell
Bullfrog Resort and Marina
P.O. Box 4055-Bullfrog
Lake Powell, UT 84533
(801) 684-2233 or (800) 528-6154

Lake Powell
Hite Marina
P.O. Box 501-Hite
Lake Powell, UT 84533
(801) 684-2278 or (800) 528-6154

Lake Mead
Echo Bay Resort
Overton, NV 89040
(702) 394-4000 or (800) 752-9669

Lake Mead
Calville Bay Resort
HCR 30, Box 100
Las Vegas, NV 89124
(702) 565-8958

Lake Havasu
Havasu Springs Resort
Route 2, Box 624
Parker, AZ 85344
(602) 667-3361

Lake Havasu
H2O Houseboat Vacations
1000 McCulloch Boulevard
Lake Havasu City, AZ 86403
(800) 242-2628

Lake Havasu
Sandpoint Marina
P.O. Box 1469
Lake Havasu City, AZ 86403
(602) 855-0549

Whitewater Rafting

Ever since John Wesley Powell led his group of intrepid explorers down the Colorado River in the mid-18th century, the white waters of Southwest rivers have held a special fascination for those who seek excitement and thrills as their rafts and boats crash through large, fast-flowing rapids.

Although the most popular rivers for rafters are the Green, Colorado and San Juan, there are dozens of smaller waterways in the region where you can enjoy this exciting sport.

For the more popular rivers, you can choose from the outfitters listed below or you can contact the Chamber of Commerce near where you wish to raft for a more complete list of outfitters.

River Rafting Outfitters

Western River Expeditions
7258 Racquet Club Drive
Salt Lake City, UT 84121
(801) 942-6669 or (800) 453-7450

North American River Expeditions
and Canyonlands Tours
543 North Main Street
Moab, UT 84532
(801) 259-5865 or (800) 342-5938

Wild Rivers Expeditions
P.O. Box 118
Bluff, UT 84512
(801) 672-2244 or (800) 422-7654

Wilderness River Adventures
P.O. Box 717
Page, AZ 86040
(602) 645-3279 or (800) 528-6154

Rivers and Oceans
P.O. Box 40321
Flagstaff, AZ 86004
(602) 526-4575 or (800) 473-4576

Grand Canyon Expeditions
P.O. Box O
Kanab, UT 87471
(801) 644-2691 or (800) 544-2691

Canyon River Outfitters
P.O. Box 3493
Flagstaff, AZ 86003-3493
(602) 526-4663 or (800) 637-4604

Utah Guides and Outfitters
3131 South 500 East
Salt Lake City, UT 84106
(801) 466-1912

New Wave Rafting Company
107 Washington Avenue
Sante Fe, NM 87501
(505) 984-1444

Sante Fe Rafting Company
and Outfitters
114 La Paloma Street
Sante Fe, NM 87501
(505) 988-4914 or (800) 467-7238

Natural History Museums and Desert Gardens

While the best way to learn about the desert is to go out into it and get the feel of the sharp, prickly plants and animals that survive there, another good way is to visit one or more of the excellent botanical gardens, zoos and natural history museums of the Southwest.

Here are some of the better museums and gardens in the region:

Living Desert Zoological
and Botanical State Park
P.O. Box 100
Carlsbad, NM 88220
(505) 887-5516

Desert Botanical Gardens
1201 North Galvin Parkway
Papago Park
Phoenix, AZ 85008
(602) 941-1217

Arizona Mineral Resource Museum
State Fairgrounds
1502 West Washington
Phoenix, AZ 85007
(602) 255-3791

Utah Museum of Natural History
and State Arboretum of Utah
University of Utah Campus
Salt Lake City, UT 84112
(801) 581-4303 (museum)
(801) 581-5322 (arboretum)

University of Nevada Las Vegas
Museum of Natural History
UNLV Campus
4505 Maryland Parkway
Las Vegas, NV 89154
(702) 895-3381

Arizona-Sonora Desert Museum
2021 North Kinney Road
Tucson, AZ 85713
(602) 883-2702

Boyce Thompson Southwestern
Arboretum
37615 East Highway 60
P.O. Box AB
Superior, AZ 85273
(602) 689-2811

New Mexico Museum of
Natural History
1801 Mountain Road Northwest
P.O. Box 7010
Albuquerque, NM 87104-7010
(505) 841-8837

Rio Grande Nature Center
2901 Candeleria Road Northwest
Albuquerque, NM 87107
(505) 344-7240

SOUTHWEST

NATURAL
AND CULTURAL
HERITAGE
ASSOCIATION

About the Southwest Natural and Cultural Heritage Association

The Southwest Natural and Cultural Heritage Association is a nonprofit organization dedicated to enhancing visitors' understanding of the natural and cultural resources of our public lands throughout the six-state region of the Southwest. We are an interpretive or cooperating association, and as such, we work with a number of land management agencies in a wide range of activities.

At present, we work with the Forest Service, the U.S. Fish and Wildlife Service and the Bureau of Land Management in support of their educational and scientific programs. We operate bookstores that provide educational and interpretive materials to the public at various sites, including visitor centers and other locations. Through our publications program, we develop and publish materials, including books, guides, postcards, posters and brochures about national forests, wildlife refuges and BLM lands in the Southwest. In addition, we conduct interpretive programs at selected Forest Service campgrounds and fund special events, research and exhibits promoting the wise use of our public lands.

SNCHA is a membership organization and you are welcome to join us. By becoming a member, you will be helping to preserve and foster understanding of one of our greatest national treasures—our public lands. Membership entitles you to receive our newsletter as well as a 15 percent discount on all purchases in our bookstores and on mail orders, as well as discounts on purchases at many other interpretive association bookstores.

Membership categories include:

Individual:	$10
Lifetime:	$500
Corporate:	$1,000

To join us, or for more information, contact the Southwest Natural and Cultural Heritage Association, Drawer E, Albuquerque, NM 87103. Phone (505) 345-9498.